History of
Heart of England Building Society

Coat of Arms, Heart of England Building Society.

TO ALL AND SINGULAR to whom these Presents shall come Sir Anthony Richard Wagner, Knight Commander of the Royal Victorian Order, Garter Principal King of Arms, John Riddell Bromhead Walker, Esquire, Commander of the Royal Victorian Order, upon whom has been conferred the Decoration of the Military Cross, Clarenceux King of Arms and Walter John George Verco, Esquire, Commander of the Royal Victorian Order, Norroy and Ulster King of Arms — Send Greeting! Whereas Thomas Donald Gumbridle Kelly Gentleman, Fellow of the Institute of Chartered Accountants in England and Wales, Chairman of the Board of Directors of the HEART OF ENGLAND BUILDING SOCIETY hath represented unto The Most Noble Miles Francis Duke of Norfolk, Companion of the Most Honourable Order of the Bath, Commander of the Most Excellent Order of the British Empire, upon whom has been conferred the Decoration of the Military Cross, Earl Marshal and Hereditary Marshal of England that the Heart of England Building Society was established on the Thirty-first day of August 1974 under and by virtue of the terms of the Building Societies Act 1962 by the union of the Rugby and Warwick Building Society with the Walsall Mutual Building Society That the said Rugby and Warwick Building Society was formed on the Thirtieth day of September 1967 by the union of the Warwick Building Society and the Rugby Building Society which were formed in the years 1854 and 1866 respectively and that the said Walsall Mutual Building Society was established as the Walsall Mutual Benefit Building Society in 1863 the name being changed on the Twenty-eighth day of May 1953 That the Board of Directors of the Heart of England Building Society is desirous that Armorial Ensigns be assigned to the said Society with lawful authority and he therefore as Chairman of the said Board of Directors and on its behalf hath requested the favour of His Grace's Warrant for Our granting and assigning such Arms and Crest and in the same Patent such Supporters and such Device or Badge as We may consider fit and proper to be borne and used by the Heart of England Building Society on Seals or otherwise according to the Laws of Arms And forasmuch as the said Earl Marshal did by Warrant under his hand and Seal bearing date the Twenty-eighth day of March 1977 authorize and direct Us to grant and assign such Armorial Ensigns accordingly Know Ye therefore that We the said Garter, Clarenceux and Norroy and Ulster in pursuance of His Grace's Warrant and by virtue of the Letters Patent of Our several Offices to each of Us respectively granted do by these Presents grant and assign unto the HEART OF ENGLAND BUILDING SOCIETY the Arms following that is to say:— Gules within a Heart voided a Chevron Or on a Chief double enarched of the last a Griffin passant of the field beaked and armed Azure And for the Crest On a Wreath Argent and Gules A demi-Bear Sable armed Gules muzzled charged on the body with a Pale couped raguly and resting his forepaws on a Heart voided therein a Chevron Or Mantled Sable doubled Or: And by the Authority aforesaid We do further grant and assign the following Device or Badge that is to say:— A Heart voided therein a Chevron Or: And by the Authority aforesaid I the said Garter do by these Presents further grant and assign unto the HEART OF ENGLAND BUILDING SOCIETY the Supporters following that is to say:— Upon a Compartment composed of Thrift growing upon a grassy Mound proper on the dexter side a Lion Or and on the sinister an Ox Gules armed langued tufted and unguled Or about the neck of each pendent from a Cord a Heart voided therein a Chevron that on the Lion Gules and that on the Ox Or, as the same are all in the margin hereof more plainly depicted the whole to be borne and used for ever hereafter by the Heart of England Building Society on Seals or otherwise according to the Laws of Arms In witness whereof We the said Garter, Clarenceux and Norroy and Ulster Kings of Arms have to these Presents subscribed Our names and affixed the Seals of Our several Offices this Twenty-fourth day of April in the Twenty-seventh year of the Reign of Our Sovereign Lady Elizabeth the Second by the Grace of God of the United Kingdom of Great Britain and Northern Ireland and of Her other Realms and Territories Queen, Head of the Commonwealth, Defender of the Faith and in the year of Our Lord One thousand nine hundred and seventy-eight.

Letters Patent granting Armorial Ensigns to Heart of England Building Society.

History of
HEART OF ENGLAND BUILDING SOCIETY

★

P. W. MARTIN
MA, (OXON)

★

Published by Heart of England Building Society
1981

Published by Heart of England Building Society
22-26 Jury Street, Warwick

British Library Cataloguing in Publication Data
Martin, P.W.
History of Heart of England Building Society
I. Title
332.3-2-0942487 HG2156.675
ISBN 0 9507414 0 X

*Set in 'Monotype' Times series 327, and printed at
The Roundwood Press, Kineton, in the County of Warwick
Made and printed in Great Britain*

To Gwen,

who shared my first mortgage

Contents

Illustrations

Acknowledgements

IN WRITING THIS book I have drawn information, illustration and inspiration from others as a bee ranging an English garden on a summer day. I am grateful for permission to quote, or to use pictorial material, as follows:-

Lord Home of The Hirsel for the quotation on page 143.

The Longman Group, Ltd., and Professor G. M. Trevelyan for the quotation from "English Social History" on pages 1 and 2.

Oxford University Press and Messrs. Carter and Mears for the maps of population distribution in 1730 and 1930.

Franey & Co., and S. J. Price for quotations in Chapter 2 and for photographs of houses at Longridge and of the memorial plaque to Ketley's Building Society.

Macmillan & Co., and J. B. Hope Simpson for quotations from "Rugby since Arnold", used in chapters 6 and 7.

Rugby Local History Group and M. S. Turpin for material quoted in chapter 6; and to M. S. Turpin for help and guidance in many ways.

C. G. Richards for quotations in chapters 6 and 7 from "Rugby Building Society 1866-1966."

John Richardson for quotations in chapters 8 and 9 from "A Century of Interest."

G. Harrap & Co., Ltd., and N. J. Bull for the prayer printed on page 60, taken from 'A School Book of Worship.'

Heart of England Press for material from The Rugby Advertiser used in chapters 6 and 7, from The Warwick Advertiser on page 49, and for the photograph of H. J. Ansell at the Banbury opening.

The West Midlands Press for material from their Walsall Advertiser files.

By courtesy of the Oxford Mail and Times, for the F. J. Powell cartoon described on page 134 and used as an illustration.

Her Majesty's Stationery Office for the quotations from the Grays' Building Society Report on page 190 and from the Wilson Report on page 192.

Walsall Borough Archives Dept. for photographs of Bridge St. and Lichfield St. Walsall, in 1895.

I have been able to meet and talk to George Smith, John Richardson and Sydney Wren – three of the leading characters in this story – and it was both a personal pleasure and a professional advantage. I did not meet Frank Pollard before his sadly unexpected death in July 1980, but he guided and corrected me in correspondence as did Mr E. A. Crane, Vice-Chairman of the Coalville Society at the time of amalgamation. Mrs Susanne Farrington deciphered my manuscript, listened to my disembodied voice on tape, and typed interminable draft pages. Miss Christine Smith, Herbert Walden's secretary, has exemplified the cheerful helpfulness of the staff of Heart of England. Arno Christiansen of Roundwood Press has been a tremendous help in putting the book to bed.

I hope that my wife has found the worries of an author a change from those of a headmaster. She has shown the same skill and understanding in dealing with them and in pointing me away from the wrong path. Herbert Walden, General Manager of Heart of England Building Society, has been my constant guide and unvarying friend and I could not have written this story without him. As I began in September 1977 and ended in December 1980, I have made a considerable demand upon him. His distinguished leadership of Heart of England and his increasingly distinguished contribution to the Building Societies Association, of which in January, 1981 he has been nominated as the next Deputy Chairman, will be his life's work. But when on retirement he looks for a change, I trust he may be as fortunate as I have been. He should certainly then consider a second career as historian or publisher.

Preface

"This be the verse you grave for me,
Here he lies where he longs to be"
(Robert Louis Stevenson)

NOT EVERYONE SEEKS Stevenson's grave, "under the wide and starry sky". But add the letter 'v' in the middle of 'lies' in the second line of my quotation and you have a basic statement about humanity. Mankind is instinctively home-loving; we are quick to make warning noises or signals if we think our home threatened. It is for example arguable that the British are more disturbed by the contemporary increase in breaking and entering than by any other social phenomenon of the late twentieth century. Man hopes to find security in the home and adventure outside it. I clearly remember the pleasure of each of my rare visits to a family home during four years soldiering in India and Burma.

The building societies have therefore a special place in the British nineteenth and twentieth century experience. They are regarded as self-help institutions, developed by individual initiative, enabling men and women to use that same initiative to build a home. They have a special position among the great financial institutions of our country. Their entry to the corridors of economic power is quite recent, and they must retain the common touch as they travel those corridors.

The story of Heart of England Building Society is intensely human. The quality of the people – their humour, initiative, courage, companionship, eccentricity and fallibility – warms and enlivens the dry bones of the minute books, annual reports, statements of accounts and newspaper commentaries which have been my source material. "We fought tooth and nail and finally emerged about 2 o'clock – only hunger separating the combatants" is a worthy minute by a secretary who was not to be deterred by the threat "to lay me one on thick and make it hot for me whenever he got the chance". I hope that, like me, Samuel Smiles smiled.

P. W. MARTIN *Kenilworth, September 1977-December 1980*

About the Author

PATRICK WILLIAM MARTIN was born at Bowness-on-Windermere in June, 1916, read modern history at Balliol College, Oxford and was a headmaster from 1952-77; (Warwick School 1962-77). In 1976 he was President of The Headmasters' Association. He held a Territorial Army commission in the Royal Artillery and was on Field Marshal Slim's staff in Burma. He is deputy leader of the Warwickshire County Council, a deputy chairman of the Warwick Magistrates, chairman of a working party based on the National Agricultural Centre at Stoneleigh, and a Coventry Diocesan Lay Reader. Who's Who gives his hobbies as books, music, foreign countries, people, and being alone in the countryside.

P. W. MARTIN, TD, MA, JP

LEONARD E. H. WILLIAMS, DFC, FCA, FCBSI
Chairman, The Building Societies Association

Foreword

CONSIDERING THE SIZE and ramifications of the Building Society Movement and the long period which has elapsed since the first society came into being in Birmingham in 1775, there have been relatively few historic accounts but those which have emerged have divided themselves between stories of the Movement as a whole and more domestic accounts of the histories of individual societies. This story of the Heart of England is one of the latter but in leading the reader along the sometimes mundane but often exciting paths which the Society and its component parts have trodden over the years, it has brought fresh light on the development of the Movement as a whole.

The mainstream of the present Society first emerged nearly 130 years ago and, since then, the number of building societies has fallen, mainly by merger, from over 1,500 to something under 300. In financial and physical terms, the business of building societies has tended to become dominated by a relatively few large national organisations whose branches are spread through the length and breadth of the kingdom. Yet this has happily done little to inhibit the continued existence and development of locally based societies and in fact has encouraged the creation of several dynamic and efficient regional societies which have continued to hold their own in the areas in which they were founded.

Among these strong regional societies, the Heart of England is one which has grown from several roots and most recently, in 1974, from the merging of three long-established and respected societies, the Rugby and Warwick, the Walsall Mutual and the Oxford Provident. These very names outline the geographic area which the present Society so successfully serves and no better name could have been chosen to describe this important region of the country than that which the Society now bears.

Regional building societies have been particularly fruitful sources of men who have risen to rank among the leaders of national building society thinking and policy and many of the men whose names are inscribed on the list of Past-Chairmen in the Council Chamber of the Association were men who lived and worked in the grass roots environment of regional organisations and were thus able to bring to the deliberations of the Council that earthy wisdom and common sense which comes from close contact with the ordinary people that societies came into being to serve. The histories of building societies, and that of the Heart of England is no exception, are stories of people – the men, and increasingly the women, who have played their part in creating and developing them and who have imprinted upon them the strong mark of their personalities. Not least of these, in the case of the Heart of England, is Herbert Walden, who alone or jointly has been leading the Society in an executive capacity since 1962. The wisdom and experience he has been able to share with his colleagues of The Midland Association of Building Societies and, since 1974, of the Council of The Building Societies Association, have made a great impression and have been highly valued. He and his Society are indeed examples of the fine contribution which strong regional societies have made. They will undoubtedly continue to make an equally fine contribution in the years which lie ahead.

LEONARD WILLIAMS
Chairman, The Building Societies Association *December 1980*

CHAPTER ONE

The English Scene: 1850-1980

1850-1914

1851 WAS A CENSUS year, the sixth since the people were first counted in 1801. At the mid-century census the population of England and Wales was 17,900,000. Queen Victoria had reigned, and very often ruled, since 1837. The Great Exhibition of 1851 in the Crystal Palace in Hyde Park was a splendid example of the initiative of her husband, Prince Albert, whose idea and creation it was. It was also a window through which the world and his wife could gaze with admiration on the energy and wealth of the first great industrial society. There is no reason to think that the building societies of the day, and their leaders, paid much attention to the building in which the Great Exhibition was housed; glass houses were a poor security for mortgage. It is to be hoped however that they had knowledge of an aspect of English life which remained hidden from foreign visitors to the Exhibition. Those foreigners were unlikely to be shown the slums which resulted from our industrial progress. Had they seen them – seen them all – they would have noted that although the nation states of Europe had slums every whit as bad, a much smaller proportion of Europeans lived in such conditions. In those sprawling British slums, spawned by the insatiable demand of British industry for man power, lay a challenge to all those who believed that men and their families should not suffer socially, should not live lives of poorer quality, because they had moved from the country to the town.

For the census of 1851 showed that, notwithstanding the continued prosperity of British agriculture, half the population of England and Wales was already urban – "a situation that had probably not existed before, in a great country, at any time in the world's history" (G. M. Trevelyan, English Social History). But future development was to show that by the middle of the nineteenth century farming had reached its high point and the acreage of land in the hands of farmers and the owners of great estates was at a maximum. This great agricultural industry was much more than a wealth earner and creator. It sustained a social system based upon owning the land, or working it, or both. It was a system which did not call for large concentrations of workers and their families in restricted geographical areas. It was a way of life in which land owners and tenant farmers alike accepted a responsibility for housing their workers on the spot – in cottages which often combined picturesque exteriors and inconvenient, even squalid, interiors. But during the summer months at least the families who occupied those cottages had easy and immediate access to the most domesticated and beautiful countryside in the world. The rural worker, experiencing the advantages and disadvantages of a patronage which was still almost feudal, had little need of the services of a building society. But when he moved to the town, as he did increasingly from 1875 when English agriculture first began to wilt under American competition, the story was very different. If he was unskilled, a drifter by temperament, he and his family found their way to the cellars, slums and tenements until a later generation was lifted clear into local authority housing. The fluctuating fortunes of English agriculture will underpin this book even though it is chiefly concerned with the systematic and persistent search of the Midlands urban dweller for a house in which he could make a good home.

In 1851 the English Industrial and Commercial revolution was still gaining strength and the increase in urban wealth and population went on decade after decade through Victoria's reign. This upsurge had begun to gain momentum during the first half of the nineteenth century. One result was that the death rate, which had declined significantly between 1780 and 1810, fell no further during the next sixty years despite the undoubted progress of medical science during that period. The advances in medicine were being nullified by the appalling standards of housing, public sanitation, and public health, which were the lot of the new generation of industrial workers who had left the countryside and sought prosperity in urban based manufacturing industries. Too often they found their homes in single rooms, in cellars, or in jerry built terraces with inadequate drains and polluted water supply. The Public Health Act of 1848 was newly on the statute book at the beginning of our period, but it was not until the 1870s that a combination of cholera epidemics and social reformers produced improvements which ended the sixty year old plateau in the death rate and set it on a downward trend once more.

During the decade from 1851 to 1861 the population of England and Wales increased by 2,160,000 and the majority of these new Victorians had to be fed and housed and employed in the towns. The Amalgamated Society of Engineers was founded, the Cotton Spinners Union was re-modelled, and peaceful picketing during a strike was made legal. The Bessemer process of steel making was patented, coal output was rising rapidly and both Gladstone's budget of 1853 and the Commercial Treaty with France in 1860 emphasised the government's commitment to a policy of Free Trade. It was this laissez-faire economic liberalism which was to convert Britain during the second half of the nineteenth century to the nation of shopkeepers Napoleon had called us fifty years earlier. The same Free Trade policies, maintained despite the flood of cheap food from the American Middle West from the 1870s onwards, was also to tip English agriculture into decline and exacerbate the rural exodus, reinforcing the need for urban housing. The building societies of England owed more than they realised to the farmers of North America. A policy of cheap food was a policy for urbanisation, a boost for manufacturing industry which gained a cheap labour force, and a blow to home produced food which could not compete in price with the fertile virgin prairies. Victoria, laird of Balmoral and future Empress of India, was riding to prosperity and greatness on a beam engine rather than an elephant.

Each Victorian decade outdid its predecessor in producing both people and wealth. In 1871 the population of England and Wales was 22,700,000; in 1881 it was 26,000,000; in 1891 29,000,000 and in 1901 32,530,000. It is always easy to succeed in business on a buoyant market. The building societies of England sold their mortgages in a sellers' market and provided a welcome home for the savings of the skilled and thrifty artisans and prospering middle classes of a burgeoning wealthy nation. Between 1870 and 1880 the average annual production of British coal was about 130,000,000 tons of which approximately half was exported. In 1870 Britain produced 6,000,000 tons of pig-iron out of a total world output of 12,000,000 tons. Of the world output of 510,000 tons of steel Britain produced 220,000 tons. Iron steamers were about to drive wooden sailing ships from the seven seas, with all that implied for the prosperity of a manufacturing and trading nation.

The enrichment of the population was not as regular and uninterrupted as its increase in number. The period from 1873 to 1896 was one of trade depression, with intermittent recoveries in the early and late 1880s. Agriculture was now meeting the full force of American competition. The period of railway construction and development was drawing to a close and Britain had been a big railway exporter. The change over from iron to steel reduced the frequency of renewals in all industries, but especially in railways and shipping. Despite the recession real wages rose by 20% between 1873 and 1888; there was more unemployment but those who were in work had a better chance of undertaking and then maintaining building society repayments.

During the final thirty years of the nineteenth century the skilled artisans and lower middle classes were not only more prosperous: they began to be better educated and better governed. First, they were politically enfranchised by the Reform Acts of 1867 and 1884 – the male half, that is. Having given them political power the politicians needed the facility of communicating with the new voters: "We must educate our Masters." The Education Acts of 1870 and 1902 created elementary and secondary education respectively and from 1876 children were virtually compelled to attend school for the first time in the history of our country. The Public Health Act of 1875 and The Housing of the Working Classes Act of 1890 both meant that housing standards must be improved, although the 1890 Act introduced Local Authorities as rivals to the Building Societies in financing the new development. By the sunset of Victoria's reign her better educated, better fed, more prosperous subjects were unwilling, and unlikely, to accept the living standards of her early days. Encouraged to be a property owning democracy, disciples of the Samuel Smiles philosophy of self-help, they turned increasingly to the building societies to enable them to buy a stake in the country of which they were jingoistically proud and which – befuddled by almost 100 years of peace (pace the Crimean War) – they were itching to defend.

The next thirteen years, principally the reign of Edward VII, were in essence a Victorian afterglow. The population of England and Wales increased by another 3,500,000 to 36,070,000 and had almost exactly doubled since 1851. The number of acres under cultivation fell by a further half million to 32 million. The majority of British families felt prosperous, fortunate compared with their parents and grandparents, and part of that successful company Great Britain Ltd. The foreign, non-English, world began at Calais and the prevalent attitude was either imperially insular, or contemptuous of foreigners, or both. The hurricane of 1914 crept up unawares, unforecast by the political weather men, but by the time it had blown itself out it had swept away the security and sense of orderly progress of the country and of the building societies. Strangely, the next 65 years were to show that the building societies did even better during a period of national economic decline (relative to other countries) and insecurity than they had during the 65 Victorian and Edwardian years. When the going is rough it is good for the snails to have a shell to shelter them and houses have proved a fine defence against inflation and insecurity.

1914-80

During the second half of our period the population of England and Wales rose by about 40% compared with the 100% increase between 1850 and 1914. The generation of girls born about 1840 had 40% more children than were needed to replace the original generation. Those born at the beginning of the present century had 30% fewer children than were needed for replacement. The figure only reached replacement level again with the generation born during the second world war. They however have either delayed or further restricted their families with the result that the school population of England and Wales is now falling fast. Couples who married in the 1850s and 1860s produced rather more than six live-born children per couple; the figure fell to 2.1 during the 1930s and rose to 2.3 shortly after the 1939-45 war. Smaller families require more homes for an equivalent national population. The increase in the number of elderly – largely responsible for the continued increase in the total population – has been accompanied by a social trend towards old people remaining in their own homes, even after the death of the marriage partner, rather than going to live with children. Demographic developments have therefore favoured house builders, house renovators, and building societies during the twentieth century no less than during the nineteenth .In 1975 there were over 17,500,000 dwellings in England and Wales of which 35% were built before

1919, 23% between 1919-44, and 42% post 1944. In 1966 85% of Britons lived in houses or bungalows, mostly with gardens; the remainder lived in flats or maisonettes, normally in blocks of from two to twenty storeys. In December 1972 51% of these properties were owner occupied and the figure is rising; 31% of properties were rented from local authorities and the sale of council houses to sitting tenants, already well under way, is gaining pace as a result of the Conservative victory in the May 1979 elections.

During this second half of our period the British national experience was much less serene that it had been in Victorian or Edwardian times. From the mid 1950s a people whose confidence at the end of Edward's reign seemed unbounded ("We don't want to fight, but by jingo if we do –") had been given good reason for uncertainty and loss of direction. We had sacrificially won two great wars and were discovering that the sacrifices were not over and were not to be made only by those who lived, and too often died, in war time. The island race went on paying the bill. The sacrifices of 1914-18 were the first massive blow to our self-confidence and prosperity. Although 1919 was a peak year for acreage under corn (8.4m acres), a decline set in almost immediately. In the same year 229 million tons of coal were raised and 1.2 million tons of steam vessels were built but ship building declined thereafter. Cotton exports totalled £154m and woollen £55m (1920 prices) and prices generally reached their peak. But the year ended in credit restrictions and depression. For the National Debt, which had been £650m in 1914 had risen 12 fold in the next six years and was now £7,435m. The economic and employment outlook in England and Wales remained variable and unpredictable until re-armament in the mid thirties began to provide work for all once more. The General Strike of 1926, the Great Slump of 1929-31 leading to the National Government of that year, the dole queues (21% of the insured population was unemployed in 1931), and the Jarrow March are all proper memorials to this difficult and demoralising period in our national history – a troubled backcloth for building society activity during the inter-war years.

The Second World War prevented true economic recovery after 1914-18. The armaments boom of the second half of the 1930s was not wealth creating although it was undoubtedly job creating. The years 1939-45 delivered another massive financial and economic blow to a still reeling Britain. Despite generous aid from the United States and Canada this second world war ran down British capital by about

£3,000m, through shipping losses, bomb damage, and arrears of industrial maintenance or replacement. Overseas investments were sold to the tune of £1,000m and new overseas debts of £3,000m were incurred. Exports in 1944 were down to a third of the 1938 volume. Between the wars the National Debt had been reduced from the £7,435m of 1920 to £7,131m in 1939. After six years of the Second World War it had risen three fold – twelve fold during the first world war – to £23,647m.

We are too near to the 1945-80 period to be able to see it in historical perspective. As this introductory chapter attempts nothing more than an outline sketch of the English scene within which the Societies which now form the Heart of England Building Society operated, certain tentative lines and colours may be sketched into the picture. The English, never neglectful of material prosperity or considerations, have been made ever more materially minded by the uncertainty of their national life. If the pound in your pocket is depreciating – spend it. If you are foolish or profligate, spend it on bingo. If you are sensible, or worried about the future, spend it on bricks and mortar and take out a mortgage. Further – and this is perhaps the most surprising reaction to inflation – save a bit against an economic downpour and keep something in your building society account. The English have shed their imperial responsibilities with an almost audible sigh of relief and if they had dared stay out of Europe they would have mistakenly done so. Northern Ireland is a sufficient reminder of the troubles overseas commitments bring. They travel abroad for holidays in ever greater numbers but their security is at home, and within the national home each family home receives more attention and more cash than ever before. Divorce may be increasing, marriage may no longer be for ever, children may be at risk from parental separation, but the house, hearth and home are well endowed with material goods, comfort and convenience. Much philosophical consideration and political time has been given to trying to bring about a fairer and more egalitarian society. There is no serious evidence that this is what John Bull wants during the final quarter of the twentieth century. There is much more evidence to suggest that he wants to be able to catch up with Mr and Mrs Jones and then pass them by in terms of house, consumer durables, car, foreign holiday and what have you. The High Streets are not full of competing building societies for nothing. There are grounds for saying that today's Englishman would be unhappy in nineteenth century expansionist, colonising Britain. If he looks overseas for a model at all it is probably to Switzerland or Scandinavia. He would like to be left in peace with his nest egg in the building society or the P.O.S.B. and his mortgage under full control. Whether the great winds which blow on world affairs – Russia, China, the third world, the micro-chip revolution, the remorseless growth of world population – will grant him that peace is doubtful, but fortunately this analysis of the English scene is historical and not prophetic. What is certain when surveying the English scene from 1850 to 1980 is that the English are now better fed, better housed, work under better conditions, have longer and better holidays, own many more material possessions including houses, and so on – even if the doubling of the population has made us uncomfortably overcrowded and the loss of our supremacy in world trade has made us dance to the tunes called by oil sheikhs or American congressmen.

CHAPTER TWO

The Building Societies 1850-1980

Introduction:- Pre 1850

THE FRENCH REVOLUTION happened in a day – the Fall of the Bastille – or, at longest, over a period of three years from 1789-1792. The English Industrial Revolution began somewhere about the middle of the Eighteenth Century and is still a force for change in contemporary English Society. At the beginning of George IInd's reign in 1727 English manufactured goods were made in villages or small towns and not in factories in industrial areas. The term "manufacturer" was applied to the workers who 'hand made' the goods. When George II died in 1760 this rural industry paradise of small local production in domestic units was beginning to give way to the concentration of industrial power and activity in particular areas and in particular industrial buildings. Birmingham was such an area; in 1760 it was already a concentration of small industries, the home of artisans deservedly famous for their skill. As it was not a corporate town it had "freedom from guild restrictions and immunity from the disabilities imposed on Non-conformists in corporate towns." During the 90 years between the death of George II and the beginning of our period Birmingham became a great industrial city. During the same period the Industrial Revolution transformed England from a largely rural and agrarian community to one in which, as we have already noted, half the population lived and worked in the towns and cities. It is not therefore surprising that Birmingham is almost certainly the birthplace of the building society movement. In 1871 J. A. Langford, lecturing on "Early Building Societies in Birmingham" under the auspices of the Midland Institute, wrote "we have large and successful land and building societies which prove that the good of co-operation has not been allowed to pass entirely to other towns, but that we have been wise enough to take advantage of the method of accumulating and increasing the savings of the industrial classes. Birmingham is in fact the birthplace of these useful institutions. Here they were first founded; here they passed through their early struggles; here they have achieved their greatest success; and from this town they have spread to almost every town and village in the kingdom."

The earliest society was probably Ketley's for which an advertisement appeared in the Birmingham Gazette of 13 July 1775. By 1825 some seventy societies had been formed in English regions as far apart as Birmingham, West Riding, Manchester, Preston, Burnley, Stoke-on-Trent, Greenwich, Liverpool, Carlisle and Gateshead. There is no reason to suppose that this is a complete list. The early societies were 'terminating'; records were destroyed on termination and a significant number sank without trace. The societies and their directors have always tried to keep out of politics – increasingly difficult for them in the final quarter of the twentieth century. It is therefore a quirk of their history that the first great parliamentary reform act of the nineteenth century – the Reform Act of 1832 – led, through political motivation, to the foundation of many new societies. The owner of a freehold estate of annual value of not less than 40 shillings was now entitled to vote. Both political parties saw an opportunity to recruit to their cause and there was a boom in the formation of freehold land societies. Large estates were bought, divided into plots, and sold to those individuals thought most likely to support the political cause of the originators. Inevitably this political franchise movement involved the building societies, for many of these land purchase societies called themselves building societies. For many decades the term building society was used for both terminating and permanent institutions and for those concerned with either land purchase or house purchase or both. Our own Rugby Society was for much of its history more involved in land purchase and development than with lending money to house purchasers or builders, but it operated under the official and legal title of Building Society. In 1847 the Birmingham Freehold Land Society was founded "for the purpose of procuring qualifications in the County for the representation of North Warwickshire." In 1858 the directors of a London building society were developing an estate in Essex. "While the directors would in no way interfere with freedom of opinion on political questions, they have pleasure in stating their belief that the votes thus created are in the hands of the persons who will use them in advancing the cause of temperance, and other movements tending to improve the conditions of the masses of the community" (quoted in 'Building Societies, their origin and history,' by S. J. Price.)

These building and land purchase societies and their members needed some legal cover and protection. Many registered as friendly societies, especially after the Friendly Societies' Act of 1834 which extended the purpose for which friendly societies could be formed to "any other purpose which is not illegal". Concern as to whether or not building societies were exempt from Stamp Duty led to the Building Societies Act of 1836. This Act extended its protection to all building societies established before 1 June 1836 as long as their rules were certified and deposited under the "Act". The registering barrister had no discretion with regard to such societies; he was bound to certify their existing rules. On the other hand societies established after 1 June 1836 had to obtain the Registrar's approval for their rules. In either case the rules could not legally be enforced until they had been certified. The new Act specifically excused the societies from Stamp Duty. The first Chief Registrar, J. Tidd Pratt, quickly contributed to the confusion of names and titles. "It doesn't matter what it is: if you want the benefit of the Act you must declare it a benefit building society whether it is one or not". The Act served as a legal umbrella for building and land purchase societies for the next 38 years.

The 14 years from the 1836 Act to the beginning of our own period proper brought steady growth to the movement. The chief purpose of the 1836 Act was to encourage the formation of societies and it succeeded. New societies appeared throughout the country – almost every one a terminating society. Housing conditions remained one of the major problems of the day. The experience of Birmingham where the population grew from 73,670 in 1801 to 146,986 in 1831, was fairly typical of the industrial and manufacturing areas of the country. For builders and building societies there was much work to do. S. J. Price ("Building Societies, their origin and history") describes the buoyant conditions as follows:- "Moreover the national outlook was now good. In the decade 1836-46 foreign complications had been few, as the country was in the midst of 40 years of peace which lasted from Waterloo to the outbreak in the Crimea. In political circles attention had been accordingly diverted from the foreign field to problems of the homeland. These were many and they persistently pressed for consideration. Fortunately 1846 ushered in a period of material prosperity, orderly progress and social peace, broken only intermittently by serious commercial disasters. In the mid Victorian heyday, Britain far outdistanced her competitors in industry, commerce and shipping. She was the world's workshop; her ships carried the world's commerce; her capital was the world's banker and clearing house. Trade figures doubled and quadrupled, and the nation was buoyed up by a general feeling of complacency and self confidence which was hardly disturbed until the Boer War of 1899-1902. It was in such conditions that the first permanent societies were born. . . ."

1850-1914

Between 1846-1856 2,000 new societies were registered, the great majority of them terminating societies. The oldest permanent societies date from 1846, but some terminating societies founded before that date changed their rules and became permanent. One hundred and thirty seven of the societies founded during the decade, including the Warwick, reached their centenary. As we have noted in Chapter 1, the population of England and Wales was 17,900,000 in 1851 and there were 3,500,000 houses. Building Societies were "a prominent part in the prosperity of a large portion of the population of our country." Their influence was well established with the middle classes and was extending rapidly within the class of skilled workmen. Samuel Smiles published "Self Help" in 1859 and five years later in a public speech went out of his way to emphasise the importance of building societies in the kind of England he advocated. "The accumulation of property has the effect which it always has upon thrifty men; it makes them steady, sober and diligent. It weans them from revolutionary notions and makes them conservative. When working men, by their industry and frugality, have secured their own independence, they will cease to regard the sight of others' well-being as a wrong inflicted on themselves; and it will no longer be possible to make political capital out of their imaginary woes . . . Building Societies are on the whole amongst the most excellent methods of illustrating the advantages of thrift."

By 1856 there were probably about 2,750 societies and the chief problems with which their leaders grappled included the continuing fight with the Treasury over exemption from various types of stamp duty, arguments with the Registrar about the power of the societies to borrow money, and the short life of many societies either through termination or failure. Parliament left the societies much to their own devices between 1836-59, except for the question of stamp duty, but on 14th April 1859 the Home Secretary reported in the House on "the condition of Benefit Building Societies registered under the Act 6 & 7 Will IV". Unfortunately his report was incomplete, for the societies had not been compelled to supply him with the necessary information and only 198 did. During the next 18 years, until the Building Societies Act of 1874, development was continuous despite some special difficulties. The Post Office entered the competition for small savings in 1863, supplementing the drive of over 600 savings banks for the surplus cash of the disciples of Samuel Smiles. The effect of the American Civil War on the Lancashire cotton trade meant hard times for building societies in the North West. When Overend and Gurney suspended payments in 1866 the financial world flew danger signals throughout England. Heavy withdrawals from building societies led to some closures. The period from 1864-72, with the adverse effects of the American Civil War compounded by those of the Franco-Prussian War, was a difficult one for the property market. Nevertheless, when the movement reached its centenary in 1875 the storms had been ridden and an important contribution made to British financial and social progress.

The Building Societies Protection Association was founded at a meeting held in London on March 12th 1869 "to watch the proceedings in Parliament in reference to Building Societies and to protect and extend their interests, privileges and advantages." At the second annual meeting held on May 12th 1871 an appeal was launched for subscriptions to the Special Parliamentary Fund; Warwick was one of the 98 societies which contributed. The particular issue on which they needed that legal protection which only Parliament could give remained exemption from Stamp Duty, for a recent judgement in the Court of Exchequer left some doubt about the cover provided by the terms of the 1836 Act. Between 1872 and 1874 leaders of the Building Societies Protection Association and their supporters in the House of Commons were extremely active in trying to ensure that new legislation was sound in principle and unflawed in detail. The major effort made by these men was well rewarded. The Act, which received the royal assent on 30th July 1874, was described by the Building Societies Gazette as "the Magna Carta of

Building Societies." It provided a legal stability which proved very important in the troubled economic climate of the final quarter of the nineteenth century.

All management tasks are easier in a period of expansion than in one of contraction. The difficulty which faced building society managers during the twenty years between the Acts of 1874 and 1894 was that property values were always unstable and often declining. The index of building cost (1930 = 100) fell from a peak of 63.0 in 1873 to 46.9 in 1896. The societies were rightly regarded as a good savings medium, offering security and a fair rate of interest. As a result they found themselves with a good deal more investors' money than they could securely lend on mortgage. Doubtful mortgage business was undertaken; the fall in property values meant that some sound mortgages were rendered insecure by the fall in the value of the equity; it is not surprising that society closures and failures were a feature of the period. Problems were not only caused by a failure amongst societies to restrict borrowing to two thirds of the total mortgage assets. They were often made worse by ignoring the requirement of the 1874 Act that those officers who had charge of money should provide proper fiduciary security. Between 1874 and 1891 the Building Societies Gazette reported 31 cases of fraud by officials. There were in addition some spectacular frauds by outsiders; in 1878 E. Downs, an accountant, pleaded guilty to forging conveyances on houses in Dulwich with the aim of obtaining nearly £40,000. Finally, during this difficult twenty year period, the development by some societies of deposit bank facilities - as a means of attracting extra funds at low rates of interest - was a source of weakness when the financial going got tough. The most unsettling crash of all was that of the Liberator Building Society in 1892. Although the activities of the Liberator were more in the field of property development and secondary banking than of normal house mortgage, the general public was unaware of such distinctions and the reputation of the whole building society movement suffered. The purpose of the ensuing 1894 Act was to restore public confidence and to provide legal safeguards against financial malpractice or eccentricity. This was achieved by insisting on the publication of financial information which would allow the investing public to judge the soundness of a society's business – for example information about those mortgage assets on which payment was a year or more in arrears or the property had actually been surrendered to the Society.

The success of the 1894 Act was one reason why the twenty years following the Act proved to be a much more stable period in building society affairs than the twenty years which preceded it.

From 1894 to 1914 the societies developed new business methods to meet increasing competition. Advertising was widely used for the first time. Investment opportunities for the public were extended and diversified – the introduction of home safes in 1910 is only one example. The importance to the movement of owner occupiers was increasingly recognised and they could normally expect a mortgage based on a higher percentage of the value of the property. The long standing argument between the tax authorities and the societies about liability for income tax was finally settled about the turn of the century. By good fortune and good management the societies reached 1914 well equipped to meet the substantial problems of adjustment caused by the Great War.

1914-1980

The First World War set entirely new problems for the building societies. They were not foreseen; there is for example a complete absence of any reference to the outbreak of war in the minutes of Directors' meetings of the Warwick, Rugby or Walsall Societies. Yet August 1914 brought a bank rate of 10% and fears of extensive withdrawals of building society funds. Initially, societies insisted on the notice provided by their rules (for withdrawals of more than £5) but it was soon clear that public confidence was sufficient to ensure orderly business. By 1915 however the societies were suffering from the higher and more competitive rates of interest offered by the government war loans; the natural patriotism of the time led to large scale investing in war stocks. Thus, between 1914 and 1918 the total assets of building societies increased by only £2.3 million from £66.2m to £68.5m despite a substantial increase in the incomes of building society investors during the same period. Nevertheless societies found themselves with considerable cash surpluses, for the volume of mortgage business fell from £9.1m in 1913 to £4.5m in 1917. These surpluses, like the funds of private investors, found a home in one or another war loan funds; such government borrowing, for which we are still paying, increased the national debt twelve fold during the four years of war. For individuals, especially owner occupiers, war service often brought difficulty with mortgage repayments. The societies gained considerably in public esteem from the sympathetic way in which they helped solve such problems and the movement emerged from the war prepared and eager to help to solve the considerable problems of providing "homes for heroes".

To the considerable disappointment of building society leaders, the Government turned to the local authorities to provide post 1918 rented homes. It was soon clear that the societies would not re-establish their pre-eminence in the provision of houses to let. But a new demand for mortgage finance quickly emerged, filling the gap created by Government policy. Landlords began to find house property for letting a much less profitable investment than it had been pre-war. It paid them better to sell their houses, either on the open market with vacant possession or even to sitting tenants, and the resulting mortgage business set the course for building societies in the 1920s. The amount advanced on mortgage rose rapidly from £7m in 1918 to £25.1m in 1920. There was a marked increase in investment by depositors and shareholders, and an even greater demand for mortgage money could have been funded. The immediate post war investment and building boom broke before the end of 1920. The government help to local authorities to build houses to let was curtailed after nearly 200,000 houses had been built. In a way which seemed strange to those living in the inflationary 1970s, the end of the boom brought a fall in building costs and therefore in house prices. The price per foot super fell from 20/2¼ in 1920 to 9/4 in 1922. The building societies found themselves dealing once again with the problem of lending money on an equity of declining value. The shortage of houses meant that the government decided to keep rent control, inevitably at the expense of landlords. But in general the societies were now clearly embarked on their major task of the inter-war years - finance to help owner occupiers buy their homes.

The 21 year period between the wars was one of major expansion for the societies; total mortgage assets increased more than seven fold from the 1922 figure of £83.7m. This expansion was fuelled by the considerable growth of owner occupation. Before 1914 it was still exceptional for wage or salary earners to own their homes; perhaps between 10% and 15% of houses belonged to the family living in them. Today more than half our dwellings belong to their occupiers and the trend continues. Since 1945 the trend has been voluntary; inflation makes property an outstanding investment. The inter-war trend was involuntary; owning houses to let was no longer a good investment and the Victorian pipe dream of retiring on the

PLATE 1

Population distribution in England in 1730 and 1930.

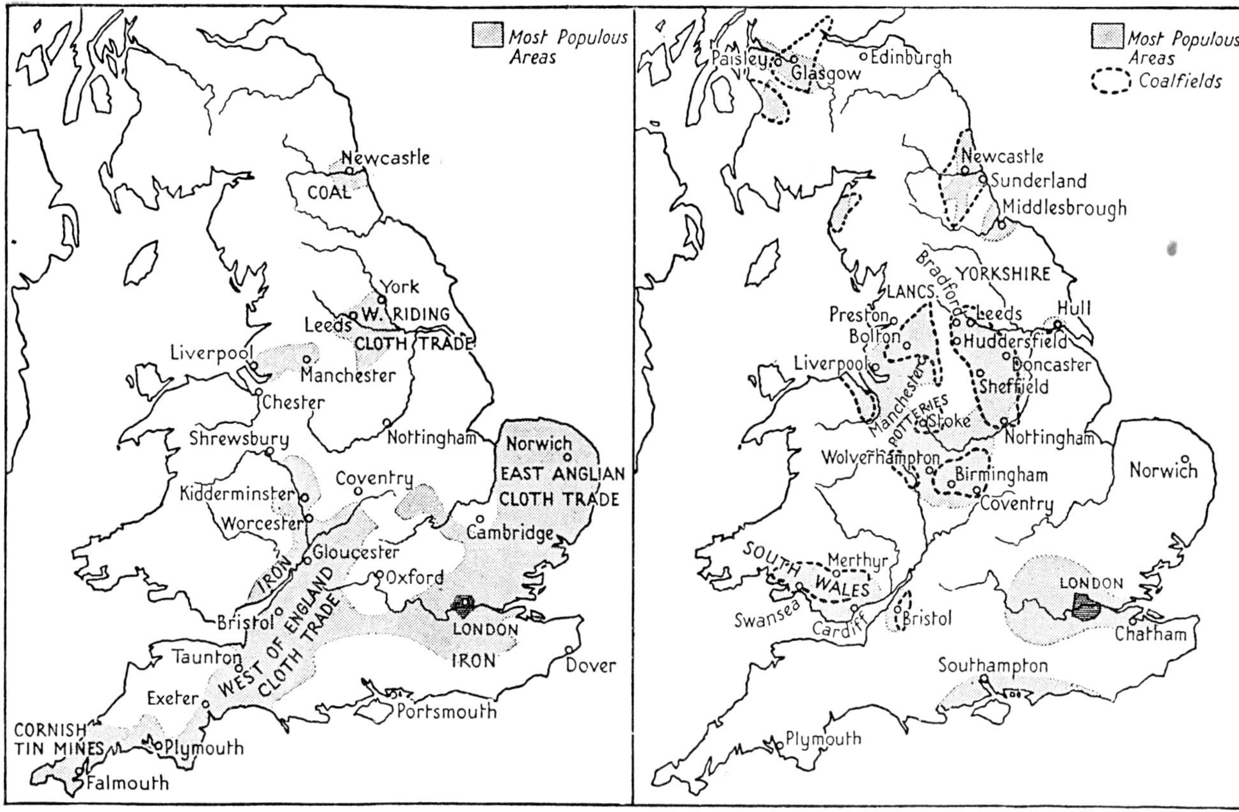

1730 1930

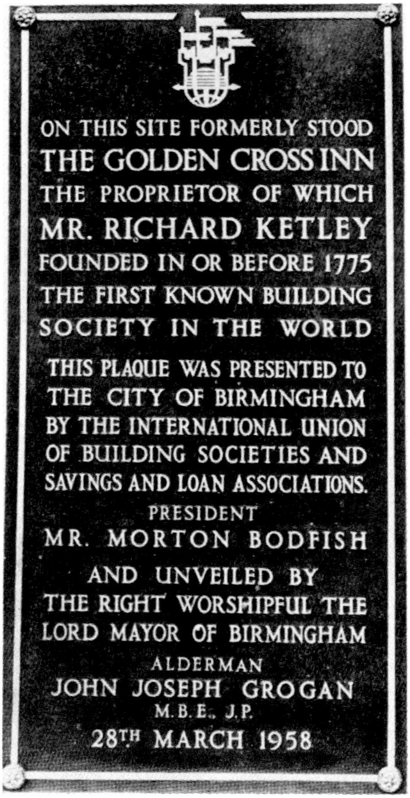

PLATE 2

Plaque marking site of first known building society.

PLATE 3

Club Row, Longridge. Built 1793. First houses known to have been built through a building society.

rents of a row of terraced houses was gone beyond recall. As the private landlord sought a better investment elsewhere, the owner occupier perforce took his place and turned to the building societies for the loan which would enable him to buy. The reluctant purchasers of the 1930s were the parents of those who in the 1960s and 70s simply could not afford not to buy. The resulting expansion in mortgage business, the spread of advertising and branch offices, the skill of many society managers, meant that by 1939 the building societies were beginning to occupy the dangerously important place in national life which is their strength and their weakness today. As so often in England, there was also a north/south dimension; northern societies with funds exceeding mortgage demand and southern societies in the opposite case. As a result southern societies began to advertise for funds in the north and northern societies sought outlets for their funds in the south. Countrywide building societies were on the way and by 1939 there was the now familiar pattern of national societies, regional societies, and local societies confined to one town and usually without branches. These latter were already under pressure from big brother.

In September 1939, as in August 1914, the first concern of society managers was the possibility of heavy withdrawals. Investors were financially more sophisticated than the small share and deposit holders of 1914. Moreover liquidity had declined from 14.3% of assets in 1934 to 9.5% in 1938. Public confidence had however been maintained by the success of the societies in meeting withdrawals at the time of Munich and in the event there was no run on share or deposit accounts. Total withdrawals exceeded new investments in 1939 and the implications of Dunkirk brought a similar outflow in 1940. But by the end of that year most societies were again financially on balance. From 1942 onwards the surplus funds of many societies led to active competition for limited mortgage business. By the end of the war – as in 1918 – the major political issue in the housing field was the provision of homes for a demobilised army, navy and air force all of record size. Again, the building societies were excluded from the government's plan to provide houses to rent: local authorities were given the task and their first pre-fabs soon spattered the land. The ex-service man, leaving his pre-fab in his demob suit, travelling to work by bus or bicycle, was happy to be finished with war but unhappy with the quality of the peacetime life his efforts had earned him. For the next six years the building societies and the

Labour government were uneasy partners and the licensing system for private building artificially restricted mortgage demand until 1953. Nevertheless the amount advanced to borrowers in 1948 (£264m) was double that of 1936 in real terms, although because houses had almost trebled in price the 1948 money bought fewer houses.

The 29 years since the election of Churchill's government in 1951 have brought continuous and continuing expansion of house mortgage finance. House prices doubled between 1946 and 1964, with falls of 2%, 6%, 1% and 2% in 1948, 1952, 1953 and 1954 respectively and increases of up to 10% in every other year. Societies had little difficulty in attracting funds and mortgage queues and chains were still in the future. This pattern was maintained in the early 1960s but the later years of that decade foreshadowed the changed circumstances of today. During the highly inflationary 1970s house prices have outstripped the ability of building society shareholders to invest, even though the societies now provide what is virtually a bank current account facility. Despite the huge increase in prices houses remain a safe, popular, capital protective investment and the continuing increase in prices has meant that all who can afford to buy do so at the earliest possible opportunity. The building society investor has done markedly less well than the borrower on mortgage, and society managers have had to meet political pressures to keep mortgage rates and therefore investment rates down. The societies are constantly searching for funds, competing with one another regionally and nationally, dominating the High Street with their branch offices. If they are in danger it is because their activities have become so essential to our national life, their finances so involved in the attempts of government to control inflation. The nineteenth century child of self help and free enterprise has grown to the stature of an economic strong man whom the politicians cannot afford to ignore, even when they are philosophically convinced that the movement should be left alone – a free capitalist activity in a free capitalist society. The Wilson Report, published in June 1980, points the finger and asks questions which must eventually be answered.

WARWICK AND WARWICKSHIRE PERMANENT BENEFIT BUILDING SOCIETY: 1853-1967

CHAIRMEN

Until the year 1904 the Society had no permanent Chairman and a Chairman was elected by ballot by the Directors and such Chairman presided over the fortnightly Subscription and Directors' Meeting.

In the year 1904 it was agreed to appoint a Chairman yearly.

1904-1906 W. J. Redfern
1906-1910 J. C. Purser
1910-1911 J. T. Chaplin
1911-1912 H. G. Alliban
1912-1930 J. C. Purser
1930-1942 P. Bailey
1942-1949 A. Tandy
1950-1951 A. H. Mercy
1951-1952 W. R. Webb
1952-1960 P. E. Kennard
1960-1967 R. S. Squires

SECRETARIES

1853-1858 W. Smith
1858-1862 R. Bromwich
1862-1875 T. I. Rose
1875-1903 J. Sallaway
1903-1920 J. Moffat
1920-1962 H. J. Ansell
1962-1967 H. R. Walden

ASSETS

	£		£
1854	1,000	1934	344,731
1864	8,000	1944	787,206
1874	16,000	1954	1,698,048
1884	65,906	1964	4,740,784
1894	59,040	1967	6,410,025
1904	70,944		
1914	92,809		
1924	138,521		

CHAPTER THREE

The Warwick & Warwickshire Benefit Building Society: 1853-1903

ALL THE EARLY building societies were 'terminating'. To the pioneers of property ownership for the non-wealthy it was self-evident that the way to emulate their economic betters was for a group to band together, help each other achieve home ownership, and then disband. This was a simple, common sense approach by men who had no particular skills in financial management and little contact with the financial institutions and network of Great Britain Ltd. The first 'permanent' societies were established in the late 1840s and 1850s and "Warwick & Warwickshire" was one of the first hundred. Warwick was of course a corporate town of national significance. The castle dominated the town in the same way that its owners had dominated important periods of English and European history. The great collegiate church of St. Mary was part of the history of the catholic Christian Church in Europe. It suffered financial and material loss at the hands of Henry VIII or his civil servants, although fortunately some of the secularised wealth was retained in the town and used for charity, including educational charity. Leycester, brother of the Earl of Warwick and Elizabeth's favourite, had left it a building of outstanding beauty which fortunately escaped the great fire of 1694 and in which ex-service pensioners could find a home. The ancient grammar school, one of the six oldest in the country, represented a history of education in Warwick as long in years as the history of Warwick itself. During the Tudor century the Bailiff of Warwick and the powerful Guild had been replaced by the Mayor and Burgesses who in most respects ruled Warwick until the Municipal Reform Act of 1835 and in many ways continued to do so until local government reorganisation in 1974. It is not surprising that a group of enterprising Warwickians saw the advantages which should follow the establishment of a permanent building society in the town. The fact that Mr James Taylor of Birmingham, a well known advocate of the political advantages of a property owning democracy, was invited to address a public meeting in April 1857, three years after the Warwick & Warwickshire was founded, prompts the thought that the local politicians joined with other men of initiative and public spirit in this move to extend property ownership and thus, as a result of the 1832 Reform Act, the franchise.

The first meeting to consider the formation of a permanent benefit building society in Warwick was held on 10 November 1853. It resolved to proceed and at a second meeting on 18 November the draft rules were settled and the Earl of Warwick was invited to accept office as President of the Society. The objects of the new body were:- "to enable any person however humble his sphere in life to become the owner of the house he inhabits or other freehold or leasehold property. To effect the erection or repair of buildings and to afford to persons who do not wish to purchase or build a greater interest for their capital than can be obtained in a Savings Bank and undoubtedly the most ample security." Much was made in these early days of the importance of paying a higher rate of interest than the Savings Banks. Borrowers should pay 5%, depositors receive 4%:- "Hence the one feeds the other." The controversial issues of 1980 were all there in those objects drawn in 1853. In these inflationary days politicians and media men seem to forget too easily that "the one feeds the other." All public discussion is about those who borrow from the Societies – borrow to invest in the best capital growth equity in contemporary British society. Yet if pressed too hard building society investors will surely vote with their feet, withdraw their funds, and leave the politicians a major housing problem. The Warwickian pioneers of 1853 went on to assert:- "The rapid and increasing progress of the benefit building societies is no doubt owing to the facilities afforded for the investment of small sums at good interest and for the acquisition of small freehold and to the protection and encouragement which is now afforded by the legislature to these institutions. The advantages of the society are far greater than could possibly be obtained under the terminating system."

By the provisions of the 1836 Building Societies Act the rules had to be approved by the Registrar of Friendly Societies, J. Tidd Pratt.

His approval was given on 9 February and the Society dates legally from 10 February 1854. The minute book for 24 February that year records that the Earl of Warwick had declined the Presidency "despite considerable correspondence with Lord Warwick and after interviews with his Steward." The Recorder of Warwick was then approached and gladly accepted: his Vice-Presidents were to be the Mayor of Warwick and the two M.P.s for the town. On 6 March 1854 the first subscription meeting was held at 7.00 p.m. in St. John's schoolroom. Fifty people attended and subscribed £17. 1. 8 towards the purchase of 194 £50 shares. The committee had met for an hour prior to the subscription meeting but this early practice lasted only two months and on 1 May, "because of the difficulty of getting a quorum" it was decided to hold committee meetings on a different day. The first chairman was Mr Thomas Davis, who also held the first share book, and the Secretary was Mr William Smith who, according to the rules that Tidd Pratt had registered, was fined five shillings if absent from a meeting and twenty shillings if he failed to pay in the money promptly. Other rules of particular interest were that subscription meetings would be fortnightly "beginning at 7.00 p.m. sharp and ending at 8.30 p.m. sharp." If any member was dissatisfied a vote would be taken by ballot. The Secretary was to be paid 1/6 for each share and 10d for each half share. The first meeting for the sale of shares was held in the Court House on 17 April 1854. Messrs. Henry and Reuben Bromwich bought the three shares on offer, each at a premium of 42/-. On 8 May 1854 the first mortgage was accordingly granted to the Bromwiches and the Society was in business both as borrower and lender.

As a result of the experience of selling the first shares, a Special General Meeting was called for 12 June 1854. The new rules then adopted governing share auctions proved more exact and therefore less controversial. Each fortnightly subscription meeting was bringing in between £25 and £30. Mrs Parsons was paid 1/- per night for getting the Court House ready during the summer months (25/3 to 29/9) and 1/6d per night during the winter months (29/9 to 25/3). In September 1854 committee members had to decide what to do with a bad half crown contributed, anonymously no doubt, at a recent subscription meeting. They balanced self and public interest nicely in deciding that "as the committee act gratuitously it should not fall on them."

In October 1854 the Society initiated an advertising policy, one of the modern manifestations of which is the lovely Heart of England rose now blooming in many a Midland town. They decided to advertise in Lacy's Almanack at a cost of 10/- plus 12/- for 2,000 off-prints. It is pleasant to record that Lacy's flourished in Warwick until 1980, spanning the century and a quarter between offprints at .072d per copy and the rose which received so much attention at the Royal Show at Stoneleigh in July 1978. In the same October 1854 a sub-committee of five was appointed to receive subscriptions; on any given night two of their number would act as Chairman and Treasurer. The same committee meeting received what must have been one of the happiest and most acceptable solicitor's letters ever written. Mr Hicks, Solicitor to the Society, wrote that "the Society is too young to bear the burthen of lawyer's charges" and declined to submit his bill. On 5 February 1855 the Committee met to organise the first Annual Meeting of the Society and discussed an improvement in pass books "so defective that a balance could not be struck." The First Annual Meeting was held on 12 February 1855; accounts for the first ten months were presented showing that 117 members had taken 406 shares which, when fully paid up, would represent a capital of £20,300. The third mortgage was granted on 26 March 1855 – the second had been agreed the previous December – and it was decided that in future the name of the mortgagor or his number would no longer be publicly announced at meetings. I wonder why we worry about the infringement of our privacy today?

It is evident from the minutes that throughout these early years you had to have collateral security in land or buildings, as well as be a shareholder in the Society, before you could get a mortgage. At the subscription meeting of 1 October 1855, when £43. 18. 4d was received, £9 was contributed by cheque, £29. 10s in gold, £5. 7s in silver and 1/4d in copper. As the Second Annual Meeting (11 February 1856) approached it was decided to pay the Auditor £2. 2s and the committee had to decide whether to recommend that a mortgagor paid interest from the time he purchased a share or from the date of the advance of the loan. These practical problems, and some important matters of principle, considered at early committee meetings must be typical of the early days of any new building society. What is evident with hindsight is that it was essential to the prosperity and longevity of the Society that its committee should get the answers right.

The Third Annual Meeting in February 1857 was chaired as previously by the Mayor. A new Auditor (perhaps two guineas was not enough) and new Surveyor were appointed and it was at this meeting that it was decided to invite Mr James Taylor of Birmingham, a great propagandist for the early permanent building societies, to speak at a public meeting in Warwick on 29 April. Warwick proved too much for Mr Taylor, or perhaps he was defeated by the cavalry. The meeting was badly attended and the Mayor adjourned it because the audience was too small. He was confident that the difficulty arose because Mr Taylor was "competing with a show of horsemanship". The Charge of the Light Brigade was of course still very fresh in the public mind (25 October 1855) and its leader the Earl of Cardigan was a great landowner in the neighbouring county of Northamptonshire. Mr Taylor was not a man to give in easily. He promised to attend on another occasion and strongly recommended "a tea party with the ladies present – this was always successful." A year later the Fourth Annual Meeting also experienced attendance problems. It was planned for 8 February 1858 but there were so few present that it was adjourned until the following Monday, when a meeting worthy of the membership took place. Unfortunately the Society was still not clear of its attendance problems. On 6 April 1858 the Secretary failed to attend a properly convened Committee meeting. It was adjourned to 9.00 p.m. the same evening at the Warwick Arms – an alternative presumably to a tea party with the ladies. The Secretary did then attend, and resigned. Mr Reuben Bromwich promptly resigned from the Committee, announcing his intention to stand for election as Secretary. He was appointed at a special meeting held two days later, there being one dissentient.

The Fourth Annual Meeting which had taken place amongst such comings and goings, or attendings and not attendings, heard news of modest progress. Subscriptions for the year ending 27 December 1857 were £599. 4. 2d on unadvanced shares and £194. 8. 4d on advanced. A total of £271. 17. 1d had been received as deposited loans compared with receipts of only £35 the previous year. Eleven shares had been sold during the year at an average premium of £3. 1. 7d. The number of shares was the same as last year – 341. This was a cause of concern to the Committee who regretted "that from various causes, but certainly not from want of confidence, several members have withdrawn the whole or part of their capital, and thus prevented sales of Shares and thereby reduced the profit." The Committee in their report to the Annual Meeting went on to affirm their confidence in the Society, emphasising "The difference moreover between Ordinary Mortgage Securities and those of the Society may be further illustrated – suppose A-B to borrow £200 and pay the interest regular for about 12 years he then still owes £200, whereas by paying a little more than 5% for the money had from the Society the principal and interest too is paid off by easy instalments." The Committee recommended that the principles of this Society should be "brought before the working classes" and observed with pleasure that "the officers had worked well together". It is abundantly clear from the report dated 29 January 1858 that the infant Warwick and Warwickshire was not yet weaned and that the committee and its officers had much work to do.

Two years later the Report to the Sixth Annual Meeting in 1860 suggested that the infant could now feed itself on the growing demand for mortgage finance and secure investment. Sales of shares were resumed; on 11 April 1859 the Committee had the interesting experience of a bid premium of £1 on the first bidding, £1. 5. 0d on the second, £1. 16. 6d on the third which also included "a ticket marked £1. 18. 6d was handed in but contained no Register Number nor would any Member acknowledge having bid that amount". Total receipts during 1859 were £1563. 5. 1d which was an increase of £360. 11. 9d over the previous year. A sum of £875 had been advanced to Members on "the security of good freehold property". By the end of the 1850s it is reasonable to deduce that the Society was firmly established, and that short of external catastrophe or internal knavery it would not terminate involuntarily.

On 21 May 1860 the Committee accepted an application from Mr and Mrs Fisher of Clifford Chambers for a mortgage of 3 shares, adequate collateral having been given: the Society's activity was extending territorially, helped by the appointment of an agent in Stratford. A special Committee met on 20 July 1860 to learn of the death of the Society's solicitor – that Mr Hicks who recognised "the burthen of lawyer's fees." The Committee adjourned for a fortnight so that the appointment could be advertised and on 31 August 1860 Mr C. G. Greenway was appointed, receiving 10 of the 14 votes cast. The choice of this member of the Warwick banking family of Greenway was to be a problem nearly twenty years later when the Bank failed with the Warwick and Warwickshire as one of their clients. In September 1860 the Committee decided that in future the Surveyor should attend all their meetings, and established a sub-committee to review the method of selling shares, still the subject of controversy and contention. Their recommendation was "that an upset price of £2. 5. od should be fixed so that any time there was an auction of shares, if the bidding did not reach £2. 5. od the Secretary would bid that sum and buy the shares in for the Society; in other words the shares would not be sold." It was further recommended that the present system of advertising an auction for shares should be abandoned and instead a set form of handbill should be printed and kept in stock; that all bidding should be in the sum of 2/6d; and that "the opinion of the Meeting is unanimously in favour of granting the application of Members applying for an advance without a sale of shares when no sale has been announced previous to such application, the premium per share to be not less than the present average of sales, that is £2. 15s." These changes in the bye-laws were approved at the Seventh Annual Meeting held in the Court House on 11th February 1861. At the same meeting the Committee reported an increase in the number of shares during the past year and announced a bonus of 3/- per share in addition to interest at 4%. Total receipts of £1239. 13. 2d during the year had been applied as shown:- £850 to Members on mortgage; £96. 13. 10d repayment of loan deposits; £443. 13. 7d to subscribers withdrawing during the year; £3. 10. 10d balance uninvested. At the end of the year there were 92 members subscribing on 407 shares.

A year later at the Tenth Annual Meeting held on 10 February 1862 the Committee reported a considerable increase in the number of shares during the year and "that notwithstanding the general dullness of trade in the district having occasioned large withdrawals, they are able to declare a bonus of 3/- in addition to the ordinary interest of 4%." Total receipts were £1425. 1. 8d. Only £350 had been advanced on mortgage compared with £850 the previous year. Members' withdrawals were about the same as in 1860 but withdrawal of deposits had increased from £96 in 1860 to £408 in 1861. There had been an increase of 48½ shares bringing the total to 455½. In their Annual Report the Committee re-stated the advantages of Building Society investment and borrowing, as they had in previous years. They needed to do so; in 1861 receipts of £1425. 1. 8d had been offset by withdrawals of £867. 19. 7d and this was an uncomfortably narrow margin for a young and impecunious society. The position was not helped by the resignation of the Secretary, Reuben Bromwich, three months later "on account of his permanent removal from

Warwick." The Committee met at the Court House to interview Messrs. Rose, Steel, Fenton, Chennell and Canner for the vacancy. Mr Rose was appointed receiving 11 of the 16 votes. Mr Bromwich attended his final Committee meeting on 30 June, 1862 and received "best thanks" for his "general attention and kindness in managing the Society." At the same meeting arrangements were made to sell by private treaty two houses in Friar's Court belonging to Mr Bullock. Bullock had been in difficulty in collecting the rents on these tenanted properties and was therefore behind with his payments to the Society. On 24 th March 1862 the Committee, through their Solicitor, had applied for a County Court summons against Bullock; the Society was very properly protecting the interests of its members.

At the Annual Meeting on 9 February 1863 the Committee had a more encouraging story to tell. The 3/- bonus per share was maintained, with the 4% interest. Receipts for 1862 were £1630. 13. 9d and total withdrawals £691. 15. 11d – a big improvement on the previous year. Mortgage lending had increased to £750, more than double the 1861 figure but still £100 less than in 1860. Shares had increased by 45 to a total of 500½. The only sad note was the death of Mr Margetts, Auditor to the Society from the earliest days. The records of the Society give no information about the 10th Annual Meeting other than the date – 9 February 1864 – and a record of those present: there is no account of the progress made during 1863. The 11th A.G.M. held on 13th February 1865 received a modestly encouraging report. Receipts were £1688. 16. 1d and withdrawals £829. 9. 10d; £755 had been advanced on mortgage to members and interest rate and bonus were maintained. The total of 556½ shares was an increase of 32 on the previous year. A year later at the 12th Annual Meeting of 12 February 1866 the equivalent figures were £2268. 5. 2d; £1092. 9. 2d; £980 on mortgage; 591 shares; interest and bonus maintained.

The 13th Annual Meeting, held on 11th February 1867, is the first for which a full Annual Statement is available in the records. As it also sets out the names of the Officers and Committee Members of the Society, it is the first available document giving detailed information about the Society at a set date. The President was still Sir John Eardley Wilmot, Recorder of Warwick, supported by the Mayor and the two M.P.s (G. W. T. Repton and Edward Greaves) as Vice-Presidents. The Secretary's address is given as Northgate Street. The Society's bankers – significant at a later date – were Messrs. Greenway, Smith and Greenway and their Solicitor was Mr C. G. Greenway. Receipts had fallen £24 to £2244. 3. 8d. and withdrawals were down by £7 to £1085. 1. 3d. Mortgage lending had decreased by £5 to £975 but the number of shares had increased by 60 to 651. The Society was successful at a modest level of activity. These circumstances remained substantially unchanged until the end of the 1860s. The Warwick and Warwickshire was fulfilling a need in an unambitious but organised fashion. It had not yet thrown up any obvious leader or driving personality. It was a local institution by now but not yet a powerful social or financial force in Warwick life. But by the end of the 1860s names which augur well for the future begin to appear in the records. Mr G. H. Nelson accepts office as a Trustee in March 1868. Mr John Purser seconds a proposal that "the worthy Mayor" be appointed Trustee: in February 1871 that worthy Mayor was called John Tibbits. The historian may begin to take a more measured and necessarily less detailed view of the years ahead.

During the 1870s the development of the Warwick and Warwickshire mirrored that of the Building Society Movement, even to the extent of providing one of the 31 cases of fraud by officials recorded in the Building Societies Gazette during the ten year period. For that reason 1875 was a difficult and dramatic year for the 21 year old society to reach its majority. The early years were more straightforward. On 25 April 1870 the Committee resolved "that meetings in Leamington for the sale of shares and receiving subscriptions be held at Mr Colley's Temperance Hall." This was on the proposition of Mr Purser, seconded by Mr Sleath. In January the following year the Auditors applied for an increase in fee: Mr Purser proposed two guineas for each auditor, but by a majority of 5 to 3 the fee was fixed at 1½ guineas each. At the 17th Annual Meeting held on 13 February 1871 the Society is recorded as having three Chairmen – Messrs. William Smith, the first Secretary, G. H. Nelson and Tibbits. Mr Smith and Mr Nelson were undoubtedly two of the three Trustees and Mr Tibbits as Mayor of Warwick was an ex-officio Vice-President. There is no record of the President, Sir John Eardley Wilmot, ever appearing at a meeting, unlike the Presidents of Rugby and Walsall who were normally in the chair at Annual Meetings.

The Society continued to extend the territory within which it was prepared to grant mortgages. Mr Hicks received a grant on property in Rouncil Lane, Kenilworth and the Surveyor, Mr Canning, "returning from surveying property at Arnesby in Leicestershire fell on the platform at Warwick Station and injured his shoulder, consequently he could not make a written report but had informed the Secretary. . . ." In 1874 the Committee considered an application from the Cooperative Society, Tiddington for a mortgage of £300 and before the end of the decade they were discussing the possibility of opening a branch in Kenilworth, or arranging subscription meetings there. "Branch" did not have its present meaning at that time, but it is still worthy of record that a suitable home was not found in Kenilworth until the opening of the present Warwick Road branch in 1979. A "branch" at Stratford was much nearer realisation. The minutes of the Committee meeting on 13 March 1876 read:- "The following report of the deputation to Stratford-on-Avon was read. Your committee beg to report that they went over to Stratford on Thursday last and met several Gentlemen interested in the formation of a branch of this Society there and discussed the matter with them when it appeared to be their unanimous wish that a branch should be established and in the event of such a course being adopted they expressed their willingness to become Shareholders."

By 1874 therefore the 20 year old Society seemed well set to participate in the national expansion which followed the Building Societies Act of the year. At a Special General Meeting held on 16 November 1874 it was resolved ". . . that the Warwick and Warwickshire Benefit Building Society be incorporated under the 37 and 38 Victoria, Chapter 42 Building Societies Act 1874 and the Secretary is requested and authorised to make application to the Registrar for a Certificate of Incorporation under the said Act. Carried unanimously." The Secretary did as instructed and the Society was duly incorporated but this was to prove Mr Rose's final major responsibility as Secretary. At a Committee meeting on 5 April 1875 it was decided that the Society's seal could only be applied to documents at properly constituted committee meetings, that deeds should be deposited with the bankers and only accessible to the Secretary when accompanied by Chairman or Vice-Chairman and "that the Secretary, Mr T. I. Rose, be suspended for one month and this was carried unanimously." The need for the first two decisions presumably explains why the third was necessary. Mr John Sallaway was then appointed Secretary "pro-tem" – he was to hold the office until 1903 – and was instructed to call in all pass books, "in order that they be checked with the Treasurer's receipt books." At an adjourned meeting on 8 April the Committee decided to call a Special

General Meeting of members for 22 April 1875 "to receive a communication from the Finance Committee as to the defalcations in the Accounts of Mr T. I. Rose, the Secretary, and to decide upon the steps to be taken."

Those attending the Special Meeting were told by the Solicitor, Mr Greenway, that the Secretary had failed to pay over all the monies received by him. The Finance Committee had already laid information against Mr Rose and a warrant had been issued for his arrest. The meeting unanimously resolved that he should be prosecuted and took another decision, brave because of unknown consequence, "that the Society do suspend all payments during an investigation of the accounts and that effect be given by Public advertisement." At the subsequent Committee meeting on 28 April Mr Stanton's offer to act as Auditor and carry out a special investigation of the accounts was accepted. The Committee agreed to appoint a Chairman for a period of three months to chair all meetings except Subscription Meetings so that the Secretary would have "someone to whom he could go with urgent matters connected with the audit of the accounts and the prosecution of the late Secretary." On 30 April Mr John Sallaway was appointed Secretary, a permanent appointment, and Mr John Purser was appointed Chairman for the coming three months. These two families – Sallaway and Purser – were to see the Society well into the twentieth century. As we know, Sallaway remained Secretary until 1903. J. C. Purser, son of John Purser, was Chairman at the time of his death in the Spring of 1930. There is in fact a clear and continuous link between 1875 and 1980 through the Pursers, H. J. Ansell the Secretary for much of the first half of the twentieth century, and H. R. Walden the present General Manager of the Heart of England Building Society. J. C. Purser (appointed Director 12.11.1888) and Ansell worked together for many years; so did Ansell and Walden. The three men span 90 years of the 125 years of the Warwick and Warwickshire, a remarkable achievement.

John Purser's first responsible duty was to tidy up the mess caused by defalcating Secretary Rose. Rose had converted £568. 1. 0d of the Warwick and Warwickshire money to his own use – small beer perhaps compared with the £2.5m Herbert Jaggard took from the Grays but a crisis in Warwick in 1875. The Solicitor's opinion was that depositors were not liable for any part of the loss which would have to be apportioned amongst shareholders according to their holdings. The

Bond of £200 was claimed from Rose's surety and the Committee decided to suspend payments for another two weeks. The definitive Committee meeting took place on 7 June 1875 when it was decided:-

"1. That the loss shown on the Auditor's report be carried to a Suspense Account, that the profits at the end of the year be carried to the credit of such account and that members withdrawing previous to the end of the year be charged 5/- per share towards the loss.
2. That certain changes in the method of keeping account, as recommended by Mr Stanton, should be brought into effect.
3. That the Secretary write to the advanced shareholders who are now in arrear that unless they pay up their arrears by Monday or Tuesday next the Society will enter into possession of the respective properties and receipt of the rents.
4. That the late Secretary be prosecuted upon other charges than the one in which he is now committed. . . .
5. That repayments be commenced to be made as from Monday next."

There the misguided Rose leaves our story. That he also left a shaken Society is evident from the withdrawals which followed resumption of payments. On 28 June depositors withdrew £637. 9. 4. On 26 July various people withdrew £521. 5. 3. On 9 August depositors withdrew £191. 9. 6. By then however the crisis was over. On 30 June a Special General Meeting chaired by the Mayor, Mr G. H. Nelson, approved all the Committee recommendations and did much to restore public confidence in the Society. On 7 January 1876 the Committee was able to report "that the profits made during the year have been sufficient to meet the loss as shown by the Balance Sheet submitted to the General Meeting in June last and leave a balance towards paying the working expenses of the Society for the past year.

During the rest of the decade the Society began to share the national experience of an excess of funds over mortgage demands. They were able to consider a loan of £2500 on the Shakespeare Hotel and other premises in Stratford. Advertisements (twice) in the Warwick Advertiser, Warwick and Leamington Times and "a Stratford paper" drew attention to money available to lend on mortgage. Between 6 June and 2 September the Directors were consequently able to approve a number of quite considerable mortgages. The Secretary warned that funds might not be sufficient to meet all these new contracts and advertisements were again organised – this time for

PLATE 4

J. C. Purser, Chairman, Warwick and Warwickshire, 1906-10 and 1912-30.

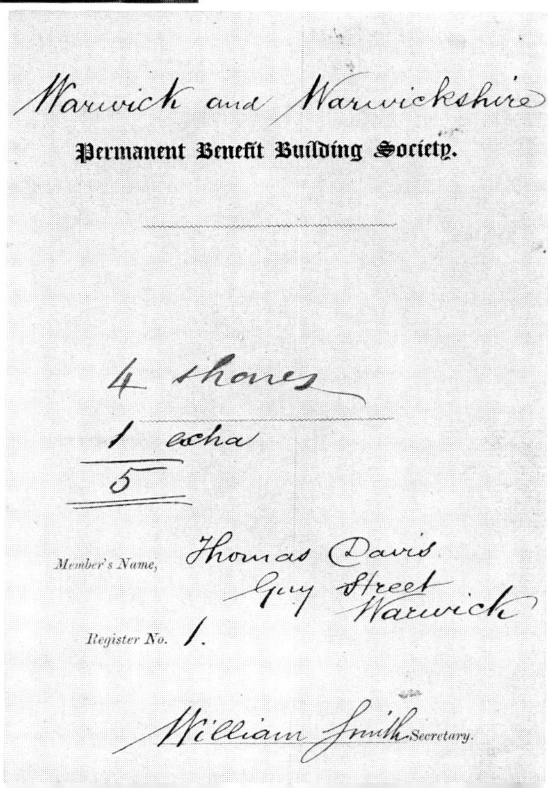

Warwick and Warwickshire

Permanent Benefit Building Society.

4 shares

1 extra

5

Member's Name, Thomas Davis
Guy Street
Warwick

Register No. 1.

William Smith *Secretary.*

PLATE 5

First pass book issued by Warwick and Warwickshire — to Thomas Davis, the first chairman.

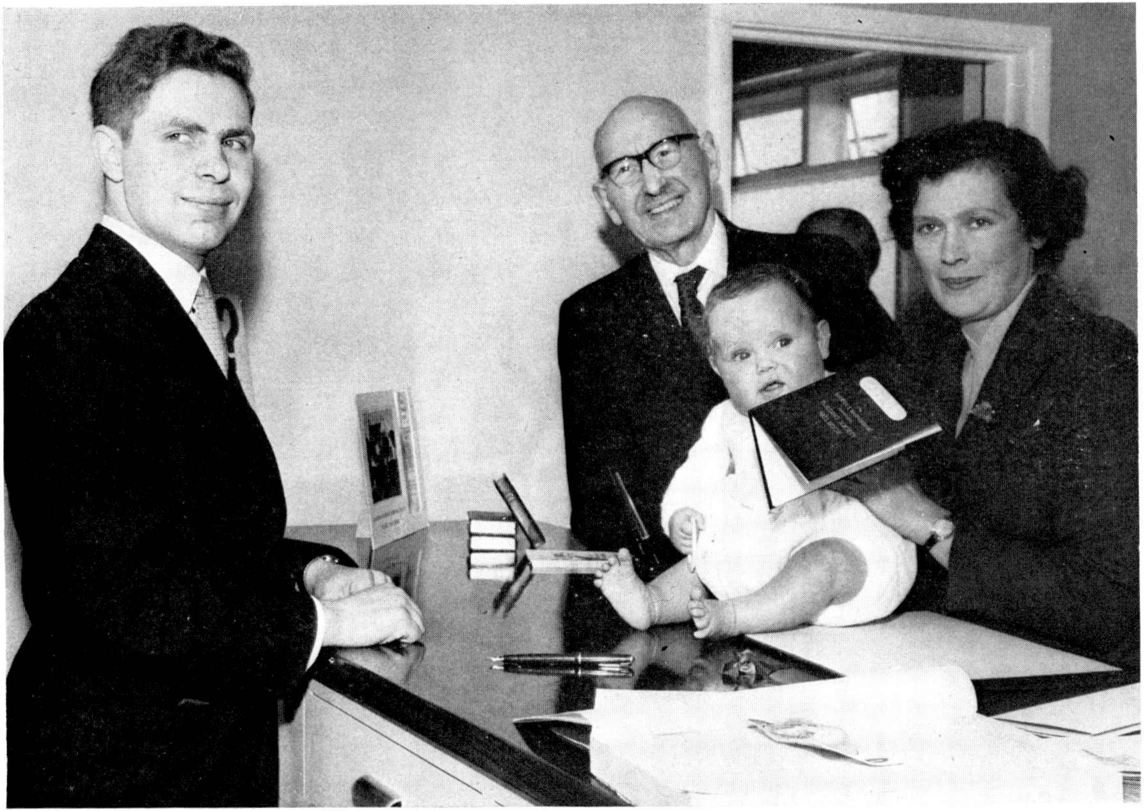

PLATE 6

H. J. Ansell introduces youngest client at opening of Banbury branch of Warwick and Warwickshire in March, 1961.

people to lend to the Warwick and Warwickshire rather than borrow from it. These advertisements were as successful as those offering money on mortgage had been and the Directors thus had evidence to support their view that the Society again enjoyed full public confidence in its own area. In particular at this time it was helping to finance new building in Coten End, Warwick and Leam Terrace, Leamington.

Contemporary committee minutes record several discussions about the insurance of property in mortgage to the Society. Mr Sallaway could only report that although he assumed that owners insured their property, he could not confirm it. At a time of falling property values, the Warwick and Warwickshire could not afford to find that in a particular case it had involuntarily been its own insurer. On 28 February 1878 the Secretary was instructed "to have all properties insured in the name of the Society and pay the premium." The 1870s were ending with every sign of a renewal of confidence and activity, the Rose affair in perspective, and the lessons learned. A branch at Kenilworth was again in the news. The mortgage records show activity throughout central Warwickshire.

Mr John Sallaway's Secretaryship continued until 1903 when his resignation due to ill-health was received at a Directors' Meeting on 15 June 1903: they resolved "The Directors wish to avail themselves of the opportunity to testify to Mr Sallaway their appreciation of his high sense of duty, of his devotion to the interest of the Society, and of his never failing courtesy; and their unbounded confidence in his integrity, his dedication and ability." During the two final decades of Victoria's reign the Warwick and Warwickshire had played a significant part in the financing of housing and commercial development in Mid-Warwickshire. It also survived the failure of its Bankers in the mid 1880s. Finally, without realising, it established the future headquarters of the Heart of England Building Society by granting a mortgage of £500 to the Secretary, with which he bought Nos. 24 and 26 Jury Street, Warwick. In fact, at the time of his death at Eastbourne on November 26, 1903 the Society was the tenant of its former Secretary and the Sallaway family were to remain landlords for some time thereafter.

A list of some of the mortgages granted during these twenty years gives a picture of the scope of activity. In April 1880 the Trustees of St. John's School, Kenilworth successfully applied for a mortgage of £150. The Society's solicitor was concerned "that the Act of Parliament under which the site of these schools was held provided that in case of the schools being discontinued at any time the land should revert to its owner which might raise difficulty in case the Society should have to enforce its security. . . .", but the Directors decided to "proceed in the matter". Two years later however, when the Trustees applied for a further £100 they had to agree to execute "a bond making themselves personally liable for repayment. . . ." In June 1880 the Directors of Cox's and King's sold their house in Stratford and paid off their mortgage to the Society – an interesting example of a major national bank borrowing from what was still a very local building society. In August 1880 Mr Bromwich was granted a mortgage of £500 on the Millwright's Arms and adjoining land in Coten End, Warwick. Later the same year Mr Meakins redeemed his mortgage by selling the Guy Tavern to Messrs. Hunt, Edmunds & Co. for £850 . . . a local example perhaps of the trend towards tied houses. In January 1881 a mortgage of £1300 was granted to Mr J. Jenkins on his "Foundry and House" in Emscote and in June of the same year £1450 was loaned on the security of the Wheatsheaf Inn, adjoining house and adjoining building land in Tachbrook Road, Leamington. In September 1881 Mr J. Woodward received £900 in respect of six houses in Avon Street and five houses in Friar Street, Warwick and the following February £1,000 was loaned to Mr H. Dadley on the security of seventeen houses at Wellesbourne.

The Society was finding funds for house purchase, house building, education, trade and commerce. In July 1882 Mr John Fell applied for a mortgage of £3,200 but this very considerable sum was too much for the Directors to stomach. When, in the same year, the Beehive Cooperative Society at Barford was wound up it is not surprising to find that the Warwick and Warwickshire held the major stake in the property. The Directors ordered "that a board be painted and affixed to the property offering it for sale by private contract, application be made to the Secretary, the selling price to be not less than £425." The pattern of mortgage advance remained very similar throughout the next twenty years and there is neither need nor space to list the details. The Society was meeting the needs of the locality and in particular was able to play its full part in financing the building of new houses in Warwick, Leamington, Kenilworth, Stratford and the surrounding area, thus keeping in line with the increasing population and growing prosperity of the area.

This ability to participate financially in local development was put at risk in the 1880s, as it had been in the 1870s. In the earlier decade the problem had been a fraudulent Secretary. In 1887 it was the failure and consequent closure of the Society's bankers, Messrs. Greenway, Smith and Greenway of Warwick. As Mr C. G. Greenway was also Solicitor to the Warwick and Warwickshire his inevitable resignation deprived the Directors of trusted legal advice at a time when they most needed it. At a Special Directors Meeting called on 6 September 1887 the Secretary reported that the Bank had suspended payment that morning and that he "had in his hands £330. 0. 3 taken at the Subscription Meeting the previous evening, less the sum of £20 previously paid into the Bank. Moreover at the said Subscription Meeting withdrawals had been authorised and the cheques would normally have been drawn on Greenways." He was instructed to pay the money into Lloyds, Barnetts and Bosanquets Banking Co. Ltd. and write the withdrawal cheques on that bank. The Directors met again six days later, received the resignation of Solicitor Greenway, and appointed Mr Campbell in his place: Messrs. Campbell, Brown and Ledbrook are still one of the firms of Solicitors advising the Heart of England Building Society. A week later the Directors met again, approved the Finance Committee's action in applying to Lloyd's for an overdraft of £1,000 and received advice from their new solicitor on their liability to meet cheques drawn by the Society, but not met by Greenways before they ceased business. Mr Campbell's written reply is worth full quotation, especially for those who are trustees of funds or those who are dilatory about paying in cheques they receive.

"Warwick, 19th September 1887. Dear Sir, *Building Society and Bank*

With reference to your enquiry about the position of the Society in connection with certain outstanding cheques viz. those given to Trevelyan on September 2nd and Murray on the same date I am of the opinion that the Society will have to pay the amounts over again since there was no negligence on the part of the persons receiving the cheques in getting them cashed, but it is otherwise as regards Wardell's cheque sent on August 26th. He will have to bear the loss and as the Committee are mere trustees for the depositors and share holders they would run the risk of someone taking advantage of the illegal act should they pay the amount over again. Probably the risk is small but trustees of funds cannot exercise the virtue of charity unless with the consent of all whose money they are dealing with. Yours faithfully, Brabazon Campbell."

The story ends with reports to the Finance Committee in December 1887 that Greenways' Bank had held £603. 8. 6 of the Society's money at the suspension of dealings; that Greenways had repaid £75. 8. 7 on liquidation in March 1889, as a dividend of 2/6 in the £1; and that a final dividend of £17. 18. 3 was received in December 1889. The shareholders had lost £510. 1. 8 and they paid for it in reduced bonuses for the rest of the decade. This was a blow, to some individuals no doubt a serious one, but to the Warwick and Warwickshire it was a minor check in a steady progress.

The third major development of these twenty years is the establishment by John Sallaway of the Secretary's position and authority in the Society, and the arrival of the Warwick and Warwickshire at 24 Jury Street, Warwick – their headquarters thereafter. As the Society prospered the method of fixing the Secretary's salary on a share transaction basis came under scrutiny and criticism from some quarters. Some members clearly considered that Secretary Sallaway was doing too well out of a system established for a tiny society in its early years. Rule 9 was the determining regulation and there was pressure to change it. On 24 April 1885 however recommendations to a Special General Meeting were:-

"1. That they are of the opinion the Rule 9 should not be altered at present.

2. The reason for this is that the Secretary receives no payment for dealing with 300 deposit accounts.

3. They are of the opinion that if the time ever does come when the Secretary's salary should be altered, the alteration should take the form of a reduction of the payment per share and not by making the Secretary's remuneration a fixed sum as proposed in the private resolution to the Special General Meeting."

The Special General Meeting held on 28 April 1885 overwhelmingly supported the Finance Committee view. Two years later, on 4 January 1887, the Secretary himself took the initiative to reduce his salary, whether in response to public outcry or to the prompting of his own conscience is not clear. The Finance Committee minutes record:-

"Secretary's Payment. The Secretary stated that in order to show his appreciation of the kindness he had at all times received from the Directors and Shareholders he would be willing to accept the following reduced payment for his Services viz. for all shares subscribed up to 3,000, 9d per share, such payment to come into operation for the year just finished and all future years."

In 1889 the Sallaway family decided to move house and by so doing brought the Warwick and Warwickshire to the prime site in Warwick which the Heart of England still occupies. The minutes of a Directors' Meeting on 4 March 1889 read "Application . . . J. Sallaway . . . £500. The Secretary submitted an application from himself for £500 on mortgage of Nos. 24 and 26 Jury Street and house in Castle Lane." The application was approved. Nearly two years later it proved fortunate that the Secretary now occupied more spacious quarters. On 15 December 1890 a Directors' Meeting minute recorded "Subscription Meetings. The Secretary reported that he had applied for the use of the room at the Court House that the Society had used for so many years, he had not received a formal reply but had been given to understand that the Society would not be allowed the use of the room hitherto occupied and that if they thought well to use the Ante Room upstairs or the Police Court (by arrangement with the Penny Bank) they could do so on payment of £5 per annum." The Directors decided that future Subscription Meetings should be held at the Secretary's Office and that he would be allowed the £5 asked by the Corporation. In a sense, Subscription Meetings have been held at that address ever since.

So matters continued until Mr Sallaway's resignation in June 1903 and death at Eastbourne five months later. Fortunately on his retirement he was willing to let 24 Jury Street to the Society as he was moving to Eastbourne for health reasons. An annual rent of £50 was agreed, on a 21 year lease with breaks at 7 and 14 years. The Society bought Sallaway's office furniture and fittings for £35 and each piece is itemised in the minutes. When Mr Sallaway died the Directors sent appropriate messages of sympathy to the relatives and arranged for Mr J. C. Purser and the new Secretary, Mr J. Moffat, to attend the funeral in Eastbourne. But they kept their business instincts alive for they were simultaneously arranging a special meeting of Directors on 2 December to consider repairs necessary at 24 Jury Street. Mr Sallaway had, "according to the lease," refused to accept any responsibility for inside repairs but wrote that "he would be willing to do a little papering and white-washing but not to the extent of the schedule sent." On 2 December the Directors resolved "having considered the question of repairs are of the opinion that the same should be carried out by the executors of the late Mr Sallaway and that the inside w.c. should be put in a proper sanitary condition by the Executors." Those Directors, worthy successors of the earlier Committee members who knew how to deal with a counterfeit half crown, had taken to heart the sixteen year old lesson of Brabazon Campbell that "trustees of funds cannot exercise the virtue of charity except with the consent of all those whose money they are dealing with." Negotiations with the Sallaway family rumble on until the Society finally purchased its headquarters, but John Moffat was now seated at the Secretary's desk in Jury Street and the next half century – and two world wars – belong properly to Moffat, Purser and Ansell.

CHAPTER FOUR

The Warwick and Warwickshire Benefit Building Society: 1903-1962

J. C. PURSER WAS Chairman of the Warwick and Warwickshire for most of the period from 1903 until his death in office in April 1930. John Moffat was Secretary from 17 August 1903 until his resignation due to ill health in February 1920. H. J. Ansell was Secretary from his appointment on 2 March 1920 until his death in office in June 1962. Moffat was a consolidator, Purser was a brake on progress, and Ansell was a moderate innovator who established the secure organisation which H. R. Walden, his successor, developed so well in the 1960s and 70s. All three were ably supported by men such as Cullis, Redfern, Chaplin and Tandy but it was the character and professional attitude of Purser, Moffat and Ansell which were to shape the Warwick and Warwickshire in the first half of the twentieth century.

John Moffat was appointed at a Directors' Meeting held on 25th July 1903. Ten candidates were interviewed and after some discussion it was decided that each Director should write down the names of three candidates. In the resulting ballot Mr Moffat gained 13 votes and his nearest rival 9; he agreed to take up his appointment on 17 August. Moffat and Purser were quickly involved with the Sallaway family, and in particular with John Sallaway's daughter, in some of the inevitable difficulties which arise between landlord and tenant – early examples of which have been given in Chapter 3. On 15 December 1903 the Secretary reported that he had had the drains of 24 Jury Street tested and they proved defective. A further letter was sent to Miss Sallaway, within a week of her father's death, asking her to complete the necessary repairs and put the drains in order. On 1

February 1904 the Directors were told of a letter from Miss Sallaway asking that the rent for 24 Jury Street for the period 17 August to 31 December be paid. The Directors agreed: one wonders why they had to be asked. But on 15 February 1904 Miss Sallaway wrote again to say that she could not accept £7. 10. 0 in discharge of the 1903 rent and the Directors offered £10. On 29 February the landlady replied that she would settle if a further 10/- were offered and the Directors agreed: horse trading indeed. On March 27th 1905 the Directors agreed to Miss Sallaway's application to remove the greenhouse at the rear of 24 Jury Street "on condition that they were not required to replace the greenhouse at the expiration of their lease and that its removal was at no cost to the Society." By June 5th 1905 the Secretary could report that the greenhouse had been removed and the lease appropriately endorsed. On 10 February 1906 Mr Moffat reported that the interior of No. 24, and his property therein, had been much damaged by water "through the defective state of the roof of the house". The Directors decided that a letter be sent to "the landlady of the property" asking her to carry out the necessary repairs.

In 1909 the landlord tenant relationship changed for the first time to that of potential vendor and purchaser – more familiar ground for a building society devoted to the virtues of owner occupation. On 8 May 1909 a letter was received from Miss Sallaway offering to sell the house and premises of 24 Jury Street for £1,000. The Finance Committee resolved "that the Committee cannot recommend the Directors to become the purchasers of the property at anything like the figure in view of the great depreciation in values of house property in the neighbourhood." It was the sort of decision they were to regret, a typical example of the expenditure brake for which Purser was responsible over a long period, keeping the Warwick and Warwickshire in Warwick when more progressive societies were going regional or national. In 1912 the roof of No. 24 was once again leaking after a January snow storm and Miss Sallaway was asked to repair it. She "expressed surprise that the roof of No. 24 needed to be put in thorough repair and she suggested that her representatives visit the property." In September 1918 negotiations were again in train to buy the property from Miss Sallaway who is reported to have refused an offer of £1600 for 24 and 26 Jury Street and 1 Castle Lane, backing on to Jury Street. She seems to have thought better of her decision during the winter and in May 1919 offered to sell 24 and 26 Jury Street for £1500. The Finance Committee held that in view of the age of the property it was too much and offered £1250.

Here for the time being the tale of the Society and its headquarters must await future developments in Ansell's time and post-Purser. There is however one episode arising from John Moffat's resignation for health reasons which belongs to his period. Like his predecessor he remained in office until his health would take no more of it. It was typical of a time when pensions were inadequate or non-existent that men worked until the end of life or the end of strength; so did Sallaway, Moffat and Ansell, successive Secretaries. The Directors accepted the resignation with extreme regret and recorded "their appreciation of his long and faithful services and it is the opinion of the Directors that this step is in the best interests of Mr Moffat in order that he should be free from all business worries." More than that, they resolved "that £100 be voted to Mr Moffat for his long and faithful services and as a token of the Directors great appreciation and warm regard." Then, like good trustees and disciples of Brabazon Campbell they began to haggle with him about the value of his bath tub. Ansell was appointed Secretary on 2 March 1920 and his conditions of service – of which more later – included residence at 24 Jury Street at a rent of £50 p.a. On March 9th the Finance Committee received a letter from Secretary Moffat to the effect that the bath, geyser and fittings at 24 Jury Street belonged to him. It was resolved "that the said bath be valued and taken by the Society." On 7 May 1920 the Committee resolved to pay Mr Moffat £20. On 4 June they received his answer that the offer was inadequate and replied that £20 was the value placed on the bath etc. by Mr Trepass, the Surveyor. On 2 July Moffat had written to say that his valuation was £30 and Secretary Ansell was instructed to tell his predecessor that the Finance Committee would pay £25 "to close the matter. If not acceptable Directors have no alternative but to allow Mr Moffat to take the bath and holding him responsible for any damage to the house." On 12 July Mr Moffat died without seeing a penny of his bath money. The Directors resolved "that it be recorded on the minutes an expression of deepest sympathy with Mr Moffat's family and our great regret at losing him." The episode of the bath ends on 27 August 1920 when Mr R. Moffat, brother of the former Secretary, accepted £25. The Society had for a short period been in negotiation with the families of both former Secretaries, Sallaway and Moffat.

Moffat seems to have been the first Secretary of the Society to have organised annual leave – another reminder that our Victorian ancestors worked until they died and did it for six days a week, 52 weeks a year, except for high days and holy days. On 24 June 1904 "The Secretary having asked the Directors to consider the question of the summer holidays – it was resolved that the Secretary be asked to take 20 days holiday and to arrange with the Chairman and Vice-Chairman as to the carrying on of the business of the Society during his absence." There is no evidence in the Society's records that John Sallaway ever had a holiday. On 13 August 1906 the Secretary applied for a fortnight's leave of absence and it was granted. This was a bonus year for holidays for it was the year of the famous Warwick Pageant in the Castle grounds. "14 June 1906. Warwick Pageant. The Secretary be authorised to close the offices of the Society each afternoon from 2 July to 7 July 1906." By 1907 the minutes of 12 August simply record that the Secretary's application for leave to take his annual holiday was granted and thereafter the matter must have become one of routine which did not need a special mention in the minutes.

In 1907 Secretary Moffat suffered personal tragedy in the death of his wife and on 2 December "the Chairman proposed that the Board tender their deepest sympathies with the Secretary in the irreparable loss he had sustained by the death of his wife and assure him how much each of them feel for him at this time." Mrs Moffat was buried at St. Andrew's in Scotland and the Chairman explained that as there was no time to consult each Director, he had ordered a wreath to be sent on their behalf. In a sensitive last sentence the minute records that a letter was then read from the Secretary "expressing his appreciation of this last tribute, and in order to spare his feelings the Chairman (J. C. Purser) was requested to enter these particulars in the Minute Book of the Society." Moffat suffered one further personal loss during his years as Secretary. On 14 December 1908 the Directors recorded "A vote of condolence and sympathy with the Secretary in his recent bereavement." No detail is given. John Moffat does not seem to have been a leader in the civic or corporate life of Warwick, as were Purser and Ansell, but it is on record that he was a candidate for the Secretaryship of the Warwickshire Chamber of Agriculture in 1908 and that at a later date he was Secretary of the Warwickshire Branch of the Red Cross. In due course he was awarded the O.B.E. for this voluntary work.

J. C. Purser was an established Director when Moffat was appointed Secretary. This seniority enabled him to dominate the activities and policies of the Warwick and Warwickshire during the whole of Moffat's Secretaryship and for the first ten years of Ansell's. On 27 February 1905 Purser was involved in a curious affair. At the first Directors' Meeting following the Annual Meeting W. J. Redfern, who had been Chairman of Directors for some years, proposed Purser as Chairman for the ensuing year. "This was seconded but Mr Purser proposed an amendment that Mr W. J. Redfern be re-elected Chairman of Directors for the ensuing year, this amendment was seconded and when put to the vote was carried, Mr Purser was then re-elected Vice-Chairman for the coming year." Purser was already involved in an annual Society occasion of some importance, started in 1904 to commemorate the fiftieth anniversary. The 8 February 1904 Annual Meeting resolved "that the sum of £20 be voted for the purpose of giving a complimentary dinner to the Directors and Officers of the Society, the Shareholders to take part in the dinner if they so desired, at their own expense." Purser was made Chairman of the dinner committee and took a leading part in arrangements for many years. It was decided that the 1904 dinner should be held at the Woolpack on Friday, 15 April – an advertisement to be published in the Warwick Advertiser. The Mayor of Warwick was invited to take the chair, or failing him, the Chairman of Directors. The Stratford Directors were allowed 10/- for a conveyance on the night. A year later Purser arranged the equivalent dinner at the Woolpack at 6.00 p.m. on 4 May; tickets were 3/6d. Complimentary tickets were offered to Mr Briscoe who had promised to act as pianist and to Mr Hicks (later editor of the Leamington Courier and father of Professor Sir John Hicks) representing the Warwick Advertiser. "The Secretary was requested to write to various gentlemen who had purchased tickets and ask if they would sing during the evening." The dinner was successfully repeated in 1906, again at 3/6d per ticket, and in January 1907 when the Directors were considering outline arrangements for that year's dinner it was resolved "that ladies be not invited to attend." Here we leave the story of this annual event in the life of the Society, and in the life of Warwick, for the early success of which Purser was largely responsible.

Redfern's proposal of Purser as Chairman of Directors in 1905 turned out to be a dummy run for 1906. In February 1906 Redfern refused to stand as either Chairman or Vice-Chairman and Purser was elected Chairman with Alliban as Vice-Chairman. On 27 February 1907 Purser was re-elected Chairman but Redfern was his Vice-Chairman. Purser was now, with the Secretary, the regular representative at Annual Conferences of the National Association of Building Societies. Purser's chairmanship of the Warwick and Warwickshire had a curious hiccough between 1910 and 1912, the more inexplicable in that in February 1910 he had recently completed two years as Mayor of Warwick. At a Directors' Meeting on 21 February 1910 Purser was proposed for re-election as Chairman and Mr J. T. Chaplin was also proposed. "The proposal of Mr J. T. Chaplin was carried unanimously. A resolution was then passed offering a hearty vote of thanks to Mr J. C. Purser for all that he had done as Chairman of the Society in the past. Mr J. W. Bissell was elected Vice-Chairman." A year later Chaplin declined to stand again and H. J. Alliban was elected Chairman with Bissell as his Vice-Chairman. In February 1912 Purser was back in the Chairman's seat. He and Bissell were both proposed, Bissell declined nomination and Purser was elected with Bissell as his Deputy, Mr Alliban "being suitably thanked." Throughout the two years he was out of office Purser continued to take a leading part in the Society's affairs. One is left with more than a suggestion – for Chaplin and Alliban each refused to serve a second year – that with Purser on the Board but not in the chair the Chairman's seat was too hot.

At a Directors' Meeting in 1907 "Mr W. J. Redfern congratulated the Chairman on his appointment as Mayor of Warwick and Mr J. C. Purser replied. At the 54th Annual Meeting of the Warwick and Warwickshire on 10 February 1908 the Mayor, J. C. Purser, took the chair. At the Building Societies Association Annual Conference in June 1909 "Alderman J. C. Purser, Warwick, asked whether it was advisable that borrowing members should be Directors of Societies and, if so, in what proportion? The Chairman in reply said that it was a matter for each Society to resolve for itself." On 27 November 1909 the Directors minutes read:-

"Presentation to Alderman J. C. Purser, Chairman of Directors. On the conclusion of the foregoing business Mr W. J. Redfern on behalf of the Board of Directors presented the Chairman, Alderman J. C. Purser, with his portrait suitably framed and asked him to accept the same as a mark of their goodwill and the high esteem in which they held him as also to commemorate the fact that during his

Chairmanship of the Society he was for two years, 1907-1909, Mayor of Warwick . . . The Chairman replied thanking the Directors for their gift which he much appreciated and said he would have much pleasure in allowing the portrait to hang in the Boardroom as desired." As we have seen, within a year he involuntarily vacated the chairmanship for two successive years. Yet when, half way through that period, a public meeting was held in Banbury to discuss opening a branch there, Purser with the Chairman and the Secretary attended as the representatives of the Directors. Moreover in June 1911 Purser and the Secretary were the Directors' representatives at the N.A.B.S. Conference in Burnley. When they were similarly elected to attend the 1912 Conference in Cardiff the Directors voted 6 in favour and 3 against – whether doubting the value of the Conference or the choice of Purser is not clear.

Thereafter Mr Purser's journey through the Society's records is regularly successful. The custom of inviting the Mayor to preside at Annual Meetings lapsed and each year, with two exceptions because of illness, Purser took the chair. At the ensuing meeting of Directors he was without exception re-elected Chairman. This happened for the last time on 20 February 1930. There is no doubt whatever that for the final ten years or more the old man acted as a brake on the Society, preventing development and frustrating Ansell. For example, he resolutely opposed the installation of the telephone in the Society's offices. The minutes of a Directors' Meeting of February 23 1928 therefore read surprisingly – "The Directors accepted the recommendation of the Finance Committee to install the telephone." The surprise is only removed when the list of those attending shows that Purser was absent ill, a very rare event. It is however within contemporary knowledge that once the 'phone was provided Purser used to march up to the office and instruct the Secretary to make telephone calls for him. Such was the man who was re-elected Chairman in February 1930, taken ill in March 1930 and died in April 1930. The minutes of 3 April 1930 record "Mr J. C. Purser. Mr P. Bailey referred to the great loss the Society had sustained on the death of Mr J. C. Purser, the Chairman, and proposed that the Board's sympathy be conveyed to Mrs Purser, her family also, and the Board's high appreciation be recorded at the excellent, able and willing services rendered by Mr Purser both as a Director and Chairman, which service had to a very large extent contributed to the successful position now occupied by the Society." The records of the Society suggest that J. C. Purser first became a Director in 1888. He worked with Secretaries Sallaway, Moffat and Ansell, he was a Director for 42 years and Chairman for 27 with a two year gap. His continuity, longevity and undoubted probity was an advantage and source of strength to the Society. His latter day opposition to change and inability to accept new ideas became a disadvantage and delayed progress and development after the 1914-18 War.

H. J. Ansell was appointed to succeed Moffat at a meeting of Directors held on 2 March 1920. They had met previously on 18 February when 32 applications and letters of enquiry were opened – "including several from ladies", none of whom reached the short list. Five candidates, including Ansell, were selected for interview and a sixth was added at a second meeting on 25 February. At the 18 February meeting a letter from Secretary Moffat was read including the following sentence; "I am also deeply grateful for the sum of money they have voted me by way of bonus for my past service." On 2 March the six candidates were interviewed in alphabetical order and Ansell appointed. His conditions of service were:- "Secretary to devote usual office hours to the business of the Society and only undertake such other duties as shall be approved by the Directors. To keep all the books and accounts of the Society and to attend Subscription Meetings at Warwick, Leamington and Stratford each fortnight and Banbury and Kenilworth each fourth week. To attend all meetings of the Directors and Finance Committee. Approximate salary (including fire insurance commission) £330-£350 p.a. The Secretary to reside at 24 Jury Street to pay a yearly rent of £50 and to provide light and warmth and heating for the office and Board Room. Office hours 9-1.00 p.m. and 2-5.00 p.m. Mondays to Fridays and 9-1.00 p.m. on Saturdays." Mr Ansell's beautiful copper plate handwriting first appears in a minute book on 18 March 1920 and he must have taken up his appointment quickly. It seems unlikely that he was in any way responsible for a decision on 26 April that the Directors would change their time of meeting to 8.00 p.m. on the Wednesday of non-subscription weeks. When in August however the Secretary had to report the resignation of his clerical assistant, Miss Happer, he received the Directors' agreement to the appointment of Mrs Ansell in her place.

From 1920 to 1962 the story of Herbert Ansell's professional career is of course the history of the Warwick and Warwickshire Benefit Building Society, of which more later. He had a separate public career of some distinction, and information about Ansell the public man will flesh out the story of his professional activities. On 16 October 1930 the Directors agreed that their Secretary might stand as a candidate for the Warwick Borough Council. When the Directors met on 26 June 1941 they resolved "Mayor of Warwick. The Chairman reported that the Secretary had received an invitation from the Town Council to be Mayor of Warwick for the forthcoming municipal year. Resolved that Mr Ansell be congratulated on the honour extended to him and that the Society make no objection to him accepting the invitation". On 26 February 1942 the Mayor of Warwick attended the 88th Annual Meeting of the Society but there is no reference in the minutes to his presence. He was there in his professional and not in his civic capacity. On 2 October 1942 the Directors heard that Mr Ansell had been invited to continue as Mayor of Warwick for a second year and gave him their congratulations and blessing; their reaction was the same a year later when he was invited to continue for a third war-time year.

He was admirably supported in that office by his wife, Annie Olivia Chubb, daughter of a Warwick business man. As Mayoress during the war she wrote some 8,000 letters to servicemen and other Warwickians.

Mr Ansell thereafter continued to be a Borough Councillor and a governor of various schools including the Warwick Schools Foundation. He had been a Justice of the Peace for some years and when he was Mayor it was still the custom of the Warwick Bench that the Mayor was ex-officio Chairman of the Bench. This ancient custom was abolished shortly after the end of the war and Ansell was then elected by his fellow Justices as their first elected Chairman. His wife, who had admirably supported all his activities, died in 1954. On 28 April 1955 the Directors congratulated him on his appointment as Vice-Chairman of the Midland Association of Building Societies. In October 1955 Secretary Ansell had for the first time the help of a fully professional assistant when Mr H. R. Walden, the present General Manager of the Heart of England, who had joined the Society's staff on leaving school and had qualified as a Chartered Secretary, became Assistant Secretary of the Warwick and Warwickshire Permanent, as the Society had now become. In 1956, when Ansell was its Chairman, the Midland Association of Building Societies held its Annual Meeting in Warwick. The Court House was booked, a 12/6d lunch provided by City of Birmingham Restaurants, and the Earl of Warwick and the Mayor of Warwick were invited as guests. On 28 March 1957 Ansell, a Director since May 1942, became Chief Executive. The Directors resolved "that the following be designated and appointed the principal executives of the Society, and that either Joint Secretary be authorised to countersign as provided in Rule 5: Mr H. J. Ansell, Managing Director and Joint Secretary and Mr H. R. Walden, Joint Secretary." During 1957 and 1958 Ansell had brief periods in hospital but, although beyond what might now be retirement age, he was still vigorous enough to accept election as Deputy Mayor of Warwick, despite his three war-time years as Mayor.

The brief final period is, deservedly, all honour. On 3 March 1960 a Special Meeting of Directors proposed "that the honorary office of President of the Society be and is hereby created; that in recognition of the devoted and outstanding services rendered to the Society over a period of forty years Mr H. J. Ansell be appointed to that office." On 5 March 1960 a luncheon was held at the Court House in honour of Alderman H. J. Ansell J.P. on the fortieth Anniversary of his appointment as Secretary of the Society. The Chairman of the Warwick and Warwickshire proposed the toast to Ansell and he responded. The Society was toasted by the Chairman of the Midland Association and the Vice-Chairman of Warwick and Warwickshire replied. The report of the occasion includes a photograph of Herbert Ansell, with his equally distinguished daughter Dr Barbara Ansell, consultant physician in Rheumatology, and of Mr and Mrs Herbert Walden. Mr Walden was later thanked by the Directors "for the efficient, excellent and smooth manner in which the arrangements were dealt with and the organisation of the luncheon." Because the organisers wished to keep the luncheon secret until the last minute it was necessary and very difficult to keep Ansell away from Villa Park or the Hawthorns on that particular Saturday.

Mr Ansell's death two years later came as unexpectedly as that of any man or woman full of years and wisdom. On 12 April 1962 the minutes record "Mr H. J. Ansell. The Chairman referred to the regret felt at the admission of Mr Ansell to hospital with a foot infection. Resolved that the sympathy of the Board be conveyed to Mr Ansell for a speedy and complete recovery." But the minutes of a Special Directors Meeting of 14 June 1962 speak of their great loss: "The late Alderman H. J. Ansell, JP, ACIS, ACCA, FBS. The Chairman referred in moving terms to the death of Alderman H. J.

Ansell and paid tribute to the outstanding services to the Society rendered by him over a period of 42 years. At the conclusion of his tribute the Chairman proposed and the Vice-Chairman seconded:- that the meeting record with very deep regret the passing in Warwick Hospital on Monday 11 June 1962 of our respected President, Managing Director and Joint Secretary, Alderman Herbert Joseph Ansell, Justice of the Peace, who, for a period of 42 years, had given his utmost in devoted and loyal service to the Society and the sincere sympathy of the Board be conveyed to his daughter, Dr Barbara Ansell, in her bereavement." The man who during the first ten years of his Secretaryship had worked under the 30 year long shadow of J. C. Purser had for many years stood clear of all others with the full sunlight of success and responsibility upon him.

On 16 June the Warwick Advertiser in a 4½ column obituary, paid him this tribute:-

> "His obvious integrity, his respect for the opinions of others, his adherence without bigotry to the principles in which he believed, his modesty and his unfailing courtesy, all allied to a shrewd brain, inspired both confidence and affection."

The Warwick and Warwickshire of 1962 was very much his creation. He might well have found it psychologically difficult to change its nature by amalgamation with Rugby, but it is quite certain that without Ansell's work the Society would not have been ready for that amalgamation and the consequent expansion which was to follow under his pupil, colleague and friend, Herbert Walden.

What sort of Society had Moffat, Purser and Ansell created? The financial and membership statistics show steady if undramatic progress. In historical perspective it is clear that the 1950s were a watershed between the local, limited, manuscript entry building society of the first 100 years and the type of Society which amalgamated with Rugby in 1967. Between 1950 and 1960 the Society's assets had grown from £1m to £2.5m; the total number of accounts had risen from 5500 to 7800 and the number of mortgages from 1050 to 2560. The number of new mortgages per year doubled and the cash turnover trebled. The remainder of this chapter sets these developments in chronological order from 1903-62.

In 1903 when Moffat assumed office as Secretary the Society had the trust and confidence of Warwick people: had it been otherwise the well known legal firm of Heath and Blenkinsop would not have placed a considerable sum on deposit in September 1903. Mr H. G.

Godfrey Payton of the well known Warwick firm of estate managers was a director of the Society. There was an active demand for mortgage money and in January 1904 the Directors borrowed a further £1,000 from Campbell, Brown and Ledbrook at 4%. The hall and staircase of 24 Jury Street was painted and whitewashed at a cost of £6. 18. 6. The Society was providing mortgages for property in Emscote Road and Humphris Street, Warwick, White Street and Shrubland Street, Leamington, and Radford Semele, but found a request for £1,100 to buy a shop and premises in Bridlington beyond the financial and territorial experience of the Directors. The Auditors fee had now risen to £25, the Annual Meeting was still held in the Court House and the Mayor took the chair. It was not yet regular policy to send representatives to the Annual Conference of the National Association of Building Societies and in April 1905 the Secretary was instructed to write to discover the cost. The minutes of 25 April 1905 record the N.A.B.S. reply and the Directors decision to send the Vice-Chairman (Purser) and the Secretary: tantalisingly the cost is not given. The Directors were still very chary of advertising – not for another 50 years did they take the sensible course of fixing a sum of money for a year's advertising and leaving the detail to the Secretary – and decided "not to insert an advertisement in the 'Daily Circular' at this time." Thirty years later they were equally opposed to advertising on the screen of the County Cinema in Warwick. They remained tough with advanced shareholders who fell in arrears with their subscriptions and threatened to sell a house in Charlotte Street, Leamington: the arrears were paid. In January 1906 Mr Standbridge wrote say to that he did not wish to be considered for re-election as a Director. The Board followed its normal practice in such matters, asked Standbridge to reconsider his decision, and on 12th February 1906 the Secretary reported an interview with Mr Standbridge at which he agreed to allow himself to be re-elected. He was so elected at the 52nd Annual Meeting the same day. The minutes of the Finance Committee on 8 May record "Investment of Reserve Funds. The Secretary reported that his attention had been drawn to the issue by the Warwickshire County Council of Debentures of £100 each at 3½% per annum and suggested that the Directors might prefer to invest £500 of the Reserve Fund in these debentures instead of Consols." The Directors decided accordingly: the Public Sector Borrowing Requirement was not even a twinkle in an economist's eye. Of such were the routine financial activities of the Society during the first three years of Moffat's Secretaryship and they may be taken as typical of the minutiae of the half century to follow. The remaining major concerns of that half century were the establishment of the Society as owner-occupier of its own headquarters, the development of branch offices, and the adjustment of policy and activity to two world wars and the housing policies of central and local government.

The Directors and Miss Sallaway had become sparring partners early in Moffat's time. In May 1919 discussions were resumed and she offered to sell 24, 26 Jury Street for £1,500. The Directors replied with a bid of £1,250 in view of the age of the property. (In January 1961 the value of 24 Jury Street alone was put at £10,250.) Finally on 30 July 1919 Miss Sallaway sold 24 Jury Street to the Society for £850 at the same time selling 26 Jury Street to E. D. Shepherd for £550. The Jury Street offices were by no means adequate for all Warwick and Warwickshire needs for in April 1921 "a Strong Room had been constructed in Pageant House with a separate part for the Building Society." Mr Trepess reported it fire proof; there could not be any collapse in case of fire. On 1 August 1924 the floor of the Board Room at 24 Jury Street showed signs of dry rot and the Secretary was instructed to confer with Mr G. J. Dean, the well known Warwick builder. On 27 August 1925 office alterations by Mr Dean were authorised at a cost of £51. 10. 0.

In December of the same year £9. 5. 0. was paid for linoleum for the alterations. In November 1933 the Finance Committee noted a letter from the Town Clerk of Warwick to say that 24 Jury Street, came "within the town planning scheme." On 15 March 1934 the Directors resolved to buy No. 26 Jury Street from Mr Shepherd for £900 inclusive of fixtures and fittings. By 10 May the purchase was complete and a sub-committee was appointed to decide how the additional space should be used. For the first time the Society was able to spread beyond the offices in 24 Jury Street which was also the Secretary's home.

On 28 September the Building Sub-Committee inspected Nos. 24 and 26 Jury Street and instructed the Secretary to see the Solicitor and Mr Trepess. Trepess attended a meeting on 22 November and produced the plans for the alterations, together with an estimate of cost. The Secretary reported his interview with the Solicitor, but after discussion the matter was deferred. On 14 December 1934 however the Sub-Committee approved its recommendations to the

Directors: these included a proposal to let the upstairs of No. 26 and part of No. 24 to the Society's solicitors, Messrs. Campbell, Brown and Ledbrook. A week later the Directors approved the scheme. There was some concern expressed by Mr H. M. Blenkinsop that the proposals would infringe the ancient lights of 28 Jury Street but this was overcome. On 25 April 1935 the Directors opened five tenders for the work and accepted the lowest for £2,013. 13. 10d. In December 1935 the Rating Authority suggested rateable values of £80 for the Building Society, £70 for Campbell, Brown and Ledbrook, and £39 for the private house. After the usual haggling, figures were agreed and it was also agreed that the Secretary would pay £40 p.a. for his private accommodation. The Directors could still not bring themselves to build him a garage, which was in fact not provided until 17 years later. They had however now successfully become owner occupiers of 24 and 26 Jury Street and provided the Society with better office facilities. The next large scale development of the headquarters in Warwick came in the 1960s and is outside the scope of this chapter.

The development or establishment of agencies and branches outside Warwick was an important feature of the first hundred years of the Warwick and Warwickshire. In February 1960, when the routine arrangements of the Society still included Subscription Meetings, the Joint Secretaries reported to the Directors as follows:

"Private and Confidential
For use of the Directors of the Warwick Building Society only

As arranged, we give hereunder a report on the position at the present time with regard to Subscription Meetings and some suggestions with regard to possible future policy.

The position at present is as follows:-

Town	*Meeting Room*	*Time of Meeting*	*1959 subscriptions received*	
			Advanced	*Investments*
Leamington Spa	G.F.S.House 3 Church Street	1st & 3rd Tuesday in month 2 to 4 p.m.	£7,100	£9,400

Stratford-on-Avon	Gladstone Chambers 55 Ely Street	1st & 3rd Thursday in month 2 to 3.30 p.m.	£10,820	£8,725
Banbury	Oddfellows Offices Bridge Street	3rd Wednesday in month 2 to 3 p.m.	£7,175	£1,650
Kenilworth	Abbey Hill Schoolroom Abbey Hill	1st Wednesday in month 2 to 3 p.m.	£1,620	£2,925

At Leamington, Banbury and Kenilworth we hire the rooms just for the period required but at Stratford-on-Avon we rent the room and sub-let when we are not using it. The rent of most rooms has remained unchanged for many years and the total annual cost is less than £50.

All the rooms are uninspiring and the facilities are, in these days, inadequate. At Kenilworth and Leamington a screen divides the table at which we work from the waiting members, at Stratford members wait in a passage while at Banbury they either wait on the doorstep or in the street, or in the small room in which we work and of course hear other people's business.

The premises afford no opportunity for advertising – in fact they would appear to be unfavourable advertisements.

Our security of tenure is almost non-existent and we could be faced with the problem of finding other accommodation at very short notice.

Looking back over the past 10 years we find that the Society's assets have grown from 1 million pounds to over 2½ million pounds; the total number of accounts has risen from 5,500 to 7,800 and the number of mortgages from 1070 to 2560. The number of new mortgages per year doubled and the cash turnover has trebled. If an attempt is made to look to the future, the next ten years must hold promise of increased activity to a similar or even greater degree and now would seem to be an opportune moment to consider future development. The subscription meetings form an excellent foundation for future activities.

We therefore recommend that the Directors consider, as a long term policy, the acquisition of premises in good positions in Stratford-on-Avon, Kenilworth and Banbury. The whole or part of the ground floor of such premises to be used as subscription meeting accommodation and the remainder of the property to be let as office or living accommodation. The exterior of the property could be used to advertise the Society and the windows may provide window display facilities. The interior would be designed to offer better facilities for members.

We emphasise that these proposals are intended to be considered as long term and we suggest that our Surveyors in the towns mentioned be asked to keep us advised as suitable properties become available in the future.

H. J. ANSELL
H. R. WALDEN,
Joint Secretaries.

11th February 1960.

Resolved:- That the Report be approved in principle."

The Leamington and Stratford Subscription Meetings had been an early development and by the time of Moffat's appointment were well established. We have seen that on the occasion of the Jubilee Dinner in 1904 the Stratford Directors were paid 10/- for "a conveyance from Stratford." On 25 April 1870 the Directors had decided to hold Subscription Meetings in Leamington at Mr Colley's Temperance Hall. They would take place "on a Tuesday evening following the Monday meeting at Warwick as adjourned meetings at the same hours as held in Warwick." We have already seen that in March 1876 a branch in Stratford was under consideration and a sub-committee of Directors had met "Stratford gentlemen" who would become shareholders if meetings were to take place there. By 1877 a separate Surveyor for Stratford, Mr T. T. Allen, had been appointed. In June 1879 he "met with an accident while journeying to Blockley to survey the property belonging to Mr and Mrs Rouse and had broken his thigh in attempting to get into a trap and proposed that he be granted a gratuity of £5. 5. 0. towards the loss and expenses." At their very next meeting on 23 June 1879 the Directors decided to open a branch at Kenilworth and "read some letters from Mr C. W. Clarke on the subject." On 16 February 1880 it was decided that Leamington members of the Board, "coming from Leamington, would be allowed 4/6 whenever they attend Board Meetings to cover the expenses of cab hire." On 20 December of the same year it was decided to pay the railway expenses of all Directors attending meetings from Stratford.

Secretary Moffat's first problem with regard to activity outside Warwick was a boundary dispute between the Surveyors. This was settled by the Finance Committee on July 6th 1907:- "The Stratford-upon-Avon Surveyor shall report on properties in Stratford, and also any place within two miles radius of the town, and that the Warwick Surveyor shall report on all other properties offered as security to the Society." Then in 1908 the Directors considered the possibility of opening a branch in Henley-in-Arden: there is no record of a decision to proceed. By 1911 the Directors had decided to seek business in Banbury. J. C. Purser, E. T. Kennard and the Secretary attended a meeting on 30 March 1911 "to introduce the Society to the town," and presented their report on 3 April. The Secretary was instructed to "enquire of other building societies their method of working branch offices" and by 8 April – such was the speed of His Majesty's mails – produced replies from Bristol, West of England and South Wales; Cheltenham and Gloucestershire Permanent Mutual; Burnley Building Society; Bradford Third Equitable and Benefit; and Halifax Permanent and Benefit.

The Directors decided that no Agent should be appointed to carry on the Society's business in Banbury "but that the Secretary and one Director attend a Subscription Meeting in the town once a month on a Wednesday evening." Arrangements were made with Mr A. E. Allen to use his office at 31A Bridge Street and the first meeting was arranged for May 3rd at 6.00 p.m. The Directors decided to ballot for "the office of Chairman at Banbury." In November 1913 the Secretary was authorised to advertise in Morland's Banbury Directory. In December 1916 the Society's tenancy of a room at the Albert Hall, Kenilworth Road, Leamington was ended and the Society hired a room at No. 39 Parade for subscription meetings at a rent of 2/6 per meeting. In November 1919 there occurred another of those personal misfortunes which seem to have happened to Directors or Surveyors from time to time. Mr Purser reported on a visit that he and Mr Alliban had made to the Mayor and Town Clerk of Banbury to gain their help in "appointing a Director to the Building Society to represent Banbury." They had left the matter in the hands of His Worship and the Clerk. The report ends:- "It is to be regretted that after our interview Mr Alliban unfortunately met with an accident by falling down a stone staircase and badly cutting his head. He has however made a remarkable recovery." The Surveyor had received five guineas for a broken thigh but the Directors did not price a badly cut head. By 1920, as we have seen in Secretary Ansell's conditions of service, the Secretary was attending fortnightly Subscription Meetings in Warwick, Leamington and Stratford and monthly meetings in Kenilworth and Banbury. In November 1920 the Notice Board in Kenilworth could not be read, the name plate at Warwick needed attention, and enquiries were being made about sites for notice boards in Stratford, Banbury and Leamington. This was the branch or subscription system which had been created during the first 70 years of the Warwick and Warwickshire, was maintained for the next 40 years, and was the subject of the unfavourable report from the Joint Secretaries to the Directors on 11 February 1960. From that report sprang the establishment of branches and the amalgamations which between 1960 and 1980 have created a network throughout the West Midland area and amply justified the title "Heart of England."

Finally, what of the effect on the Society of two world wars and of Government housing policy? We have seen in Chapter 2 that building societies pre-1914 were more involved in financing the building of houses to let than with owner occupation but that from 1920 to the present day the emphasis has been on owner occupation. The Warwick and Warwickshire shared that experience. The most startling fact about the outbreak of war on 4 August 1914 was that, as far as the minutes of Directors' Meetings are concerned, it did not happen. There is nothing minuted before August 1914 to suggest that the Board envisaged the possibility of war. The Directors actually held a routine meeting on the day war broke out, but the event is not recorded in their minutes. On 12 September they told the Banbury Rural District Council, who were soliciting investments, that "at the present time the Society has no funds available for investment," but on 12 October they were sufficiently flush to grant the Woolpack Hotel Co. Ltd., a mortgage of £500 to buy 17 Market Place, Warwick. This decision had to be reversed in November, on the Solicitor's advice, because the Woolpack was a limited liability company. The war perhaps first reaches the minute book on 19 December 1914 when the Directors expressed their sympathy to one of their members, Mr R. U. Ivens, "in the unexpected loss of his son." The minute of 18 January 1915 leaves no doubt – "that the Board desires to express its sympathy with Mr B. Campbell and his family in the bereavement they have recently sustained by the loss of his son, killed in action." Mr Campbell was of course Solicitor to the Society. The B.S.A. Conference in 1915 became one day (June 4th) non-residential because of the war, and Purser and the Secretary attended as usual. The Finance Committee considered selling their Consols in June 1915, and investing in 4½% War Loan, but were advised that Consols "were practically unsaleable at the present time." In July 1915 the Society increased its interest rate to 5% – perhaps to compete with War Loan and start that competition with National Savings which still exists today. The National Savings Movement was founded in 1916 and over the years has been a formidable rival to the building societies when funds are in short supply. In October 1915 the Consols were sold for £1410. 9. 4.: their nominal value on 31 December 1914 had been £2014. 19. 1d. The proceeds of the sale were invested in War Loan. In February 1916, after almost twelve months of discussion, the Directors decided "that all properties in mortgage to the Society be insured under the Government Scheme against any loss by aircraft damage, if not already covered, and that the premiums be charged to the borrowers accounts."

Economy was even more necessary in war time and on 10 May 1917 the Secretary was told that "because of the cost of fares he should attend Banbury meetings on his own in the future except that at quarterly meetings he would take a Director with him." In August 1918 the Secretary was medically examined by the National Service Medical Board and placed in Grade 2 and B2. The Chairman was asked to support an application for Mr Moffat's exemption from military service; six months' exemption was granted. The final reference to the Great War in the minutes reads: "Owing to the large balance to the credit of the Society's Account at Lloyd's Bank – £5,000 instead of £4,000 was invested in the 5% War Bonds during Warwick Gun Week."

In 1939 the record suggests rather more anticipation of the holocaust. On 1 September the Finance Committee minuted:- "Air raid precautions. The question of the protection of the Society's records against war damage was considered: resolved that the strong room be sandbagged and strengthened and divided, the deeds placed in one half and certain office records placed in the other half and the remainder of the office records kept in the Whitfield safe; also that dark blinds be fitted to the office windows." On 7 September the

Directors reacted to war time black-out by cancelling all evening subscription meetings. They discontinued the Warwick Meetings – presumably subscribers could get to 24 Jury Street in office hours – and moved the Leamington, Stratford, Banbury and Kenilworth meetings to the afternoon. In July 1940 the Secretary submitted a copy of "The Defence (Building Societies) Regulations 1940". At the same meeting it was decided the £5,000 should be invested in the Post Office Savings Bank. Throughout the six years of war there is a steady record of investment in various kinds of war loans – Heart of England Spitfire Fund, Banbury Weapons Week, Kenilworth Warships Week, Kenilworth, Warwick and Banbury Wings for Victory Weeks, Salute the Soldier Campaign, and finally in October 1945 the Thanksgiving Weeks. From September 1940 permission to erect air raid shelters was being given to those with property on mortgage to the Society. There are reports of mortgaged property damaged by air raid – in November 1940 (the Baedeker raids) and June 1941. Economy was in the air again:- "30 April 1942. Important. Special Notice. The Directors have decided in order to conserve paper and thereby help the war effort that for the time being quarterly reminder notices will not be sent to members." The Secretary reported generally "on his action as to salvage of old papers in the Society's possession" – not too much to the detriment of this history one hopes. In July 1942 it was more than paper that was asked. The minutes of a meeting on 24 July read:- "Home Guard. A letter was submitted from the Commander, Warwickshire Zone, Home Guard, asking whether certain accommodation at 24/26 Jury Street could be made available to him in the event of mustering taking place if invasion had commenced or was imminent. Resolved that the Chairman and Vice-Chairman meet the Zone Commander and report on the matter." No further report appears in the minutes; perhaps it all became Top Secret. At the same meeting a letter was received from the Building Societies Association suggesting that Societies should not transact mortgage business unless the standard of liquidity was not less than 10% of the total assets. Finally, the relief which greeted the end of war in Europe was evident in the minute of 24 May 1945. "Resolved that Messrs. J. Dean and Son be requested to remove the sandbags on the roof of the strong room." As far as the 1939-45 war went, the directors minutes started with the strong room and ended with it and that seems as it should be in a property owning democracy.

A general study of the Society's records during the two world wars shows one major difference between them. Between 1914 and 1918 it does not seem that mortgage business declined anything like so markedly as between 1939 and 1945. The decline during the first war would of course have been from a lower base than that during the second. But by the Spring of 1940 mortgage business had almost completely dried up. Not until the Directors Meeting on 21 June 1945 is a long list of applications for advances once again recorded. During both wars the Society co-operated with the generally enlightened Building Society Movement attitude that Directors should be patient with those for whom war time conditions made full regular repayments difficult. In August 1917 the Directors discussed "The Housing Question" – more familiarly known as homes fit for heroes – and wished to co-operate with any local committee appointed for the matter. In February 1919, encouraged by the Building Societies Association, they wrote to local M.P.s to call attention to "the large amount of liquid assets the Building Societies had available at the present time for financing the purchase of houses for the occupation of purchasers, as soon as building starts again." As we have seen in Chapter 2, the Government of the day was not very forthcoming, but the Warwick and Warwickshire, like the other societies, was soon busy helping those who had the initiative and the cash to buy their own houses. Those who lacked them turned perforce to the Warwick Borough Council where no doubt J. C. Purser played a prominent part in housing matters, as must H. J. Ansell have done after the 39-45 War. In 1946 the Attlee Government had a clear policy of encouraging local authorities to build council houses to let, and of restraining private building by a licensing system. In February 1946 the Directors nominated Mr A. B. Blower as a member of the Leamington Consultative Committee which would advise the Borough Council Housing Committee. They do not seem to have got nearer than that to the council house scene, but they did not need to do so. Mortgage demand was buoyant; liquid funds accumulated during the six years of war could now be released to increase the number of mortgages approved – on 28 January 1947 for example the sale of £35,000 of 3% Savings Bonds was authorised by the Finance Committee.

Mr Ansell, who was Mayor of Warwick for three war time years as well as Secretary of the Warwick and Warwickshire, must have reached the autumn of 1945 with his full share of that tremendous sense of relief shared by all who lived through those years. For Moffat and Purser of course 1914-18 had been the Great War: Ansell served in 1914-18 and laboured professionally and as a civic leader in 1939-45. But Moffat, Purser, Ansell and their contemporaries gave their professional energies to ensuring that men should have the opportunity to be well housed in buildings and on land which they could be proud to call their own. They would have found no difficulty of any kind in saying amen when people prayed:- "O Lord God, our Father, guide, we beseech Thee, all those who bear authority in our towns and cities, that there may be noble streets and open ways therein, that all the skill and beauty of art and craft may be drawn into the service of the common people, for the glory and the delight of men. Give them inspiration and courage, O Lord, to sweep away all mean streets and unworthy habitations, that men and women may be finely bred and taught and trained, and that Thy kingdom may come on earth."

CHAPTER FIVE

The Warwick & Warwickshire Benefit Building Society: 1962-1967

THE WARWICK AND Warwickshire Benefit Building Society – a title he had thought too long and tongue tying – survived Herbert Ansell by only five years and three months. Thanks to Ansell's foresight there was immediate continuity of top management. His pupil, friend and Joint Secretary, Herbert Walden, was appointed Chief Executive and a Director on 28 June 1962. The Directors used the opportunity to rationalise and simplify the leadership structure. The main feature of these revised arrangements was to give the Chief Executive increased authority to take decisions on expenditure within the policy agreed by the Directors. The other principal features of what proved to be five dynamic final years were the alterations to head office, the opening of branch offices, a complete alteration of the rules, and the amalgamation with Rugby.

The movement from subscription meetings to branch offices began in Banbury. At a meeting of Directors on 28 April 1960 the Joint Secretaries reported that the previous Banbury subscription meeting had had to be cancelled as the normal room had not been made available to the Society. The owners had subsequently given notice to terminate the hire of the room to the Society for such meetings. It was also reported that a suitable property on the corner of George Street and Broad Street could be bought for £4,100. The Directors resolved that "authority be given for the purchase at the price mentioned." Subscription Meetings were a well tried method of going to the public to collect their money instead of waiting for them to approach the Society. The infant Warwick and Warwickshire developed as it did because of them and throughout the nineteenth century most building societies held such meetings. But the joint Secretaries had already reported unfavourably on 11 February 1960 and the time for change was overdue. Subscription Meetings must have been both fascinating and irritating for Ansell and Walden. On the day of the fortnightly Leamington meeting for example they had to get themselves and all their books and documentation to the Urquhart Hall which was on hire to the Society at that time. The queue would form well before opening time and at the busiest period would stretch from the hall, down the main staircase and into the street. For many of those in the queue this was a regular occasion and there is no doubt that Herbert Ansell and Herbert Walden were doing the job of social workers as well as building society officers. The routine of the Warwick Subscription Meetings became so dear to one customer that when the new banking hall was opened and the meetings discontinued she still attended on her regular day and insisted on entering and leaving the building as she had always done, despite changes which produced a much simpler alternative used by all clients. Money could be invested at a subscription meeting; it could not of course be withdrawn. Notice of withdrawal could be given and a cheque would be sent later, by post. Those were the days when even the Hatton Garden jewellers still thought that the safest way to deliver their goods was by registered post.

By 1960 the British public was outgrowing its patient war-time addiction to queuing and there is no doubt that branch offices were becoming essential if Societies were to attract the big money they needed. The customer could then go in his own time, as part of a shopping trip perhaps, with a reasonable expectation that he would not have to wait too long. On 27 October 1960 the Directors accepted a tender from Messrs. Hinkins and Frewin for improvement and repairs to Nos. 52/54 Broad Street, Banbury. In January 1961 the Finance Committee decided that the new Banbury branch would be formally opened on 11 April. They also decided that the member of staff living at Banbury should have his travelling expenses paid when attending at Warwick. On 9 March 1961 the Directors invited the President to chair the luncheon to be held at the White Lion Hotel after the official opening of the new branch. The photographs, press cuttings, menu and toast list all suggest a happy and successful occasion. One especially delightful photograph shows a customer of no more than a year old sitting on the counter of the new branch holding a pass book, and supported by the beaming President, H. J. Ansell. One hundred and eight years after its foundation the Warwick and Warwickshire had opened its first branch. Eighteen years later the Heart of England Building Society has thirty branches.

The only other branch office to be opened before amalgamation with Rugby was in Stratford-upon-Avon. On 11 May 1961 the Directors decided to buy No. 53 Henley Street, Stratford for £17,750 exclusive of furniture and fittings. By 25 January 1962 planning and bye-law permission had been granted for the necessary development. Arrangements proceeded smoothly. Sir Denys Lowson, President of the Chartered Institute of Secretaries and High Steward of Stratford, accepted the Directors' invitation to perform the opening ceremony on June 20th and a lunch was arranged at the Red Horse Hotel. Tragically, President Ansell died less than a fortnight before an opening ceremony which would have given him great pleasure.

Apart from the radical revision of the rules and the rationalisation of the management structure, the other major development of these five years was in Jury Street, Warwick. As we have seen, top management was strengthened and the General Manager given more authority in the changes resulting from Ansell's death. The new draft rules were submitted to a Special General Meeting of shareholders held at the Court House, Warwick on 28 March 1963, at the conclusion of the Annual Meeting. After answering questions R. S. Squires, the Chairman, announced that in accordance with the Building Societies Act the motion must be passed as a special resolution. Mr E. J. Nettle (Auditor) and Mr B. D. Hill, (Solicitor) were appointed scrutineers and the motion was carried by 28 votes to nil. There is no doubt that the decision of the 28 shareholders was right, but it remains an alarming feature of our political, industrial, commercial and financial scene that most members or shareholders prefer to avoid annual meetings, and the risk of office, and leave important decisions to the committed few.

On 13 September 1962 the Directors received "a plan for alterations to the Head Office premises incorporating Nos. 22, 24 and 26 Jury Street." They approved the outline plan "subject to the modifications suggested" and asked the Architect to meet them on September 27th to discuss the front elevation treatment of No. 22. This is one of the fine old Warwick houses which escaped the fire of 1694. The Directors and their Architect achieved a harmonious restoration of No. 22 and of the whole of their new headquarters.

Internally the building is well suited to its financial and administrative tasks, even if you do "pant for cooling streams" by the time you reach the top step of the top flight of stairs. Externally it stirs the imagination and enhances the appearance of Jury Street. It is a visual reminder of the history of the heartland of England. The Directors decision, taken on 27 September 1962, that the external beams of 22 Jury Street should be exposed on both the first and second floors was the key decision. Herbert Walden's contribution of visual and verbal imagery, in addition to his exceptional personal and administrative qualities, had begun to stamp itself on the future 'Heart of England'. When on January 24th 1963 the Finance Committee decided to allow the General Manager an annual sum of £800 for advertising, thereby ending the system whereby the Directors exercised control over each item, they released an imagination which has served the Society's image well.

Meanwhile the adaptation of 22, 24 and 26 Jury Street moved from the field of policy decision to matters of detail. On 12 March 1964 a Building Committee was formed comprising the Chairman (R. S. Squires), H. B. Duggins, B. A. Tandy, and the Chief Executive (H. R. Walden). These four directors turned the plans into reality. There was considerable argument about the proposed plan for the front entrance and the architect was asked to draw fresh plans. Consideration of "an external clock" was wisely deferred until the building was completed – and then properly abandoned. On 19th October the four members of the Building Committee turned their attention to door fittings, floor coverings and internal decorations and took the imaginative decision "that a glass panel be inserted in the Assistant Secretary's Office to reveal a portion of the original lath and plaster work of the old building."

A new Document Store was considered and arrangements made: the source material of this history is now stored and guarded there. The Directors themselves did not escape inconvenience for on 30 March 1965 "it was reported that it would not be possible to remove the machines from the Board Room until the present temporary accommodation occupied by the office was available. . ." As the completion date, 30 June 1965, drew near the Building Committee became increasingly occupied with matters of detail and in early May the General Manager reported that progress was satisfactory. It seemed safe to assume completion by the middle of July at latest and arrangements were made for an official opening on 29 July

PLATE 7

Presentation to H. J. Ansell to commemorate 40 years service to Warwick and Warwickshire. Left to right:- Mrs Kennard, P. E. Kennard *(Chairman)*, H. J. Ansell, Dr. Barbara Ansell *(daughter)*, H. R. Walden, Mrs Walden.

PLATE 8
Stratford-upon-Avon branch, first opened by Warwick and Warwickshire in 1962.

1965, at 11 a.m. Mr John Richardson, Chairman of the Midland Association of Building Societies – and by chance General Manager and Secretary of the Walsall Mutual Building Society with which the Rugby and Warwick was later to amalgamate – formally opened the new headquarters in the presence of a distinguished local company. The contemporary photograph of the banking hall, showing a complete absence of protective screens, is a reminder that as recently as 1965 banks and building societies did not think it necessary to put a physical screen between their officers and the general public. The contrast between the screenless banking hall of 1965 and the screened banking hall of today is a visual socio-criminal history of the past 15 years. The key and the lock remain one of the basic comments on human nature.

The Warwick and Warwickshire was 112 years old when the new headquarters was opened; there remained only two years of separate existence. Their President, Mr P. E. Kennard, who had succeeded Herbert Ansell, celebrated his golden wedding in 1963 and he and his wife were presented with a cut glass vase. Financially the Warwick and Warwickshire was at full stretch. On 8 July 1965 the Directors heard from the General Manager that there was an improvement in the net inflow of funds and agreed "(a) that the existing waiting list of mortgage applications totalling approximately £93,000 be dealt with in the immediate future. (b) that monthly quota figures, excluding the above applications, be increased to £60,000 and that in addition eleven applications per month should be accepted in connection with the sale of houses on certain local estates which were in process of development." In 1966 it was necessary to switch the Annual Meeting from the Court House to Head Office because of the General Election: this was only the second time in the Society's history that the A.G.M. had not been held in the Court House. By 1966 preliminary discussions had begun "regarding a possible merger with the Rugby Building Society." The first reference in the minutes of a Directors' Meeting is in March 1967 when Mr B. A. Tandy suggested that "a photograph of members of the Board should be taken prior to the proposed union with the Rugby Building Society." He also successfully proposed that the final Annual Meeting on 30 March 1967 should be taped "as long as no objection is raised at the meeting." At a Directors Meeting on 13 April 1967 Mr R. S. Squires was re-elected Chairman and Mr L. J. Twigger Vice-Chairman. The General Manager reported the current position with regard to the union with Rugby "and that the next formal stage, the completion of the Instrument of Union, had been reached." The necessary resolution to ensure progress were passed, and a Special General Meeting arranged for 1 June 1967. At that meeting the proposal in favour of the merger of the two Societies was passed by 73 votes to nil. The resolution now required the approval of the Chief Registrar, and if that approval were given the union would become effective on 30 September 1967. On 31 August 1967 the Directors formally resolved "that as the meeting of the Directors held on 28 September 1967 would be the last meeting of the existing Board before the union with the Rugby Building Society arrangements be made by the General Manager for a dinner party for Members of the Board and the Assistant Secretary and that an invitation be extended to the President, Mr P. E. Kennard, to attend". The final entry in the minute book, dated 28 September reads:- "Chairman's concluding remarks . . . he was convinced that the decision was a very wise one, linking the Society with a local neighbour of comparable size and outlook. . . . The Chairman . . . expressed to all his colleagues his sincere thanks for their support, courtesy and encouragement and in particular mentioned the assistance he had always received from the General Manager (Mr H. R. Walden) who he was sure would prove to be a great asset to the United Society. . . . The Board adjourned to an informal dinner party – each of the members present added their contribution in short reminiscent speeches."

The pioneers of 1853/54, Thomas Davis, William Smith, Henry and Reuben Bromwich, would surely have been well content. Rugby was not quite Warwick to them, but Rugby was Warwickshire and – most certainly – Heart of England. The men who ran the middle laps in this hundred years race, Sallaway, Moffat and Purser, would have rejoiced to see their team strengthened by good Rugby brain and financial skill. Ansell of course was the team member whose long, strong run for home set up Herbert Walden to finish the course in such style and assurance. It was great loss that he did not live to make his "informal, reminiscent speech" on September 28th. One hopes that a certain former Headmaster of Rugby and Archbishop of Canterbury would have blessed these good and faithful servants. They had neither hidden their talents nor buried them. The Society which received its first £17. 1. 8 on 4 March 1854 had assets of £6,410,025 at the time of amalgamation. More important, thousands of people had homes which otherwise might have been denied them, and thereby a stake in the country.

RUGBY BENEFIT BUILDING SOCIETY: 1866-1967

PRESIDENTS

1866-1902	Dr. Frederick Temple (His Grace The Lord Archbishop of Canterbury)
1903-1920	C. J. B. Cooke, J.P.
1920-1922	S. J. Dicksee
1923-1937	W. W. Vaughan, M.V.O., M.A.
1938-1943	Dr. William Temple (His Grace The Lord Archbishop of Canterbury)
1943-1955	P. H. B. Lyon, M.C., M.A.
1956-1967	Major-General Sir Hubert Rance, G.C.M.G., C.B.E., C.B.,

CHAIRMEN

1866	Rev. F. Temple. D.D.
1866-1874	W. I. Tait
1874-1878	P. Simpson
1878-1891	J. Alcott
1891-1914	H. Miller
1914-1925	E. F. Barnwell
1925-1926	T. W. Willard
1926-1927	W. J. Warner
1927-1945	J. W. Darby
1945-1959	C. G. Richards
1959-1962	E. R. Marshall, M.A.
1962-1965	W. C. Everard
1965-1967	L. T. Goodway

SECRETARIES

1866-1876	B. H. Fisher
1876-1877	H. Lister
1877-1889	B. H. Fisher
1889-1926	W. T. Fisher
1926	W. J. Warner
1926-1928	E. E. Howarth
1928-1950	W. J. Warner
1950-1967	George Smith

ASSETS

1866	£3,980	1906	£101,867	1946	£1,687,003
1876	£15,257	1916	£139,518	1956	£3,548,382
1886	£32,209	1926	£307,051	1966	£9,679,095
1896	£36,742	1936	£1,061,260	1967	£10,937,524

CHAPTER SIX

The Rugby Benefit Building Society: 1866-1914

ON WEDNESDAY, 21ST February, 1866 Frederick Temple had been Headmaster of Rugby School for eight years. In "Rugby since Arnold" J. B. Hope Simpson describes him as "Granite on fire". From Blundells he went up to Balliol and gained a double first in classics and mathematics. Although intellectually privileged he was materially ill-provided and his start at Oxford was only made possible by an anonymous gift of £50. In a sense he was intellectually 'self-made' and his habit of hard and independent work must have given him some sympathy with the Samuel Smiles philosophy, and with the self-help ideal of building societies, "We were not made merely to listen to a teacher", said the Headmaster of Rugby, "but to learn – there is real and special value in throwing a boy on his own resources and allowing him to learn." He was a reforming headmaster, a tremendous worker, a games player, walker and tree climber who was reputed to have climbed every elm tree on the Close at Rugby School, and very good company. When Arthur Hallam was invited to stay with him in the Lakes he wrote "Dr. Temple's company would make a coal cellar a pleasant sojourn, but Temple and the Lakes together. . . !"

The author of this history – a native of the Lake District, a Balliol historian and a former Headmaster of Warwick School – feels an immediate affinity with the Rugby Benefit Building Society through its first President, Temple. For it was Temple, future Archbishop of Canterbury, who took the chair at a public meeting in the Court Room of the Rugby Town Hall on 21st February, 1866. The purpose of the meeting was "to consider the propriety of establishing in the town a freehold Land Society." That famous propagandist for land

and building societies, Mr James Taylor, who had been defeated by the cavalry in Warwick and advocated "tea parties with the ladies", was chief speaker. He and Temple must have been a strange contrast. Temple the mathematician, classical scholar, Anglican clergyman headmaster who spoke and looked like granite on fire and Taylor of whom it was written "his language is that of the people, his illustrations homely and striking, his gesticulations graceful and his eyes and countenance betray an earnest and sincere heart". In his opening speech Temple offered three reasons why the best investment for savings was in land. His "granite" reason was that land would never drop in value. His "fire" reason was that other things were the produce of the human hand but land was from the hand of God. His third and most interesting reason was that a man can love his land but "An investor could not have any great affection for his Post Office Savings Book". Taylor began with some knock-about stuff about "doing" the lawyers, but the essence of his creed was that a Land Society "should buy the land wholesale and sell it wholesale at retail prices (cheers and laughter)".

It says much for Taylor's pleasant manner that his materialistic approach did not upset Temple, who agreed to be President and held that office for the rest of his life. Nor did "doing" the lawyers prevent T. M. Wratislaw, a prominent Rugby solicitor and son of Count Wratislaw, accepting the office of solicitor to the Society. For the meeting was entirely successful. "At the conclusion of Mr Taylor's address a working-man stood up and asked permission to bear testimony to the sterling worth of all that Mr Taylor had advanced saying that seventeen years ago another man and himself had been induced to take the way so admirably set forth by Mr Taylor, and he might say that all he possessed was owing to the kind and energetic labours of that gentleman (loud cheers).

"Dr Temple expressed his delight at having heard Mr Taylor, and said he had no idea of the wondrous amount of good that had been effected by these institutions, and that though those who moved in the upper walks of life might express approval of and sympathy with those engaged in it, the work itself could best be done by the working men themselves, and he should be happy to see such work vigorously carried out.

T. M. Wratislaw, Esq., moved "That a Freehold Land Society be established in Rugby." Mr William Gilbert seconded the resolution, and it was carried unanimously.

"The Rev. H. Angus moved the thanks of the meeting to Mr Taylor for his able address, and to Mr Gilbert for obtaining that gentleman's services. A vote of thanks to Dr. Temple for presiding terminated the meeting. Upwards of sixty names were entered of persons willing to join the Society, which we have no doubt will be found an admirable co-operator with the Building Society."

The formation of the Land Society was completed in March 1866. Its title was "Rugby Freehold Land Society, enrolled as Rugby Benefit Building Society". Here is local proof that after the Building Societies Act of 1836 Tidd Pratt, the Registrar practised what he preached: "It doesn't matter what it is: if you want the benefit of the Act you must declare it a benefit building society whether it is one or not!" With a ringing statement such as that for guidance from the Barrister with chief responsibility, it is no wonder that the Rugby Benefit Building Society acted as a Land Society for the next 60 years without knowing that it did so illegally and 'ultra vires'. There are already two short histories of the Rugby Benefit Building Society and I am grateful to the author of each for permission to draw upon them and quote from them. C. G. Richards, director and former Chairman of the Society wrote "The Rugby Building Society, 1866-1966 onwards" sub-titling it "A Review to Commemorate 100 years service to the Community". M. S. Turpin, a local and well respected solicitor and some time senior partner in T. M. Wratislaw's former firm, wrote a six page article "Rugby Benefit Building Society" which is printed in "Rugby Aspects of the Past" published by the Rugby Local History Group. It would be ridiculous to write the Rugby section of "The History of the Heart of England Building Society" without drawing on these excellent publications, and I make no apologies for doing so. I hope that I can match their authors' high standards.

One of the interesting features of the Heart of England Building Society is that the history of each constituent Society is so different. In M. S. Turpin's words "so far as the writer can discover, the town of Rugby is unique in that during the period of about 60 years from 1866 onwards a Building Society played the major part in laying out and developing estates – Although Land Societies functioned in other towns, and particularly in Birmingham, in no other town do they appear to have carried out anything like so high a proportion of the total development as in Rugby". C. G. Richards included two invaluable maps in the history of the first hundred years. The first is of "Rugby as it was at the time of the Society's inception", and the second is a "Diagrammatic map of Rugby illustrating parts of the town which owe their development to the Rugby Building Society between 1866 and 1928". They are printed side by side elsewhere in this book and a regular reference to their visual image will give body to the story. I built the history of the Warwick and Warwickshire Society on a framework of people: the framework of the Rugby Society will be land.

Rugby has always interested me as a place. The railway which has played a large part in its history during the past 125 years had already come to Rugby when the Rugby Freehold Land Society was founded. Before the railway age Temple once walked, in a day, the 48 miles from Oxford to Rugby to keep an appointment with Arnold. I first knew Rugby as a railway station on my way each term from Westmorland to Balliol. During my war-time years in the Royal Artillery, before I went overseas to the Far East, I often drank a cup of tea on Rugby Station in the middle of the night. The railway has brought many people to Rugby and much business to the Rugby Benefit Building Society. Arnold had already made Rugby School nationally and internationally famous nearly 50 years before Temple chaired the public meeting which launched the Society; I have made many journeys to Rugby to headmasters' meetings at the school or to watch Warwick play Rugby on the Close. Industry came to Rugby in the nineteenth century and the town is the home of nationally and internationally famous firms which have brought people, employment and prosperity to Rugby and Warwickshire. The Church – Anglican and Nonconformist – has made a strong contribution to the life of the town. Rugby, like Warwick, is of British and European, as well as of Warwickshire significance. The growth and expansion of Rugby is the history of the Rugby Benefit Building Society. Acting as land speculators and property developers the Directors of the Society effectively built large areas of the town. As we have seen, although enrolled by Tidd Pratt as a Building Society, Rugby was in practice a Freehold Land Society. The difference between the two is admirably described by M. S. Turpin.

"The distinction between a Land Society and a Building Society is that a Land Society buys land with the funds contributed by members of the Society and then divides the land among them. On the other hand, a Building Society advances to its borrowing members sums of money derived from subscriptions and deposits which the borrowing members themselves lay out in the purchase of land or buildings and then mortgage to the Society by way of security (per Romilly Master of the Rolls in Grimes-v-Harrison 1859 reported in 26 Beav.p.435). In other words, a Building Society does not buy land and develop it as a building estate; it only lends on mortgage of land or buildings. In the early days of Building Societies this distinction between a Building Society and a Land Society was not clearly understood and a number of Societies which intended to operate as Land Societies were enrolled as Building Societies in order to obtain the legal and other advantages enjoyed by such Societies. The Building Societies Act of 1836, which controlled the activities of Building Societies up to 1874 did not – unlike the Act of 1874 by which it was superseded – expressly prohibit investment in land by a Building Society and this no doubt contributed to the failure to distinguish clearly between Land Societies and Building Societies. It was, however, decided in the year 1859 in the High Court case of Grimes-v-Harrison that it was not one of the functions of a Building Society to buy a freehold estate and divide it among its members (although it would be a function of a Land Society) and that if a Society did purchase an estate the Directors would be personally liable in damages to the members of the Society for a breach of trust. This decision of the High Court prevented Building Societies from buying land in their own names for development as building estates. A scheme was, however, devised by one James Taylor of Birmingham which in effect enabled a Building Society to operate as a Land Society without actually infringing the legal prohibition against the purchase of land for development. This scheme became quite well known and was described by a Solicitor, Mr Henry F. A. Davis, on p.75 of the Second Edition (1874) of his book "Building and Freehold Land Societies" as follows:

"If it is desired to carry on the business of a Land Society incorporated under the Act" (i.e. the Building Societies Act 1874) "the only plan will be to let the purchase be taken in the names of Directors or Trustees and then mortgage the property to the Society for the full amount of the purchase price. So then, in effect, a Building Society may with consent of all its members become a Land Society, but if any member should at any time object to such a course he will have a remedy in a Court of Equity." (i.e. by means of a Chancery action).

"It was the practice of the Directors or Trustees in whose name the land was purchased to execute a Deed at the same time as the mortgage to the Society declaring that they had purchased the land with the object of dividing it into lots and selling the lots to members of the Society and that they relinquished to the Society all profit which might accrue to them from the sale of the lots. The Society thus obtained for the benefit of its shareholders and depositors any profit made from the Development of the estate and in this important respect it was placed in the same position as a Land Society."

The new Society, born at Temple's public meeting on February 21st was registered and in business by the end of March, 1866. Funds came in rapidly and by November the Directors had completed their first purchase of land at New Bilton which they bought for £694. 9. 0d. The Society was able to provide £590 and the balance was borrowed from their solicitor, Mr T. M. Wratislaw. The Committee decided "that no lot or lots of land shall be conveyed to the allottees until at least one fourth of the purchase money has been paid by them into funds of the Society." The Directors judged correctly that the acquisition of this land was an important development in the life of Rugby. They decided to organise a soirée to celebrate it, hired the Town Hall for a fee of £3. 5. 0d, arranged to supply tea at 6d per head, and invited the ubiquitous and itinerant Mr James Taylor to attend. In January 1867 the Committee was told that an opportunity had arisen to meet the executors of the late Count Wratislaw (father of T. M. Wratislaw) to discuss the possibility of buying his land beyond the union workhouse, lying between the upper and lower Hillmorton Roads. The Executors were said to be willing to sell the seven acres at £240 per acre, accepting payment in instalments of £100 with interest at 4%. Houses built on the land should be of not less than £400 value. The latter restriction would certainly maintain standards in the town. The roads in question are now Temple Street and Caldecott Street. On 30th November the Committee decided to buy the Wratislaw land, despite a warning from their Surveyor, Mr Henry Manning, that "the town sewer will not take further drainage in the area and so it may not be possible to build houses on the land immediately. This led the committee to consider whether it might nevertheless be desirable to put the streets in at this stage". They were already involved in land development decisions very different in nature from the sort of decisions confronting the Directors of the Warwick and Warwickshire.

Within 18 months of this purchase a small piece of adjoining land came on the market lying between Lower Hillmorton Road and Clifton Road. On 7th April, 1869 the Committee decided "that considering the high price asked for the land situated on the Clifton Road and also its disadvantages being adjoining the workhouse and the cemetery and that the land on the other side of the road was sold at 1/- per yard it would not be advantageous to purchase at £1,050." Between April and September 1869 however the market turned against the Committee and they were warned that even the full £1,050 might not now be sufficient to secure the land. On September 16th, 1869 they resolved "that the Secretary call upon Dr. Temple and inform him that the Committee will be glad if he will see Mr Wratislaw and ascertain if it is possible to effect an arrangement, so that the land lately Mr Highton's could be purchased by the Society at the price first named viz. £1,050." The future Archbishop undertook the mission and was successful. How many Archbishops of Canterbury, one wonders, have negotiated a real estate deal on behalf of a building society. "Granite on fire" was a powerful ally. Meanwhile, the Third Annual Meeting was held on 15th October 1868. The Committee reported total receipts of £2,558. 15. 11d. since the formation of the Society. Count Wratislaw's land had been divided into 59 plots, 56 of which were now allotted. The three remaining were being "cultivated by the Committee", not personally one imagines, "from which they hope to realise a profit." When the Fifth Annual Meeting was held two years later, the President could not take the chair and the Chairman since foundation, Mr W. I. Tate, deputised for him. The President was no longer Headmaster of Rugby but Bishop of Exeter: the change was in the office but not the man. "At Rugby his time drew all too swiftly to an end; his last Chapel crowded with Old Rugbeians, where he preached his last sermon as Headmaster, described by Thomas Hughes, who heard it, provided a tense scene, and the last concert a few days later, when he said a less formal farewell to the School was an occasion of deep emotion." Thomas Hughes was of course the author of "Tom Brown's Schooldays". During the next 12 months the Society was busy consolidating. On 22nd December 1870 the Committee decided that the Secretary's salary should be £30 per annum. Two members of the Committee would attend fortnightly subscription meetings in rotation. In March and in May 1871 committee meetings had to be abandoned: " no meeting; quorum not being present". The Warwick Society had passed through similar difficulties. On September 6th

1871 the Committee took an important decision "to negotiate for the purchase of a piece of land situate near the footpath leading from Rugby to Newbold at a price not exceeding £250 per acre." At the Fifth Annual Meeting on September 23rd 1871 the report confirmed that the receipts for the past year were £1,413. 11. 3d. that the total profit since foundation was £802. 12. 8d. and that purchase of the third Rugby estate had been completed during the year. Only one lot from the third estate remained unallocated. Committee meetings during December 1871 were chiefly concerned with negotiations to buy land belonging to Mr Caldecott adjoining Railway Terrace. He asked £425 per acre. The Committee opened their bidding at £400 per acre, moving via £405 to £412. 10. 0d. Mr Caldecott held firm however and on 21 March 1872 the Committee bought the land – Rugby Estate Number 4 – for £425 per acre. Spring Street, Arnold Street and Charlotte Street were the result. A letter to the Committee about the same time gives an idea of the detailed responsibilities they had undertaken as land purchasers and developers. "I am obliged to ask the Trustees of the Land Society what I am to do for a drain to take away the water from my premises. I have no drain to take away even the rainfall. Will you be kind enough to lay my difficulty before the proper parties and ask them to find out wherewith to get away the surplus water and you will much oblige, Your Humble Servant George Green." At their next meeting the Committee resolved that Mr Green's letter be entered on the Minutes but that he be told their regret that according to the Conditions of Sale "they can give no assistance in the matter".

At the Committee Meeting on April 13th 1872 the Surveyor, Mr Henry Manning, reported on the development of the land adjoining Railway Terrace; the streets were to be 30 feet wide. The Committee decided to advertise this new estate (Rugby No. 4) in the two Rugby papers. In September 1872 they were negotiating for an additional piece of land adjoining Railway Terrace (Rugby 4) belonging to Mrs Horner for the sum of £1,551 "including the timber". On October 15th 1872 the Society paid £1,629. 2. 6d. towards the cost of the Railway Terrace (Rugby 4) estate, leaving the balance of £1,000 at 4% until completion. Mrs Horner's land was developed as Rugby Estate Number 5, immediately adjoining Number 4, and in the autumn of 1872 the Committee was making arrangements to grub up hedges, build roads and lay drains. The countryside with the fields, hedges and trees was being converted to urban streets to accommodate the migration of country workers to the towns. That was an easy conversion. It will be much more difficult when the silicon chip reverses the migration and we have too many urban houses and streets and too little accommodation in the villages.

As when writing the history of the Warwick and Warwickshire, I have deliberately given a fair amount of the detail of these early years. A broader brush is now essential if interest and brevity are to be maintained and the history of the Rugby Society kept to its proper share of the whole. During its first six years the Rugby Freehold Land Society had bought and developed, wholly or partially, five estates. Each was small; with one exception all are now near the centre of modern Rugby, although on the edge of 1866 Rugby. For the map of Rugby in 1866 not only shows fields, hedges and trees over large areas of modern Rugby, but trees on the Close of Rugby School where William Webb Ellis had picked up the ball and run with it in 1823. That famous run resulted in the formation of the Rugby Football Union in 1871. The trees on the Close formed an integral part of early Rugby Football and "the chance of severely imparing the physiognomy in a long tight scrum against one of the three trees was considerable". 'Hacking' had been forbidden by the first President of the Rugby Benefit Building Society but many still considered it a virtue because "it promoted running scrummages which were the beauty of the game". But the last of the three trees fell in 1891 and new and proper goal posts came into use between 1866 and 1891. Many other trees fell in and around Rugby as the Benefit Building Society provided the streets and houses so vital to the growing industrial and commercial prosperity of the town.

Large areas of modern Rugby are as they are because of decisions taken by the Committee of the Building Society. A letter from the Chairman of the Law Society to the Committee in June 1873 leaves no doubt that at that time it was the Committee which determined the direction and appearance of the roads they were building on the estates they were developing.

In July 1873 the Society paid £3,800 for 39 acres of land at Newbold-on-Avon. It was developed as 17 lots varying in size from 1 acre to 6 acres, and for committee purposes designated as Rugby No. 6. Before the land was developed the Committee charged 1/6d per week for grazing cattle on it and 6d per week for sheep. At the Annual Meeting on November 23rd 1873 the members decided that progress was so satisfactory that they could vote a bonus of 1.25%

to members and to those who had bought land between 1866 and 30th September 1873. On 6th November 1874 at a special meeting the Committee took the important decision to instruct their solicitor (T. M. Wratislaw) to negotiate with Mr Allibon for the purchase of his land north of Clifton Road at a price of £6,000. Negotiations were protracted, Mr Allibon's sisters who were co-owners held out for £220 per acre and the Society bought at that price on 6th April, 1875. The result was Oxford and Cambridge Streets, showing today the wear of one hundred years invaluable service to the citizens of Rugby. The Committee again took great care to guarantee the appearance of the new estate. Houses fronting on to Clifton Road were to cost not less than £300; £120 on the other plots. The Local Board of Health, Rugby and Urban Sanitary Authority, also intervened to ensure a good development. A letter from their Clerk in December 1875 required "that General Conditions of Sale of estate No. 6 should provide for the repair and maintenance of the streets falling upon the owners or occupiers of the lots abutting on the streets respectively in the same manner as the cost of construction to the full width and that a definitive arrangement should be made for superintending and repairing the streets and roads by providing the appointment of a Surveyor". Delicate negotiations were necessary with other local Committees and Boards. On 12th October 1876 for example it was resolved "that the Burial Board have permission to put the cemetery water into the sewer in the 15 foot back road as per plan, on condition that the Board lay the Society's drain for surface water with 9″ best socket pipes to the middle of the said back road".

At the Eleventh Annual Meeting on November 17th 1876 a new problem was reported, one which was to remain with the Society for some years. Money was coming in too fast for "5% money at call is higher than can now be generally obtained." It was decided to reduce the rate of interest to 3.75% but neither this nor the purchase in 1877 of 3½ acres of land off Clifton Road – the eastern side of South Street – had the desired effect. At the Annual Meeting in 1877 therefore the Rugby Freehold Land Society, enrolled as a Benefit Building Society, went almost involuntarily into the Building Society business. On the recommendation of their Solicitor they initiated mortgage business, offering loans on houses or land at rates varying between 4.5% and 5.25%.

The history of the Society between 1877 and 1914 is so admirably summarised by C. G. Richards in his Centenary History that I cannot do better than end the chapter with an extensive quotation and my grateful thanks for such an excellent account. Before drawing on Mr Richards' words however the following matters which he does not include may add to the human interest of the story. Between 1876 and 1878 there was keen rivalry between Mr B. H. Fisher and Mr Harry Lister for the Secretaryship of the Society. At the Annual Meeting in 1876 Fisher lost the Secretary's appointment to Lister by two votes. On December 22nd 1876 the new Secretary, Lister, reported "that on Monday the 18th at about 7.00 p.m. he had attended with an Assistant at the late Secretary's house to receive the books and property of the Society and saw Mr Fisher who handed him some books of rules and pass books but refused to deliver anything more and used language not justifiable towards him." The Committee instructed the Secretary to send a letter to Mr Fisher telling him that unless he delivered all the Society's property to the Secretary "they would take steps to compel delivery without further application to him." This had the desired effect and there then followed a petty wrangle over Mr Fisher's final account for his salary. One guinea was deducted on the grounds that "entering the names of members in the contribution book is a charge – for which he is paid in the commission and that the bill be paid, less such amount."

On June 12th 1877 the new Secretary refused to inform his predecessor "during what hours he conducted the Society's business" and told him that if he required an interview he must adopt the same course as other members. On August 7th 1877 the Secretary was told by the Committee to write to Mr Fisher "that he is instructed by the Committee to decline further correspondence on the subject". But Fisher was to triumph in the end. At the Annual Meeting in November 1877 there was again an election for the Secretaryship and Fisher won by 90 votes to 42. Moreover he then discovered discrepancies in Secretary Lister's accounts for his year of office. "I have discovered an error of 9/5d in page 7 of the allotted ledger and another of £6 in page 16 of the unallotted ledger". The affair rumbled on for 12 months, bringing about the resignation of the Auditors who were not easy to replace. At the Annual Meeting in 1878 revised accounts from the 1877 A.G.M. were submitted and approved. Fisher was again elected Secretary, an office he was to hold for many years, and this time only Mr Lister, Mr Lister's son and two others voted against him. Rugby may not have had a defalcating Secretary, as Warwick and Warwickshire did, but it certainly had two turbulent ones.

Moreover the Treasurer could be awkward. On 17th November 1878 the Committee resolved that one of their members should accompany the Treasurer to the Bank after each subscription meeting. The minutes of 17th December 1878 read:- "With reference to the refusal of Mr Waite (The Treasurer) to allow a member of the Committee to accompany him to the Bank the Solicitor be asked whether in the event of the Treasurer being robbed he, the Treasurer, would be held responsible for any loss of money and that the Chairman and Secretary call upon the Solicitor with reference to the matter". After trouble with the Secretary and trouble with the Treasurer, the Auditor could hardly be expected to keep a low profile. The minutes of the Committee Meeting on 6 March 1879 tell the story. The Auditor, Mr Gilbert, had refused the payment of £5 for his work on the previous year's accounts. The Committee decided that that was all they were going to pay him and that the cheque should be returned to him together with the Secretary's original letter "endorsed in red ink".

The other personnel matter of chief interest arose from the purchase of the Bullfield Estate in Coventry. It certainly mopped up some of the Society's surplus money when it was bought for £9,500 in June 1879, but its development brought the Committee untold worries and problems. On 16th April, 1880, the Secretary pointed out that because of the development of Bullfields he had been much overworked and his son (W. T. Fisher, who later succeeded his father as Secretary) had worked full time for the past six weeks. Moreover the Secretary was having his troubles with the Local Board of Health in Rugby and in March 1881 told the Committee – "I shall certainly not be deterred by the threat of the Board's Surveyor to 'lay me one on thick and make it hot for me whenever he gets the chance." There were endless negotiations with the L and N.W. Railway about their development in Coventry, adjoining the Bullfield. Many visits to Euston were necessary. A Parliamentary Bill was involved and the effect on the Society's investment in Coventry could have been disastrous. "Mr Wratislaw however added that we must not allow our hearts to sink within us as he had no doubt it would all come right in the end" (13.5.87). The difficulties were by no means over however. Miss Fisher, the Secretary's sister, be-

PLATE 9

The Rt. Revd. Frederick Temple, D.D., President, Rugby, 1866-1902.

PLATE 10

Temple St., Rugby, in the 1960s.

PLATE 11
The first office of the Rugby Society – small annexe on left of then Secretary's house in Clifton Rd.

PLATE 12
Interior of Sheep St., Rugby, office in 1980.

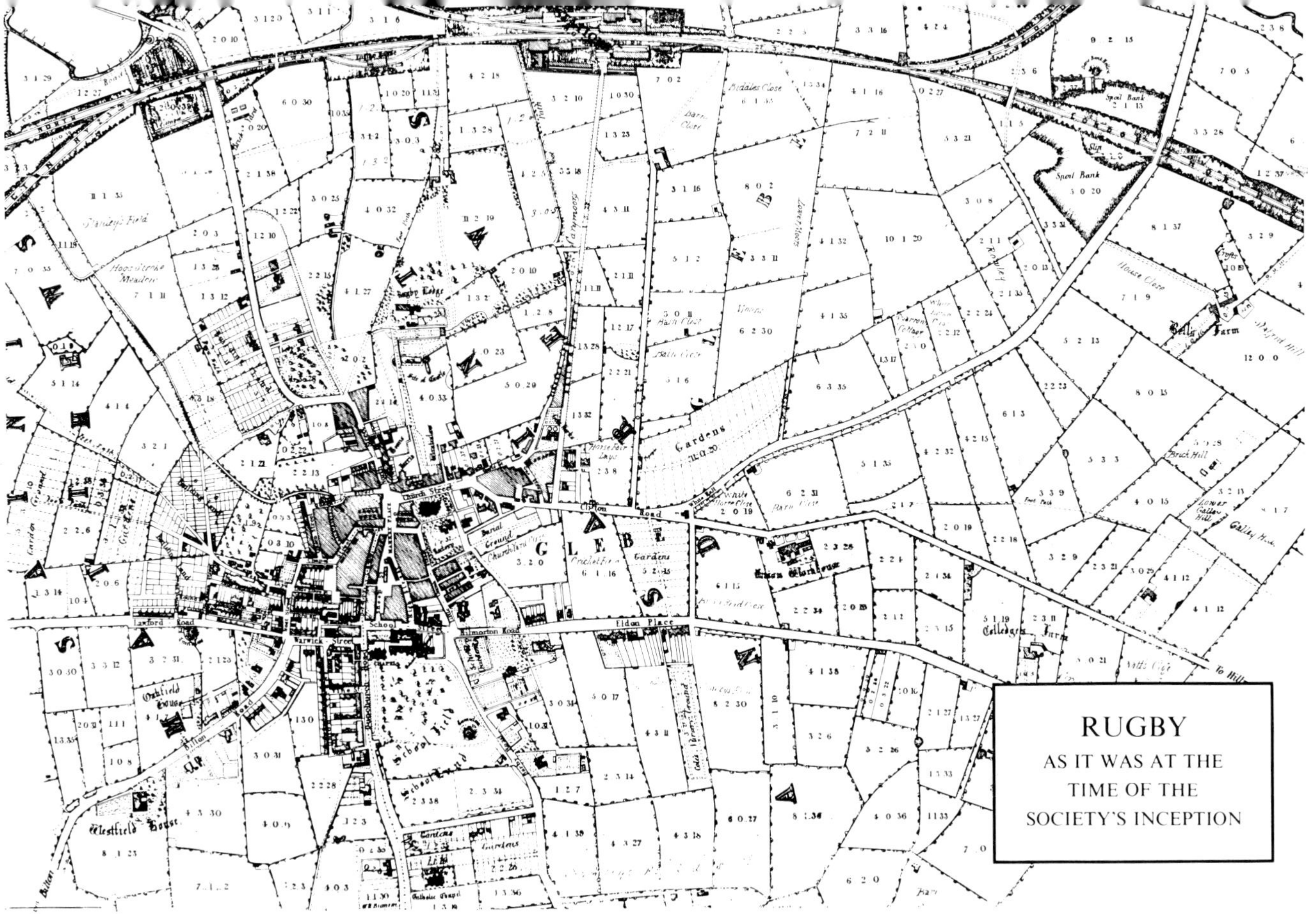

PLATE 13

Rugby in 1866 when Benefit Building Society was founded.

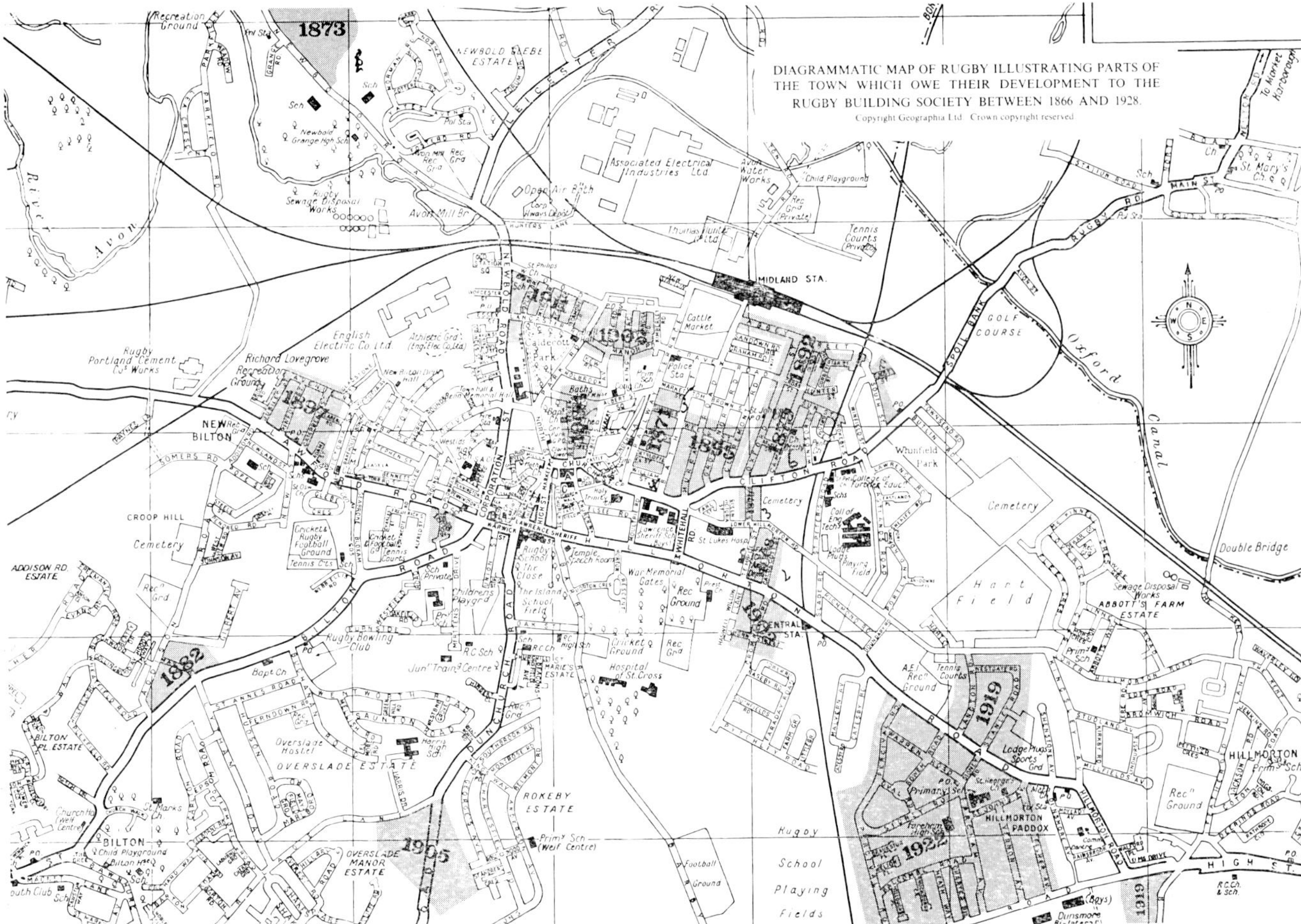

PLATE 14

Diagrammatic map showing area of Rugby developed by the Society between 1866 and 1928.

came involved as she owned Bullfield Lots 13 and 14 which were much affected by the railway development. In February 1888 the Society and Miss Fisher jointly agreed to brief Counsel and through their Solicitor chose Mr Howe whom they then exhorted and pressurised to such an extent that on 25th June 1888 he wrote:- "I should have been very glad indeed to have declined the papers and had them removed from my Chambers for from the time they have occupied they have been a serious loss and inconvenience to me by obstructing other matters." The Committee properly decided that it would be "suicidal" to retain Mr Howe further and he was succeeded by Mr B. F. Lock who happily for the Society brought the negotiations to a successful conclusion. Sadly, on 22nd March 1889, the Secretary (B. H. Fisher) died; he was succeeded by his son, W. T. Fisher, whose temporary appointment was made permanent at the next Annual Meeting. Fisher Junior conducted the important negotiations with the Rector for the Glebe Fields, reporting on 24th November 1882:- "I am very pleased to say that the Rector's bark had proved worse than his bite." The land was bought for £360 per acre and the question of a contribution to the Church school left open. So through the minute books we see the human face of the Building Society and its Committee:-

"We fought tooth and nail and finally emerged about 2 o'clock – only hunger separating the combatants".

"I fear their thoughts were not parliamentary".

"Mr Seabrook's monkey having by this time curled up his tail and gone to sleep".

(Negotiations with the Local Board; February 1893).

"The spirit of Huxter and Barter is unworthy of a Body having the direction of public interest but unfortunately it reigns supreme at Windmill Lane".

(Negotiations with Local Board; February 1894).

"The Committee inspect the Bullfields Estate and then partake of a good spread (August 1895).

"The Jubilee Committee have leave to light a bonfire on the vacant Lots in Clifton Road" (1877)."

One reads these records with pleasure and leaves them with regret but it is time to return to Mr Richards' excellent account and take the story to 1914, noting en passant that in 1883 Rugby had absorbed the former Daventry Building Society thus opening what is now the oldest branch office of Heart of England. The remainder of the chapter is an extensive quotation from "The Rugby Building Society; 1866 to 1966 onwards" by C. G. Richards.

"In 1877 some relief was found from the curiously embarrassing financial position by the purchase of 3½ acres of land off Clifton Road which ultimately became South Street and East Street. But this did not go far enough and the Committee asked their solicitor to advise on "what to do with unemployed money". On his recommendation the Committee launched out on mortgage business, offering loans at from 4½ per cent to 5¼ per cent interest on land or houses.

Enquiries for land in and around Rugby were still unproductive so the Committee turned their attention to Coventry and there in June, 1879 they purchased for £9,500, 17½ acres of land known as Bullfield, lying near Warwick Road and the railway station. At the annual meeting on November 14th Committee reported their relief in this utilising a "large sum of unemployed capital which had been for a long time a source of considerable anxiety".

An estate of about 8 acres on Bilton Hill was purchased for £1,050 in February, 1882 and within three months it had all been allotted in building plots.

Both mortgage business and membership were now increasing steadily. In March 1883 the Committee decided to make advances on mortgage for periods "not exceeding 15 years" and by the end of the year 90 new members had joined. Interest on share investments was maintained at 5 per cent, and money was coming in fast. Towards the end of 1884 many more applications were being made for mortgage loans on houses in course of erection on new estates and in November the Committee decided, "under present circumstances" not to advance so large a sum as £1,250 to one individual. Subscriptions for the year amounted to £8,687 and as no fresh land had been secured the Committee had to rely on advances on mortgage for the employment of funds. £5,162 was so advanced but the Committee had to take £152 from the reserve fund to help out. To stem the inflow of money, however, the Committee decided again to reduce the rate of interest on investments from 5 per cent to 3¾ per cent. This evidently had the desired effect for during 1884, subscriptions dropped considerably, and there was a restricted enquiry for loans, only £1,295 being advanced.

No great development occurred for some little time. The Committee had to look afresh into the financial position, and they hoped for an improvement by reducing the mortgage period to ten years.

In the annual report for 1888, they rebuked members for investing too much and not borrowing enough. They warned such depositors that they might be asked to take their money elsewhere, and £20 was fixed as the limit to be deposited in any one year.

The money situation continued to be perplexing. Many members withdrew their money, but there were fewer new borrowers. There was "a large proportion of funds unemployed" at the end of 1891. The Committee had tried to get another estate at the south end of the town but were unsuccessful and apparently they were not drawn towards any other form of investment. Realising, however, that the number of railway workers was increasing and that houses would be needed in greater numbers for newcomers, the Committee maintained its search for land and in April 1892, when the L. & N.W.R. erecting shops were opened, it was resolved to buy about 12 acres at the north end of Oxford Street and Cambridge Street and near to the railway, for £3,150. In October of the same year the Committee secured from the Rector of Rugby about 4½ acres of Glebe land for £1,518. 15s. 0d. All this was important because it enabled the continuation of Abbey Street into Mill Road (now Murray Road), thus improving traffic facilities to the railway station and also creating a way to what is now the A.E.I. works for a considerable number of people who were destined to become owner-occupiers of houses in the area. The Committee soon had both these estates laid out and in April, 1893 applications for plots were invited and allocations made, all but two reserved lots being disposed of "at a very handsome profit to the Society", the Committee reported. The profit appears to have been about £1,000, plus the value of the two reserved lots.

For some reason not recorded, the Committee failed to entertain a tentative offer of Brookside, Dunchurch Road, for £5,000, but in March, 1894, they secured land belonging to St. Matthew's Church for £885 and turned it into a pleasant residential property of 18 lots including Vicarage Road.

At the annual general meeting in December, 1894, when mortgage advances had amounted to the improved total of £3,500, and some years after the first decision to advance money on mortgage, the Committee in their report stated sorrowfully that some members had gone elsewhere "because they did not know the society advanced money upon mortgage".

The Society took a big leap forward, however, in January 1895, when a further stretch of Glebe land became available, and it was purchased for £13,500. It fronted Clifton Road at right-angles to Bath Street "from a point little below Spring Street and passing eastwards to the rear of property fronting Oxford Street".

The subsequent lay-out made provision for hundreds of artisan-type houses on roads now known as Murray Road, Grosvenor Road, Claremont Road and Wells Street, which have always been in popular demand on account of their proximity to town, railway station, and engineering works. The deal evidently impoverished the society, for despite their desire to advance money on mortgage for house purchase they had to tell an applicant for £1,000 that they were unable to advance so large an amount "in consequence of our recent purchase". The allotment of lots so increased the work of the Committee on the fortnightly subscription nights that in January, 1896 they voted themselves 5/- each per attendance instead of 2/6.

On several occasions during the preceding years, the question of the incorporation of the society had been brought to the committee's notice but no serious consideration had been given to it because incorporation was not compulsory upon a society which was in existence before the passing of the Building Societies Act 1874. Subsequent to that year, however, there were several building society failures and measures were tightened up, with the ultimate result that in 1894 another Act was passed giving the Chief Registrar sterner control over societies. It was then in the interest of the members that the society should fall into line and on July 24 1896, the Committee called a special general meeting at which it was resolved to apply for a Certificate of Incorporation.

In 1896, 30 years after the society's inception, assets amounted to £36,741. The Committee considered it "of vital importance if the society was not to fall into the background" that terms of business should be revised. Accordingly they reduced the rate of interest to borrowers to 4 per cent and extended the period of repayment to 21 years (instead of 10 or 12). In their annual report the Committee oddly described mortgage loans to owner-occupiers of houses as "a branch of the society's business".

The real industrialisation of Rugby began in the following year when Willans and Robinson's electrical engineering works (now English Electric Co. Ltd) were established on the north-west side of the town and adjacent to New Bilton. This contributed largely to an increase in the population of about 5,000 by 1900. The society rose to the occasion by acquiring land at New Bilton (embracing

Campbell Street, Pinfold Street and Clarence Road) and advancing loans on land and houses both there and on other estates at Bilton and Rugby. The demand was continuous. By the end of 1899, the society's assets had risen to £53,000.

At the turn of the century the society was faced with its greatest challenge. The British Thomson-Houston Co. Ltd. had bought 27 acres of land north of the town in 1899, and rapidly established works for the manufacture of electrical equipment. This resulted in an influx of highly skilled people, the majority needing houses of a good standard.

Within two or three years the society had made available for building purposes some of the most desirable land in the town. This included the Moat Estate and the Lodge Estate. The Moat Estate cost £16,000. It was occupied by Capt. Beatty, later the famous Admiral Beatty. The society got on with its development so quickly that when the captain's groom was caught stealing apples (on land over which he had not so long since had the freedom), it was decided to prosecute him for theft "as a warning". The apples were later divided among members of the Committee "at wholesale prices".

The Committee were justifiably pleased with their purchase of this estate "right in the heart of the town", and in their annual report spoke of it as the "most valuable which has ever come into the market in Rugby".

The truth of this is more manifest today when it is realised that, Captain Beatty's residence demolished and the moat filled in, the site is now Regent Street, Regent Place, Bank Street, Henry Street, and other important business thoroughfares. The Lodge estate adjoined it and hard bargaining went on before the society secured this too. It contained about 15 acres for which the society paid £10,500. Later an additional 16 acres of the Lodge estate were bought at £800 an acre. Notable adjustments of these two properties included the sale of a portion of the Lodge estate to the Urban District Council to give access to Caldecott Park from Manor Road; the sale to the Urban District Council of a triangular plot of the Moat Estate, at first intended as an open space but now occupied by the public baths; and the sale of two acres of the Park estate to the council for an extension of the park (now Caldecott Park).

The Committee were now watchful concerning land southwards of the town and Naseby's field off Hillmorton Road was bought in 1902 for £2,250 and divided into 80 lots which sold quickly.

A number of other potential building sites were secured from time to time the most notable being the Westfield House estate off Bilton Road for which in October, 1904, they paid £15,000. The Committee regarded this as "undoubtedly the best situated estate in the neighbourhood of Rugby", and they marked their pleasure by having a dinner at Westfield House. But they sold the estate as a whole in the following year at a handsome profit. The Committee's sagacity was not so pronounced when, in February, 1906 they rejected an offer of The Lawn, a residence with extensive grounds, now occupied by the Town Hall and its adjuncts. At an offer of £4,600 the site was refused as not "likely to prove of advantage to the Society".

The expansion of the B.T.H. (A.E.I.) works naturally gave an impetus to the demand for houses, especially of the smaller type. From 1911 onwards the society pressed on with the building of houses in pairs in the groves and other sites adjoining Caldecott Park. In 1912 plans were presented for 180 houses on the Lawford Road estate, now Northcote Road, Frederick Street, Charles Street, and Alfred Street, and the society itself built houses in Sycamore Grove in 1913, nine with bathrooms to be sold for £325 each, the remainder without bathrooms for £300. These houses were sold so quickly that the Committee proceeded to build more in the other groves.

CHAPTER SEVEN

The Rugby Benefit Building Society: 1914-1967

EXCEPT FOR THE one year Lister interregnum either B. H. Fisher or his son W. T. was Secretary to the Society for the first sixty years of its existence. Their years of office coincided almost exactly with the period when the Society was acting principally as a Freehold Land Society. Shortly after the death of W. T. Fisher in 1926 the Auditors suggested that the Committee was acting ultra vires in buying and developing land. One of those Auditors was Old Rugbeian Mr H. W. L. Reddish who was later to have a distinguished career as leader and inspirer of the Rugby Portland Cement Co. The correctness of the Auditors' submission was established by legal opinion and the Society had thereafter no alternative but to discontinue its Land Society activities, dispose of any property and land it owned and "confine future activities to the business allowed by the Building Societies Act". All this however, was fourteen years in the future when W. T. Fisher recorded the end of the Committee Meeting held on 7th August, 1914 in the following terms:-

"A special meeting was suggested but nothing decided – the fog of war settling down upon the meeting".

This meeting on 7th August 1914 had reacted immediately to the outbreak of war, much more so than the Warwick and Warwickshire or than Walsall; their first action was to rescind a decision of July 24th to grant a mortgage of £1,000. As this was for two shops and premises in course of erection on Clifton Road, the Committee's decision highlights the impact of war on those who needed to borrow money. On the other hand, it was decided on the 21st August that a mortgage of £150 to a mobilised soldier should be subject to a moratorium during the war and "for the debt to be spread over say five years in equal instalments after conclusion of peace, meanwhile carrying interest of say 5%".

The 49th Annual Report presented at the Annual Meeting on 27th November 1914 included these loyal sentiments "At this crisis in the history of our nation and empire, your committee think that it would be only right and fitting that members should be able to express their views as to what contributions should be made for the relief of distress, and to what fund or funds it should be allotted". It was decided to give £50 to the Prince of Wales Fund, £25 to Queen Mary's Fund, and £25 to the local Belgian Relief Fund. The Society's chief concern was that there might be a run on the funds. In April 1915 therefore they were disturbed to find in the Rugby Advertiser an announcement by the Market Harborough Building Society offering "money at 4% on balances and repayments at 5/-d per £100 per fortnight". Mr Willard, a director, agreed strongly that "it behoves our Society to be up and doing". At the Annual Meeting on 26th November 1915 the Committee reported with pleasure that withdrawals of £19,229 were only £428 more than in the previous year. The following year the withdrawal figure was £14,748 – business was generally at a low ebb – but the 52nd Annual Report presented in December 1917 showed withdrawals of £23,171 "as the motive was a desire to assist the Government by subscribing to National War Loan the Society is to be congratulated on possessing such a large body of patriotic citizens among its members." In fact towards the end of the war business began to pick up quite significantly and like the rest of the Building Society Movement the Rugby Benefit Building Society was eager to play its part in "homes fit for heroes".

The impact of the 1914-18 War on the Society was both various and particular. On 23rd July 1915 "Our Society seemed to the Secretary particularly vulnerable to an aircraft raid, in as much as, so much of our property and mortgages clustered around this important railway junction and the works of Messrs. Willans and Robinson and the B.T.H., and bombs aimed at them could not very well fail to inflict damage upon us. The range of action and powers of destruction of aircraft were growing rapidly and would continue to do so".

On 29th October, when everyone was digging for victory, the Committee was told "the purchasers of potato plots said they were turning out a very poor crop, that half the amount they were asking for them would be quite enough. It was necessary to act quickly as many tubers were going diseased". They decided to dispose of them at the best price they could get. In September and October 1916 it was decided that in view of the earlier closing of the shops on Saturdays, Subscription Meetings should be held from 6 p.m. to 8 p.m. and "that a taxi cab be ordered at the last moment to take the money to the bank on Saturday night". Autres temps, mêmes moeurs; Securicor was yet to come. In March 1917 the Surveyor reported that he had been offered a commission in the Army. The Committee's generous decision reads "After considerable discussion it was resolved that a Building Committee be appointed to carry on the work of the Surveyors during Mr Newman's absence, the fees accruing to belong to him". The Committee, however had little sympathy with those whose troubles seemed self-induced and not the result of the war. In September 1917 Mr X of Manor Road complained "that the state of his front wall was that it was likely to fall right out into the street before many months were up and that the back wall is starting to go again". Resolved "that in as much as Mr X has been for a long time under notice to quit, the Committee would recommend him to clear out before anything happened". In February, 1918 the same tenant was still in residence and expressed his intention of only paying half rent. "Some said 'go for him' and others said 'go warily'." The Secretary was left to look into it.

In September 1918 the Society adapted quickly to peace time conditions. They bought the Water Tower Farm for £3,000 and its timber for £525. They were considering purchases of land on Barby Road and Bilton Road. The Freehold Land Society was 52 years old and had 10 years to run in that role. In 1919 and 1922 the Committee acquired valuable land in the Hillmorton Road and Hillmorton Paddox area and its development is the major story of the immediate post war decade. The Committee presented their 53rd Report to the Annual Meeting on 6th December, 1918. Subscriptions during the year had been £42,525, advances on mortgage were £12,058 and withdrawals £9,859. Considerable progress had been made with the sale of land on the Park Estate – ready for development in 1914 and delayed by the war – and the Water Tower Farm Estate of 43 acres was being divided into lots. It was A. David, Headmaster of Rugby from 1910-21, who prevented houses going up on those 43 acres. When he urged the Governing Body to secure it for the school, they decided that their existing commitments prevented more spending. David raised the money himself, borrowing extensively from Housemasters, and bought it on his own responsibility. Later the Governors repaid the loan and bought the land. There is no doubt that had this not happened the school would have eventually become so hemmed in that it would have had to move out of Rugby to a more spacious site, and the citizens would have lost their green lung in the centre of town. The Building Society shared in the general post-war local contentment. They bought Water Tower Farm for £3,000 in September 1918 and sold it for £4,000 in May 1919. Between 1919 and 1922 the Committee made the final land purchases already mentioned. They bought Brown's Farm for £8,100 and an adjoining 16 acres for £1,500 – a total of 55 acres. They then bought three neighbouring farms totalling 87 acres. These formed "an extensive block approximately extending from the Great Central Railway line to Hillmorton Paddox and from Hillmorton Road to Ashlawn Road." There was a considerable demand for building plots and this was good both for the land development activities and the mortgage business of the Society. Some of the plots sold were extensive. On 8th April 1921 the Committee decided that "although the additional areas added to some of the front lots materially increased the size of those lots it was not proposed to increase the number of houses to be built thereon, which was still restricted to one house per plot. It was thought that with such large areas provision should be made for a gardener, chauffeur or other servants and it was resolved to allow rooms for them over a garage, stable or other building for use with the house on the front".

The Society shared the need of many Rugby citizens for a new home. At their meeting on 5th October 1921 the Committee confirmed their purchase for £5,250 of "the Market Hall and shops fronting Sheep Street at present occupied by Messrs. Spencer, Whittaker, Ponting, Steele and Underwood". This proved an inconvenient headquarters however and in 1926 it was sold for £8,000. It was later to become part of Woolworths. For three years the offices were at 12 Henry Street; finally in 1929 the Society bought Nos. 1 and 3 Railway Terrace and on 9th March 1931 their President W. W. Vaughan opened the new headquarters there – named Temple Buildings after the first President, one of Vaughan's predecessors as Headmaster of Rugby. Vaughan was Headmaster from 1921-31, being 57 at the time of his appointment. He was one of three Headmasters of Rugby to be President of the Society; Hugh Lyon was the third. Vaughan was succeeded as President in 1937 by another Temple, William, who also became Archbishop of Canterbury. The Society was blessed with some very distinguished Presidents.

The Hillmorton land was the last the Society was to purchase and develop. The clear ruling that the Committee of a Building Society could not legally so act left them no alternative but to sell off their existing holdings as soon as sound commercial practice allowed. For some years the minutes of meetings record decisions on the sale or development of building land but all new business was normal building society investment or mortgage. Total assets first passed one million in 1935. On 4th November 1932 the Directors, as they were now styled in the Minute Book, decided to buy property in Banbury (46 High Street) for £1,100 and open a new branch there thus improving the branch facilities they had first developed elsewhere in Banbury in 1927. The Directors held a meeting at the Banbury branch on 23rd March 1933 and expressed their pleasure at the way the alterations had been carried out. Two other branches at Lutterworth and Leamington were opened in 1945 and 1962 respectively. Surprisingly, the Committee was actively looking for branch offices during the final 12 months of the 1939-45 war. The minutes of the Directors' Meeting on 20th May, 1944 read "After discussion, the Secretary is directed to enquire whether there was property for sale suitable for conversion to Building Society Offices at Stratford-on-Avon, Daventry, Lutterworth and Southam, in which towns it is intended to open branch offices of the Society". The Daventry branch was acquired by taking over the small Daventry Building Society. No. 40 High Street, Banbury, a derelict building, was bought for £250 within the next two months. Property in Lutterworth was inspected in the early autumn of 1944. At the same time "the death of His Grace the Lord Archbishop of Canterbury on 26th October is reported, the Directors standing in silence as a mark of their great sorrow and of their appreciation of the association which the Society has enjoyed during the sixteen years of his Presidency". For once the Secretary had got it wrong; Temple had been President for six years. In April 1961 the Directors considered a branch office at Ealing but finally decided upon an agency. On 26th September 1961 they instructed the Secretary to attend the auction at Birmingham on September 28th and to bid up to £17,000 for 18 Victoria Terrace, Leamington Spa The bid was successful and the Society established a branch there, after spending £5,800 on the conversion.

Between 1963 and 1965 the Directors were also anxious to acquire additional property in Rugby, to be used as a central collection office. Several possible sites were considered and each time there was a difficulty – building unsuitable, price too high, or out-bid at the auction. In the meantime on 4th February 1964 a lease was taken on 27 Wood Street, Stratford-upon-Avon and a branch subsequently opened there on 3rd February 1965. Finally, in November, 1965 the Society found a suitable property in Rugby. Fleet's the Chemists at 24 Sheep Street came on the market and the Directors agreed that negotiations to buy at £24,000 should be opened. The Secretary was given authority to increase the offer to £25,000 if necessary but by 12th November the deal was complete and, subject to contract, the Society had found its central office. Two further building developments took place before the amalgamation with Warwick and Warwickshire in 1967. No. 26 High Street was bought and developed as a much better Banbury branch office; it is still the Banbury Office of Heart of England. By the end of November 1966 alterations to Head Office in Rugby were complete and the new banking hall was ready for occupation. Sadly, it was the management of three of these branches which was to bring much anxiety to the Directors and General Manager during the final two years of the Society's separate existence. Following almost immediately upon one another there were financial irregularities at Banbury, Stratford and Rugby with all the worry and suffering that such human weakness brings. The police were brought in and prosecutions followed. The General Manager and Secretary who had held office since 1950 had a difficult and worrying time in discovering the full and detailed truth.

Although it has been convenient to see this history of the Rugby Society in terms of land development rather than of people and thus to emphasise the contrast with the history of the other societies forming Heart of England, the men who inspired the Rugby Benefit Building Society for one hundred years made no less a contribution than those who led the others. The Presidents were men of outstanding quality, two of them Archbishops of Canterbury, three Headmasters of Rugby School, and one a distinguished soldier. The Directors deliberately maintained their connection with Rugby School. In October 1948 they invited the new Headmaster, Sir Arthur fforde, to become a Vice-President; his predecessor P. H. B. Lyon was by now President. When Lyon left Rugby and suggested that there might be good reason to resign the Presidency he was asked to continue. Fforde's successor, Dr. Walter Hamilton, in turn became a Vice-President. The Chairmen were essentially Rugbeians, for the Society needed ready access to them as decision makers. C. G. Richards, who was Chairman for 14 years made a major contribution, including the centenary history which by its excellence has made my task both easier and harder. After publication Sir Halford Reddish sent a letter of congratulations, and a reminder that as a young man he had taken part in the audit of the Society's accounts.

Like the Warwick and Warwickshire, Rugby was most fortunate in its Secretaries. In 100 years there were only four if you ignore Lister's one year hiccough and the two years of Howarth. The Society was therefore effectively controlled on a day to day basis by the two Fishers, by W. J. Warner, who was the first Secretary to be elected a Director, and by George Smith. Mr Smith, who is now Chairman of Directors of the Heart of England, was Assistant Secretary when W. J. Warner died in office in 1950. The Directors had no hesitation in appointing him to succeed, without advertising the post, and his ability and considerable experience were of great value to the Rugby Society in the final 17 years and to the Rugby and Warwick Building Society in the early days when he was Joint General Manager with Herbert Walden. His personal qualities, and the quality of his contribution to the Society are distinguished. They have enabled a man who joined the Rugby Society as a junior clerk in 1928 to assume the office of chairman of Heart of England two years before he must retire as a director under the age rule. These men brought much benefit to Rugby. Another look at the two maps will show how much of the Borough of Rugby they urbanised. In 1866 Rugby was a small country market town surrounded by rural and leafy Warwickshire. The arrival of the railway, the coming of the engineering industry, necessarily transformed the town; the country came to Rugby, gobbled up the surrounding fields and woods and settled down to live and work there. It was Rugby's good fortune that much of the development was in the hands of local men who took decisions without having to consider how much money they personally stood to gain or lose.

Houses were provided within the financial reach of skilled workers and within easy travelling distance of the new industries. At a later stage came the agreeable development at Hillmorton, a development which might so easily have been nearer the centre, shutting everything in, but for the prescience of Headmaster David. Much of the earlier work of the Rugby Benefit Building Society is of course now old property and its future is one of the problems of today's civic leaders. But Frederick Temple has surely been proved abundantly right by 100 years of Rugby history. A man "cannot have any great affection for his Post Office Savings Book", but he can "love his land". The keen sense of belonging of modern Rugbeians, their strong local pride in a town which at one time had the highest per centage of owner occupation in the country, leaves no doubt that the Directors of the Rugby Benefit Building Society gave Rugby what it both needed and wanted.

THE WALSALL MUTUAL BUILDING SOCIETY: 1863-1974

PRESIDENT

None appointed

CHAIRMEN

1863-1891	John Smith
1891-1893	William Smith
1893-1911	Joseph Dixon, Junior
1911-1938	John Shaw Shaw
1938-1951	William A. Homer
1951-1955	Arthur W. Cotterell
1955-1968	B. Baker
1968-1972	A. Fox
1972-1974	A. L. Wiggin

SECRETARIES

1863-1889	Joseph Dixon
1889-1892	Joseph Dixon, Junior
1892-1939	A. J. Llewellen
1939-1949	A. J. B. Llewellen
1947-1974	John Richardson

ASSETS

1863	£1,500	1923	£93,523
1873	£10,000	1933	£266,249
1883	£22,000	1943	£462,786
1893	£28,273	1953	£1,020,867
1903	£52,956	1963	£4,433,748
1913	£65,446	1973	£20,122,267

PLATE 15

Joseph Dixon Snr., Founder Secretary of Walsall, 1863-89.

PLATE 16

Joseph Dixon Junr., Secretary of Walsall 1889-92. Chairman of Directors 1893-1911.

PLATE 17

J. S. Shaw. Chairman 1911-38

PLATE 18

John Richardson, Secretary 1949-71; General Manager and Director, 1971-74; Joint General Manager (HEBS) 1974-76; Director (HEBS) 1976–.

PLATE 19
Bridge St., Walsall, 1895.

PLATE 20
Lichfield St., Walsall, 1895.

CHAPTER EIGHT

The Walsall Mutual Building Society: 1863-1914

THERE WERE NO future Archbishops of Canterbury in Walsall in 1863; nor was there any equivalent of Warwick Castle and its influence. There was however a community of skilled and semi-skilled work people living in an historic town which had been an important centre of communication since the early days of English history. The Industrial Revolution brought great social and economic changes to the West Midlands; Walsall, a leading Staffordshire community, was at the heart of them. For example, in 1801 the population was 10,400; fifty years later it exceeded 40,000. The people of Walsall had long had particular skills in making saddlery, spurs, bridles, stirrups and buckles of all kinds. Manufacturing industry in the town developed and diversified throughout the first half of the nineteenth century, as it did in several English regions, but housing development did not keep pace in "the Town of an Hundred Trades." The stocks were not taken from High Street until 1854 and the cottage hospital opened as late as 1863, the year in which the Walsall Mutual Benefit Building Society was founded. The Society produced a valuable brochure, anonymously written, for its centenary in 1963 and I am indebted to the writer, in particular for information about the foundation and first ten years of the Society's life.

"On the evening of 19 February, 1863 a meeting was held in St. Matthew's Hall when Rules were read and adopted. They began:- 'The Society shall be called the Walsall Mutual Benefit Building Society. Its objects shall be to enable members to purchase or erect freehold or leasehold property, or to invest their contributions upon interest.' The Society's offices were registered as No. 2 Bridge Street, Walsall, (where the Gaumont Cinema now stands). The subscriptions of members were to be received fortnightly, on alternate Monday evenings commencing 9th March, 1863". (Centenary Brochure, published 1963.) The new Society elected three Trustees, a Board of Directors, Surveyor and Auditor, and Mr Joseph Dixon as Secretary. Mr Dixon and his son, Joseph Dixon Junr., held leading positions in the Society from 1863 to 1911 and had greater influence on its progress and development during the first half century than had anyone else.

In 1913 the then Mayor of Walsall said of Joseph Dixon Senr. that he was "one of the grandest old men he could remember, who used to teach a night class of boys at the Unitarian Church, Stafford Street, and he (the Mayor) was a lad in that class." Dixon evidently personified the spirit of nonconformist self help, self education and thrift, which was such a driving force in England during the second half of the nineteenth century. But he clearly did not think of his written record as source material for a future historian. The minutes of the early Warwick and Warwickshire are informative, clearly and legibly written, and provide most of the information an historian needs. The early minutes of the Rugby Society are so good that they might well be published verbatim, and the historian's problem is one of selection and condensation. The early records of the Walsall Mutual are in comparison very uninformative.

As a result the history of the first twenty years of the Society is a matter of inference rather than of certain knowledge; the Centenary Brochure uses only two sentences to move from 1863 to 1883. A minute of 27 August 1880, one of the few entries adding flesh to bare bones, gives a glimpse of the elementary level at which the young Society was probably operating:- "A member of the Society of the name of Edward Chetland accompanied by Mr.——— attended the meeting of the Board. Mr Chetland had withdrawn £2. 6. od from the Society on March 17, 1879 and had signed the receipt book by a cross and his name was written by the Secretary, but he now declared that he never received it. After a long conference and examination of the books Mr—— was quite satisfied that the money had been paid to him and at last Chetland confessed that he must be mistaken but that he never remembered receiving it." The blank name is not because the gentleman was anonymous but because only a lexicographer could decipher the Secretary's handwriting.

The general tone of the first twenty years can however be inferred and the inference begins with a meeting of the Board on April 21st, 1882:- "The Board then considered the suggestions made by Mr Lees (Annual Auditor) for the better management of the affairs of the Society." Arrangements were made for the safe custody of deeds, the Solicitor was asked to prepare a security book, members were to produce the receipt for ground rents paid, a separate account would be kept for each member, and the Society's books would in future be kept in double entry. Improvement was not immediate. Fifteen months later, on October 12th, 1883, the minutes of a special Board Meeting explained:- "All deeds belonging to advanced members were brought out of Mr Cotterell's strong room and placed on the table in the office. They were there carefully compared with the security book and the whole found to be there. The Trustees complained that the deeds had not been kept in the Society's chest as was originally intended. It was then resolved that at the close of the meeting the deeds be replaced in the Society's chest which was accordingly done the Secretary having two keys pro tem but for the future the Trustees have a key each." Shortly afterwards the Directors decided to keep the deeds in the Bank, and there was a call for the Solicitor (Cotterell) to resign – not seconded.

The Society's difficulties were by no means over. They continued and deepened during the next five years and it was not until March 1887 that the Auditor (Lees) began to express any real satisfaction with the effect of the financial discipline for which he had repeatedly called. In October 1883 the Directors were asked to make themselves personally responsible for the balance due to the Bank and "respectfully declined." A month later, no doubt as a result of backstairs activity, the Solicitor wrote to say that he was "most reluctant to resign." The Directors pressed him and received his resignation. One wonders why they were surprised when it proved difficult to find a successor. On December 20 1883 the Secretary reported that "when all the demands upon the Society are met there will be a balance of £1,700 owing to the Bank.." The year ending March 1885 was apparently more successful. Receipts were £10,132. 7. 2 making a total of £174,419. 2. 4 since foundation. Withdrawals during the year had been only half the amount of deposits and no member had been "inconvenienced" when he wished to withdraw any money. But a year later the Auditor reported that "considered on a proper basis I find the profit for the year amounted to about £50 only, the operations of the Society being so seriously crippled by accounts which cannot fairly bear the charge of interest." The problem was essentially that the value of the property was depressed, the majority of the shareholders were skilled and semi-skilled workmen with no financial reserves, and many of them had been allowed to become well behind with their payments. The Auditor recommended the drastic step of writing down the accounts to "such figures as the securities may be held at." In Chapter 2 I mentioned the difficult years between 1874 and 1894 when property values were always unstable and often declining. The Warwick and Warwickshire and the Rugby Societies came through that period with little real trouble, but it looks as if the Walsall Mutual Benefit nearly capsized. That they survived is largely due to the realism of their Auditor and to a brave decision by the Directors. They decided unanimously to receive the report of the Auditor, write down the property values, and thus write off £1,857. 5. 9. They had of course not only to make the correct financial decision; they also had to retain public confidence. The wording of the 23rd Annual Report, dated March 1886, was carefully chosen. The standard so surpasses the standard of minute taking that it seems unlikely that the Secretary wrote the Report. The Directors reported a successful year: £8,739. 14. 5 had been received: no one who wished to withdraw money had suffered any delay: this surely was the reason why so many people were anxious to invest with them that the Directors had had to decline some large sums. Nevertheless depression in trade had prevented some advanced shareholders making good their payments to the Society and the Directors, had been obliged to take possession. They had now decided to use the entire reserve fund to write down the value of those properties to a realistic figure.

That decision marked, and probably caused, the turn of the tide and the Society never again seriously faltered. It was saved by a wise Auditor who restored financial rectitude when the Directors and their Secretary had failed to impose it. In March 1888 he suggested another improvement:- "In some cases where the intrinsic value of the security is noticeably less than the shareholder's indebtedness, strong measures should be taken to enforce payment of arrears. If it is found that this cannot be done without interfering with the Society's interests I would suggest that the members be required to assign to the Society policies on their lives. . . ." A year later the Auditor again expressed his satisfaction with the financial trend, and the strength of his relationship with the Directors is emphasised by an item one would not expect to find in an Auditor's Report. The Secretary, Joseph Dixon Senr., was resigning because of advancing years and declining health. "I trust", says the Auditor, "that you will not think that I am going beyond the proper scope of my office in giving my opinion that if the shareholders appoint Mr Joseph Dixon Junior they will secure a Secretary in every way competent to discharge the duties, and of the value of whose services they have already abundant proof." The last few words imply that Joseph the son had already deputised for his father and helped the Auditor and Directors restore control. It is not clear whether or not the shareholders were ever told of their Auditor's opinion, but they certainly shared it and unanimously appointed son to succeed father.

The early 1890s brought important changes in the leading officers of the Society. Joseph Dixon Junr. was Secretary for only three years, resigning in 1892. He was succeeded by Mr A. J. Llewellen who was Secretary for the next 47 years and whose son held the office for ten years after that. Joseph Dixon Junr. became a director on his resignation as Secretary, and was Chairman from 1893 to 1911. Mr G. R. Ridsdale of Ridsdale, Macintosh and Ridsdale was appointed Auditor in 1890 and he and his firm maintained the high standard of service and advice set by Mr W. E. A. Lees who now lived in Birmingham and could no longer undertake the Annual Audit. The Society was blessed with continuity of leadership from 1890 to 1950 – only four chairmen and two secretaries – and the difficult days of 1870-90 were not to recur, or rather not to find the Society weak and ill-organised when they did. Let Mr Ridsdale, presenting his Auditor's report in March 1892 have the final word on this period of the Society's history:- "At the same time we would issue a note of warning. This position can only be achieved by strict adherence to the lines which have been followed in the past few years, which have resulted in the transforming of a somewhat sickly child into a healthy, if not a very plump one."

In their Annual Report of the same year the Directors paid tribute to their previous Chairman, John Smith, who had died during the year. He was the founder chairman, holding office for 28 years. Within two years he was succeeded by Joseph Dixon Junr., the former Secretary who remained Chairman until 1911. By then A. J. Llewellen had been Secretary for 19 years and was to continue so until 1939 when his son succeeded. In effect the Dixons and the

Llewellens took the Walsall from its foundation in 1863 until 1949 – little more than 20 years from amalgamation with Rugby and Warwick. By 1949 the strong support of John Richardson – A. J. B. Llewellen's successor as secretary and a present director of Heart of England – was available to see the Society through the final years of its separate existence; a remarkable secretarial succession of two fathers, two sons, and one other.

The remaining years of the nineteenth century brought steady, undramatic, and reassuring progress. There were moments of humour and even of excitement. On November 25th, 1892:- "The Revd. Peter Dean made a suggestion which had come across his mind for setting out the benefits of the Society before the public by means of lantern slides. . . . The matter was deferred for consideration." On November 16th, 1894 "a suggestion was thrown out by Mr Thomas Bayliss at the close of the meeting as to the desirability of calling the members in arrears to appear before the Board." But no one rocked the boat too hard; there were no major excitements. In March 1900, at the 37th Annual Meeting, the Directors reported a gross profit of £1,348 for the previous year, less £1202 paid or allowed to investing members as interest. The amount received during the year was £19,306 making a total of £355,153 received since foundation. There were 609 members compared with 559 in 1898.

The fourteen years between the 37th Annual Meeting and the outbreak of war in August 1914 brought the Society increased recognition in Walsall and reasonable financial progress. Leading citizens began to take a more active part in Building Society affairs. The Town Clerk, Mr J. R. Cooper (father of Mr Frank Cooper, Solicitor and Director for 50 years), was a frequent speaker at Annual Meetings or other public occasions and strongly supported the aims and objects of the Society. The Walsall Advertiser gave prominence to these public occasions and as a result the history of the Society is very well documented during the period. Through the press and from their public platforms Building Society leaders commented on the progress of the Society, or the state of the building industry in Walsall, or the importance of self-help or the duty of patriotism. In March 1905 the Directors "announce with pleasure" that the Society has no properties in its possession and no advanced accounts twelve months in arrears. In 1907 the Walsall Adertiser congratulated the Borough Council on reducing the rate by 4d in the £1 to 4/- (1/8d General District rate, 1/3d Borough rate and 1/1d Poor rate), expressed satisfaction with the state of Walsall and added "further evidence of the satisfactory state of things financially in Walsall is afforded by the perusal of a report of the meeting of the building society. If trade has been bad in Walsall, certainly this society has not felt it; year by year it has been able to show a record of sound, substantial progress; its securities are all what might be termed gilt-edged." In 1908 the Chairman had an interesting point to make. He reported steady progress, but took a nostalgic look a few years back when the building trade in Walsall was prosperous and the Society was "advancing by leaps and bounds." He then explained that the heavier weight of cash withdrawals was probably explained by the great age of some of the members:- "Early that month he had helped the Secretary to pay out the interest on the paid up shares, and three members who came were between 80 and 90 years of age; there were others of a similar age who sent to withdraw their money, and they could only expect that when members got to that age they would naturally wish to withdraw their savings." Can you take it with you?

Despite the depression in the building trade there were those who recognised the improvement in housing in Walsall since the Society was founded. At the 50th Anniversary Dinner in February 1913 the Chairman reminded his audience:- "few of them could realise the difficulty an ordinary working man had fifty years ago in finding a decent house to live in. In his time, in Park Street, now the most important shopping centre in Walsall, there were six courts which contained upwards of sixty tenements of the one room up and one room down class, and where lived the forefathers of our Walsall families." Three years earlier Mr W. T. Cotterill, seconding the adoption of the Annual Report, had urged the "working man" to identify himself with such an excellent Society so that "a good deal of the difficulties they heard of would soon disappear." He added, "When a man owned his own house he took a deeper interest in the affairs of the town or district in which he lived; with the result that they not only secured improved sanitary conditions but also many of the things which they were told would be the result of town planning and better environment which they heard of so much." About the same period Mr J. Shaw Shaw, a future Chairman, was appealing to national rather than local pride. The Walsall Advertiser reports him as saying:- "He was told the other day by a gentleman that as soon as things improved he should sell all his property and invest the proceeds in some foreign securities which paid a better rate of interest without any trouble. He (the Speaker) remarked that the idea was not a very patriotic one, for if all Englishmen did the same what would become of the good old country? It would soon lose its prestige." The 1980 Chairman of British Leyland would surely say 'Amen'. The Society was by now a Walsall institution and on its own terms a successful one. In 1900 the Assets were £39,657, the Reserves £1,280 and the membership 609. When war broke out in 1914 the equivalent figures were £65,446; £3,290 and 776. In 1912 the Chairman claimed to have heard of several building societies which had been unable to meet their engagements. He "considered that all this would have been avoided if the Directors of such Societies had exercised the same judicious care as the Directors of their Society had done." One of their problems was that the decline in value of all kinds of property had continued during the year:- "according to the last census there were no less than 1,076 uninhabited houses in the Borough, whilst there were only 15 houses in the course of erection." The sort of property on which the Society was chiefly lending money was rented for 6/-, 6/6d and 7/-d per week. "The working man was undoubtedly beginning to realise that he was entitled to live in a much better house than he used to do."

The increasing prestige and membership of the Society would probably have justified a new headquarters. But intervention from above precipitated action and the Directors did not have to invent reasons or excuses. On 17 June 1901, at a special meeting of Directors:- "The Secretary reported the circumstances under which the meeting had been called, namely the nuisance and annoyance of the electric motor and sewing machines above the Society's offices." Walsall, "the town of a hundred trades", had infiltrated one of those trades too near to the Building Society's think tank. The Secretary suggested that the Walsall Club in Bridge Street might provide good alternative premises and the Directors decided to inspect. This was on June 17th, the inspection took place on June 19th and by June 25th 45 Bridge Street had been bought from Messrs. W. Brooks and Sons for £1,500 and the lease of the offices in Leicester Street terminated. In addition the Society paid £100 for a piece of land in front of the new offices, belonging to Walsall Corporation. The necessary alterations, including the name of the Society in large gold letters, cost £350 and the two front rooms on the second floor were let to Mr C. Frankham, Architect, for £20 p.a. to include electric lighting. The first Directors meeting at 45 Bridge Street took place on 8 November 1901.

The Society celebrated its 50th Anniversary with a dinner on 19th February 1913. The report in the Walsall Advertiser of 22 February 1913 recalls the occasion so vividly, and is so typical of that period in our history, that I cannot do better than quote extensively from it:

"Growth of the Society.

Mr John R. Cooper submitted the toast of "The Walsall Mutual Benefit Building Society," and said it afforded him the greatest possible pleasure to do so. A week or so ago a gentleman asked him the very pertinent question, "Why on earth are you having a dinner in connection with the Building Society?" and his answer was, "Why on earth shouldn't we, if we so think fit?" (Hear, hear, and applause.) But there was every reason why they should hold a dinner on that occasion. Fifty years, to that very day, their society was founded, and during the whole of that period it had been doing good work in our town, and had been the means of many thrifty men becoming the owners of their own homes. It had encouraged many hundreds to follow their example, and done much to promote what today is more needed than ever – thrift. (Applause.) Mr Cooper went on to refer to an "exceedingly interesting document" – the first annual report which was made in connection with their society. From that it appeared that during the first year the society was in existence there were 72 members, and the total amount of money received was £654. 8s. 10d. In that report there was a paragraph which he thought he ought to read to them, because it summed up practically all that could be said with regard to their society. It read, "It will be seen by the following statement of accounts that the society has quite fulfilled the expectations of its promoters, and has borne out its right to be called a mutual benefit building society." The writer of that report might have been a prophet, for had he been writing today, he could not have better expressed what the result of the work had been. Their society was a mutual benefit society, particularly in this way: it was composed of two classes of persons – those who had money to lend and those who desired to borrow – and the principle underlying its work was that while the man who lends should have a reasonable and fair return for the money he lent, the borrower should obtain it at the lowest possible rate of interest. (Hear, hear.) Today, the total number of members was 775 – (applause) – and the total income last year was no less a sum than £17,000 (Applause). While the first annual report of the society recorded a profit of £11. os 9d., the report for last year showed an undivided profit of £3,199 1s. 4d (Applause). These figures, he thought, showed the remarkable growth which the society had made during the last half century, a growth which could undoubtedly be attributed to the fact that the public had confidence in the management and the working of that society – (applause) – because they knew there was nothing speculative about it. (Hear, hear.)

NO SPECULATION

The society did not deal in speculative securities, and took care that every one of their securities should be fully investigated. They only lent money on mortgage, and not on speculative deals which would be likely to yield a high rate of interest. Furthermore, the public knew that those who found the money had a voice in the management of the society, and that none of the directors were self-elected, but were appointed annually by the members themselves. When one looked into the management of the society, one was bound to admit that the directors proceeded on a very wise and cautious policy. (Hear, hear.) He found, from the printed statement of the accounts, which were audited by auditors elected by the members, and further audited by a chartered accountant, who exercised the closest supervision, that the total number of securities, all of them mortgages on property, which the society held, was 218, only two of which were for sums over £1,000, and no less than 188 represented mortgages of less than £500 each. From this they would quite see the wide field over which the operations of the society were spread. Another feature was the small cost of management, which worked out at something less than a ¼ per cent of the total amount of estate which the directors mortgaged, and which stood at a sum of no less than £65,000. He thought everybody must admit that the directors were most economical in the manner in which they conducted the business of the society. Speaking of the origin of the society, Mr Cooper said that it followed the Walsall Freehold Land Society, which was formed with a somewhat different object, both the Mutual Benefit Building Society and the Freehold Land Society being founded by the late Mr Joseph Dixon the elder. (Applause.) He founded them not for any personal benefit, – and those who knew him were perfectly well aware that this would be one of the last things he would think of – (applause) – but for the benefit of his fellow-men, in whom he took the greatest possible interest. (Hear, hear.) The Freehold Land Society was established long before town-planning was dreamt of. It bought up freehold land, laid it out in streets, allotted it to the members at the actual cost, so that while no profit was made for the society, the members were able to obtain small quantities of land at wholesale prices."

SHORTAGE OF WORKING-CLASS HOUSES

Mr John S. Shaw, responding to the toast . . . said . . ."Few of them could realise the difficulty an ordinary working man had at that time in finding a decent house to live in. In his time, in Park Street, now the most important shopping centre of Walsall, there were six courts, which contained upwards of sixty tenements of the one room up and one room down class, and where lived the forefathers of our Walsall families. The White Horse Yard, Pig Lane, and Hazeldine's Yard, all now wiped out of existence he was happy to say. In High Street, which years ago was one of the most important streets of Walsall there were also tenements at the back of most of the principal shops, all this being due to the difficulty of obtaining land upon which to build houses fit for people to live in. Today things were very different. There was plenty of land within easy distance of the town, and any-one who desired to build a house of his or her own, would find the funds of that society at their disposal. It was one of the happiest things in life for a man to possess a house of his own, and he could do it by joining that building society. Continuing, Mr Shaw said that having acquired his own house through the help of that society, a man would be unable to go to church and sing in truth the well-known hymn of John Wesley, "Not one foot of land do I possess in this barren wilderness." Rather should he inform his friends by what means he had obtained it, and induce them to join the society and do likewise. He felt he could not close without mentioning the lady members, some of whom, he was very pleased to see, were present; and whilst thanking them for their co-operation, he would like to remind them that their society was one of the most forward pioneers of their cause, for it gave them the right to vote."

Song, "She alone charmest my sadness," Mr Arthur S. Brittain.

THE MAYOR ON THRIFT

The Mayor, in proposing the toast of "The Trustees, Directors, and Officers, both past and present of the Society, "thanked the committee for the kind invitation to the Mayoress and himself to be present at that important gathering . . . Concluding, Councillor Venables said he was afraid that the young men and women of to-day were not as thrifty as they might be. He hoped he should prove a bad prophet, but he thought the present-day tendency was in the direction of less thrift. For the past forty-three years he had been associated with a building society in the town, and he described how the payments he made in his younger days had been the means of his acquiring land and property. He hoped his remarks would act as an incentive to the younger people of the town to do likewise, and he did appeal to them to become associated with a building society of that description."

The toast was heartily drunk.

Recital, "The Telegram," Miss Fanny Mason.

SECRETARY'S RESPONSE

Councillor Llewellen (secretary) also responded, and cordially thanked the Mayor and Mayoress for the honour they had done the society in being present that night. . . "He had been secretary of the society for twenty-one years and he felt proud of it, the members were proud of it, and the town of Walsall ought to feel proud of it. (Hear, hear.) . . . He was connected with many commercial institutions, but there was not one in which he had more confidence than the Mutual Building Society. Its affairs were conducted in a business-like manner, and although the directors were not paid, they gave of their best, and attended the meetings very regularly. Much of the success of the society was due to the judicious management. Concluding, Mr Llewellen spoke of the valuable and useful work which the society was doing, and said he felt sure it would continue to develop and share in the prosperity which would come to our good old town. (Applause.)"

That Anniversary dinner was held little over a year before the lights began to go out all over Europe. The 1914-18 war created new conditions and new challenges for the Society, as we shall see in Chapter 9. The flavour of the first fifty years is well captured by extracts from two speeches. On March 31st, 1908 the Chairman, Joseph Dixon Junior, "did not care how much help a man had from outside, there was no help so efficient – none that gave him more comfort of mind or greater pleasure – than self help. Some were too apt to expect others to try to help. . . . The very foundation of the Society was self help; they helped themselves and at the same time helped each other." Four years later the Town Clerk, a Trustee of the Society:- "felt in difficulty about speaking to them, but when in difficulty he always turned to Holy Writ; so he was reminded of the Egyptians who compelled the Hebrews to make bricks without straw. As he had listened to the various speeches he felt that bit by bit his straw was going until at last it became almost as scarce as fuel was today. He recognised that he was speaking to an audience who were all of them savers and not spenders – and that was the class of men which was the very backbone of English society today. They would find many men who would spend as much money as they could lay hold on, and were not particular if they spent other people's money."

CHAPTER NINE

The Walsall Mutual Building Society: 1914-74

ON THE OUTBREAK of war in August 1914 the Walsall Mutual experienced the same early anxieties as other building societies but eight months later, when the 52nd Annual Meeting was held, the Chairman (J. Shaw Shaw) was able to report:- "That night they were meeting under most exceptional circumstances; a war which had practically engaged the whole of Europe and part of Asia, in which thousands of men were engaged in fierce battles involving, as it did, the enormous loss of the bravest and best soldiers and the deplorable destruction of valuable property, as well as costing the nations engaged in the terrible conflict millions of money. When the war commenced and some people became panic stricken that Society, like others, had a few members who became affected by a nervous complaint and wanted to withdraw their money immediately. He was pleased to say, however, that they were able to accommodate those members and also to make advances at the same time." By the end of 1915 however the tragedy of war had affected the Board more personally and the Chairman expressed his sympathy to fellow director Mr M. H. Harrison on the death of his son in action on the western front. By February 1916 the war was extending its grim clutches even nearer home:- "an air raid by Zeppelins in the Midland counties and in Walsall which took place on Monday evening, January 31st, 1916" persuaded the Directors to arrange insurance against air raids for all properties mortgaged with the Society. In the same year the Walsall Mutual had its first experience of a different kind of warfare:- "The Secretary reported that the Solicitor of the Society, Mr T. Harrison-Evans, had unfortunately met with an accident through a motor car knocking him down, and was now progressing satisfactorily." The Annual Report for 1917 recorded sound and re-assuring progress. The auditors pointed out that when a balance was struck the amount owed to the Society was £1,263. 14. 8d. Ten years earlier the equivalent figure had been £15. 16. 6d. The Directors were already looking ahead to post-war reconstruction – to homes fit for heroes – and sent a resolution to The Building Societies Association urging that Societies be well represented in any scheme that might be discussed for post-war housing. At local level they wrote to the Town Clerk of Walsall to emphasise that they wished to be represented on any local committee established to consider such matters. At the same meeting the Directors decided that the Secretary's salary should be a minimum of £200 p.a.; the impression is given that the method of paying him according to the business transacted was not working too well in war time. During the final year of the war the Society was investing quite heavily in war loans of one kind or another – £3,000 in War Bonds for example and £6,000 in National Securities. The Secretary, A. J. Llewellen, was rendering more particular service to King and Country. On October 25th, 1918 the Directors congratulated him on his election as Mayor and Chief Magistrate of Walsall.

The Walsall Mutual moved from war to peace with the declared aim of being fully involved in the national housing building programme. They shared their ambition with the Building Society movement as a whole, and like all other Societies they failed. The failure was probably a blessing in disguise for it forged the still unbroken link between building societies and owner occupiers. But the failure was deeply regretted by the contemporary leaders of the National Association of Building Societies and by their counterparts in Walsall. The NABS national policy was expressed as "every man is his own landlord – an ideal good alike for country and for individual." The Walsall Directors agreed with Ezra Naylor, Chairman of the B.S.A., urged that the houses so desperately needed should be built through the concerted efforts of small builders and local building societies rather than by local authorities:- "The small builder is a specialist, acts as his own architect and clerk of works, his own agent, both in buying and selling and has no establishment expenses, can vary his fitments to suit different tastes, and can adapt any house during erection to the wishes of the prospective purchaser at little or no extra cost. He usually arranges to have a few nearing

PLATE 21
Headquarters, Walsall Mutual, in 1960s.

PLATE 22

Board of Directors, Walsall Mutual, in 1960s. Left to right:-
H. W. Bonner *(Trustee)*, G. Harvey, G. L. W. Bradbury, C. F. Ballinger, Austin Fox *(Vice-Chairman)*, B. Baker *(Chairman)*, J. Richardson *(General Manager and Secretary)*, G. W. Richards *(Asst. Secretary)*, C. C. Gray *(Architect)*, E. H. Page, Sir J. Cliff Tibbits *(Trustee)*.

completion all the time, so as to save interest. By such economies he can build at a price with which the local authorities could not compete. Building Society managers especially know and appreciate this point. The houses will be purchased for occupation by the owner, and one cannot but feel that a few thousand people owning their own houses would be a better asset to a town than the same number of tenants occupying municipal houses." Such sentiments have a contemporary ring in the 1980s when the policy of selling council houses seems partly inspired by the heavy burden of public housing upon public expenditure, and partly by the view that independence should be encouraged and dependence limited to those who genuinely cannot help themselves. But although the Chairman and Vice-Chairman of Walsall Mutual were invited to a meeting in the Town Hall – chaired perhaps by their Secretary, the Mayor – nothing came of it. Houses for letting between the wars would in the main be built by local authorities and building societies would enter into partnership with potential or actual owner occupiers.

By March 1920, when the 57th Annual Meeting was held, there was evidence of that developing partnership. The Chairman reported a greatly increased demand for money on mortgage during the past year. The Directors had therefore to sell their 5% War Loan which "they did at very satisfactory figures." It is sad to remember those countless individuals who were less prescient than the Directors and left their money in War Loan when they could have moved it to bricks and mortar. During the next three years, 1920-23, progress was steadily unspectacular, although it is encouraging that the first annual meeting of the newly formed Midland Association of Building Societies was held in the Mayor's Parlour, Walsall, on 7 April, 1921. The Walsall Mutual celebrated its Diamond Jubilee on 21 February, 1923. Sixty years earlier they had gathered in St. Matthew's Hall to adopt rules and a constitution. Now 120 members and guests enjoyed a Town Hall dinner over which their Chairman, J. S. Shaw, presided, supported by the Chairman of the Building Societies Association, Mr Enoch Hill. The theme of the speeches following an excellent meal was "self help instead of coddling."

Very shortly after the Diamond Jubilee the Directors made a wise property purchase. For £9,000 they bought a corner block adjoining the Bridge Street offices of the Society. This block of six shops, with offices above, had a valuable frontage on Lichfield Street. It was another 34 years before the business activity of Walsall Mutual outgrew its Bridge Street headquarters, but expansion into the adjoining Lichfield Street block in 1957 and 1958 was by then fundamental to the rapid development of the Society in the 1960s. If the Directors had not bought Lichfield Street in 1923 their successors in 1957 would have been in serious difficulty. For the rest of the 1920s the progress of the Society was sure and purposeful. A protest made at the 61st Annual Meeting has, again, a contemporary ring in the early 1980s. The Society expressed the opposition of members to the Government's rent restriction legislation. They objected to the owner's limited right of obtaining possession and the reduction of rentals from 40% above to 25% above the standard pre-war level. They argued that a distinction should be drawn between "the owners of blocks of tenement houses and owners of cottage houses."

Finally, before deserting the 1920s for the 1930s, the progress of the Society during the previous fifty years is admirably summarised in the retirement speech of one of its officers. Mr A. J. Fryer, who retired as Cheques Steward in May 1924 and had been associated with the Walsall Mutual for fifty years said:- "I always look upon the upward turning point of the Society's career as being the year Mr A. Lees was appointed auditor, as he put down ruthlessly a number of inflated activities and placed the Society on a sound financial basis. Next came the advent of our present Secretary (A. J. Llewellen) who from the first outset threw himself heart and soul into the work which is now carried out on sound business lines which are a credit to the Town and to the Board of Directors." Mr Fryer concluded:- "In my early association it was a very precarious affair but now it has attained greatness." In 1939 "our present Secretary" (A. J. Llewellen), was succeeded by his son (A. J. B. Llewellen) and a three man continuity was established from Llewellen Senior who became Secretary in 1892 through Llewellen Junior who in 1949 handed over the Secretaryship to John Richardson who in 1980 holds office as a director of the Heart of England Building Society.

By the end of the 1920s Alderman A. J. Llewellen, former Mayor of Walsall, Secretary of the Walsall Mutual, Senior Partner in his firm of Auctioneers, Valuers, Accountants and Estate Agents, friend of Sir Enoch Hill (Chairman of the National Association of Building Societies) had another ten years ahead as Secretary. He was a senior and leading figure in the Building Society movement. In July 1931 he had leave of absence to attend the International Conference of

Building Societies to be held in Philadelphia. He also attended the centenary celebrations of the Building Societies of the United States as one of the delegates of the British Building Societies. In September the Walsall directors congratulated him on his safe return and on the fact that "the visit had been undertaken without any expense to the Society." The 69th Annual Report for the year ending February 28th 1932 showed further progress towards establishing a good financial base. Assets were £234,829 and liabilities £218,505. "The Home Bank Department continues to grow. The Automatic Recording Safes are highly appreciated and many new members are being enrolled. A savings account can be opened with an initial deposit of 5/-d or more, which sum is credited to the depositor's account, and interest is given at the rate of 4% on all amounts of ten shillings and upwards." This was Walsall's reply to the National Savings 6d stamp.

Although the 1930s – the Great Depression – were a period of recession and unemployment, they were remarkably stable years for those who had work and therefore money. Prices hardly changed, and if they did were as likely to go down as up. The building societies were encouraged to play their part in stimulating trade. They could "lend money at interest" to those who had "creditable accounts" and wished to improve their property. The Walsall Directors considered:- "It is probable also that were funds available numbers of house owners would like to effect desirable improvements in their property, such as central heating, equipment of bedrooms with basins of running water, replacement of old fashioned ranges and grates by more modern types, installation of gas and electrical appliances etc." Here surely are the germinating seeds of "Mr 1970", that centrally heated man who needed few clothes in the house or office, leading in his inevitable turn to the energy crises and electricity and gas price increases of the late 1970s and 1980. On 28 February 1933 the Assets of the Society had risen to £315,096 and the liabilities to £294,241. Trading margins were very narrow by modern standards and in the ensuing year the profit was only £1,500, enabling £2,000 to be transferred to reserves. By February 28th, 1939, the last Annual Report before the Second World War, Assets had further increased to £414,914; reserves stood at £26,549 and there were 2,683 members and depositors. In the 20 years between the wars membership had increased from 756 to 2,683, reserves from £3,921 to £26,549 and assets from £69,337 to £414,914.

A. J. Llewellen and his directors could well be satisfied with their stewardship during these twenty inter-war years. As recognition the Secretary's salary was increased to £700 p.a. in 1936 and that of the Assistant Secretary to £175 p.a. In 1937 the Auditor's fee was increased from 85 guineas to £100 and in April 1939 the Directors were invited by the shareholders to divide £165 amongst themselves. In June 1936 the Secretary reported:- "that the Strong Room of the Society was now completed and asked for authority to purchase a small safe to be kept in the Strong Room so that all monies belonging to the Society could be placed therein and paid into the Bank the following day." The decision taken by the Directors is one of the many changes of detail which were to take the Society from the stool and quill pen methods which predominated from 1863 to 1945 to the systems we know today. On June 26th, 1936, the Secretary's minute continues, "this was approved and authorised by the Board and the Directors decided to discontinue the practice of attending at the Bank on each Pay Night, after office hours, and that the sums received on such pay nights should be deposited in the safe kept for that purpose and paid into the Bank the following day."

With such minor streamlining of systems, the Society moved towards September 3rd, 1939. Sadly, a number of Directors and their Officers did not complete the journey. In July, 1936 the Society joined the newly formed Building Societies Association, successor to the National Association. The Vice-Chairman, W. T. Cotterell, was reluctant to be re-elected to that office after the 1937 Annual Meeting because of ill-health. The Directors procrastinated and did not appoint his successor until twelve months later. But unfortunately the Chairman, J. S. Shaw, also missed many meetings that year so that on November 26th 1937 the Directors decided:- "That in the absence of the Chairman of Directors at any meeting of the Board, the Director taking the chair at such meeting shall be empowered to sign any deed or document that may be required", and on December 17th:- "That Mr W. A. Homer, Director, be authorised by the Board to witness the sealing of documents in cases where the Chairman and Vice-Chairman are not readily available." In February 1938 the Surveyor, Mr Sam Wistance, died and was succeeded by Mr C. C. Gray. Chairman Shaw missed the 75th Annual Meeting in April, 1938 and at the Directors' Meeting held on April 29th resigned as Chairman after 27 years in that office and 58 years as a Director. He, too, had been an element of strengthening continuity in the affairs of the Society, reaching back to the 17th Annual Meeting and to the first Secretary, Joseph Dixon. W. T. Cotterell, the Vice-Chairman, brooked no shilly-shallying this year, and resigned with his Chairman. Shaw was succeeded by W. A. Homer and Cotterell by his son, A.W.

Between April 1938 and September 1939 four great servants of the Society died in depressingly regular succession. The first to go, in August, 1938, was Alderman J. A. Leckie, JP., MP., who had become a Trustee in 1935 and was the Borough Member of Parliament. J. S. Shaw, whose 58 years on the Board we have already noted, died the following month. He, also, was a Trustee and the two vacancies were filled at a Special Meeting in April, 1939 by the election of Sir William Talbot JP and Councillor (late Sir) Cliff Tibbits, JP. Four new Directors Mr B. Baker, Mr Austin Fox, Mr H. W. Bonner and the Society's solicitor, Mr Frank Cooper, all appointed in June 1939, were to become leaders of the Society in the post-war years. Their leadership was needed for in April 1939 the Secretary, A. J. Llewellen, a widower for some years, died still in office. He had been Secretary for 47 years and if any one individual is to be regarded as the corner stone of the Society's edifice, he is the one. Fortunately for the unsettled Directors a new Secretary was ready, fully trained, and A. J. B. Llewellen was appointed to succeed his father on June 20th, 1939 at a salary of £550 p.a. His place as Assistant Secretary was taken by A. E. Gough who had been the Cashier. In the meantime, W. T. Cotterell died on May 16th: he had been a Director for 29 years and Vice-Chairman for 10. In fifteen months the Society had lost two of the three Trustees, the Chairman of 27 years standing, the Vice-Chairman of 10 years service, and the man who had been Secretary for 47 years.

The Directors took quicker and more urgent action in September 1939 than their predecessors had judged necessary in August, 1914. They met in Special Meeting five days after war was declared and decided that withdrawals of up to £25 would be paid without notice, that in cases of extreme urgency withdrawals of up to £50 could be authorised by Chairman or Vice-Chairman and that all other withdrawals would be subject to 28 days notice. The immediate impact of war on the building industry is shown by a decision on September 14th to reduce to £8,000 a loan of £10,000 granted to a local firm of housebuilders shortly before war was declared. On September 29th the rate for new mortgages was increased to 5.5% and by February,

1940 the Secretary was wisely arranging to deposit elsewhere copies of the abstract of ledger balances. But in all the financial and human confusion of the early months of the greatest war yet the Directors retained their human touch. On February, 1940:- "The Secretary read a letter from ——— explaining that owing to the continued illness of his wife he found himself in straitened circumstances. He requested that an application for withdrawal of £16 made by his son should be paid, although his son was only 14½. The Board authorised the withdrawal."

Mortgage business was at a low level during 1940. At the 77th Annual General Meeting the Secretary expressed his thanks for the kind reference to his late father. Duplicate sets of the ledger balances were with the Walsall and Shrewsbury branches of Lloyds' Bank. A proposal of a merger from Brighton and Sussex Building Society was politely rejected. Brighton was about to become an invasion area but it is hard to believe that they thought of Walsall as a safe evacuation teminus. In June, 1940 the Surveyor could not comment on a £3,000 mortgage application on property in London "because of difficulty in travelling" and he was asked to brief a responsible local architect. In January 1941 it was made clear that the Fire Watching (Business Premises) Order applied to the Society's offices in Bridge Street, and a joint scheme was worked out with the other tenants. The 78th Annual Report dated February 28th, 1941 showed a drop in membership and a very modest increase in reserves and in assets.

By April 1941 however the drop in new mortgage business and the steady repayments on existing mortgages meant that liquid funds were increasing uncomfortably. B. Baker, one of the new generation of Directors and a future Chairman, suggested that the Finance Committee should consider investment. This was the beginning of a steady flow of funds into the Government's war chest. In June £8,000 went to the Post Office Savings Bank; in October £3,000 was invested in 3% Savings Bonds 1955/56. In January 1942 it was decided to invest £12,000 during Warships' Week and by December, 1942 the Society had £20,000 in Savings Bonds. The 80th Annual Report in February 1943 confirmed that the Directors had experienced great difficulty in obtaining mortgage business during the year (the total was £23,000) and in March 1943 another £12,000 was invested, this time in "Wings for Victory". In May 1943 a further £6,000 was invested in War Weeks, but mortgage business was now increasing and in February 1944 the Directors reported that £45,000 had been advanced on mortgage during the past twelve months. The final Annual Meeting of the war took place on March 25th, 1945. The Directors reported curtailed mortgage activity, coupled with investments of £171,897. 4. 3d which could be made available for mortgage business when demand increased. Building Societies, including the Walsall Mutual, had played a valuable part in financing the war. Not only had they loaned their corporate funds to the Government but of course many individual members had withdrawn their savings from the Society and re-invested in war stocks. Before leaving the war years, and in a lighter vein which nevertheless emphasises the necessary strictness of control, in June 1944 Walsall Mutual was in serious trouble with the Ministry of Supply because too much paper was being used in the Annual Report. The Registrar of Friendly Societies was consulted. He ruled that an abbreviated report could indeed be published as long as it was borne in mind that every member was entitled to a full report in the form prescribed by the Registrar and if any member requested such a report, he must be given it.

The end of the war gained no foothold in the Directors' minutes. Soon however they found themselves at war with the new Labour Government. In October 1945 a special sub-committee was formed "to consider the implications of A. Bevan's remarks as Minister of Health." On November 30th the committee recommended, no doubt with regret, that no further action should be taken. In December the mortgage rate was reduced to 4%, investment rates to 1.75% and 2.25% and income tax to 9/-d in the £1. From January 1946 onwards the Society began to realise investments – £10,000 in January and £5,000 in February – and lend the money on mortgage. Once again the Societies were lending to owner occupiers and local authorities were building for tenants. The Directors were therefore properly concerned to find that the building licence system meant that private building was virtually at a standstill. But the 83rd Annual Report dated 28.2,46 showed that £75,013 had been advanced on mortgage during the year, and reserves and assets had both increased. The Vice-Chairman, seconding the adoption of the report "thought that as the Society had paid over £6,000 in income tax and defence contributions they were entitled to a little more respect from certain Ministers of the Crown. More encouragement should be given to people to own their own houses." A year later, at the 1947 Annual

Meeting, the Directors reported that building activity had been further restricted and that all mortgage business was limited to change of ownership. "The Society had again advanced over £70,000 to mortgage business but a noteworthy item in the accounts was the repayment of advances and interest amounting to over £88,000, easily a record for the Society which showed a striking testimony to the prosperity and thrift of the citizens of Walsall." The Vice-Chairman commented that "A benevolent Government tried to provide houses for everybody on a more or less stereotyped pattern."

At the Annual Meeting on 29th April, 1949 the Chairman reported that the Society's activities were seriously curtailed by Government controls. But the end of this frustrating period was in sight. By the time John Richardson succeeded as Secretary at the end of 1949 the Walsall Mutual was poised to take part in the tremendous building society expansion which has changed the face of so many towns and villages during the past thirty years. Mr Richardson's arrival in Walsall was indeed a local harbinger of that change. In April 1949 the Directors decided, wisely as events were to prove, that the Society should have a full-time Secretary. They offered the job to A. J. B. Llewellen at an annual salary of £900. He could not give up his flourishing private practice and regretfully declined. The appointment was then advertised in the Building Societies Gazette, the Manchester Guardian, the Daily Telegraph and the Birmingham Post and on October 7th, 1949 John Richardson was appointed from a short list of seven. His warm personality, administrative ability and clear, firm financial control were to be major factors in the above average progress and expansion of the Society during the next 25 years. A. J. B. Llewellen resigned as Secretary on November 25th 1949 and was elected to the Board. Office accommodation in the Bridge Street block was re-arranged and the firm of Llewellen moved to the first floor.

As the Society left the war-time decade, it moved into a quarter century of vigorous expansion and development. In 1949 the Assets were £548,146 and the Reserves £45,190. In 1959 the comparable figures were £2,491,586 and £102,357 and in 1969 £10,626,137 and £388,827. At the 1974 Annual General Meeting, the last before amalgamation with Rugby and Warwick, the Assets were £22,842, 920 and the Reserves £863,000. The other comparison of interest is that, compared with an average of £70,000 immediately after the war, the amount loaned on mortgage reached a peak of £4.95m in

1972. Office stool and quill pen could not handle financial growth of this order and it is not therefore surprising that John Richardson's other contributions during this period of continuous expansion included mechanisation followed by computerisation, and a take-over of the Lichfield Street premises to house the Society's steadily increasing staff. The opening soliloquy to the drama was spoken by the Vice-Chairman A. W. Cotterell – at the Annual Meeting on 28 April 1950. He "emphasised that the Society was a small Society but a sound Society, with a high degree of liquidity in its funds, low expenses of management and a hidden reserve in its office premises." He might well have added, but did not, that there was also a hidden asset in the goodwill and virtually voluntary support of the Board. Each Director was voted £25 for his work for the Society during the past year.

The story of the Walsall Mutual during these final 25 years is one of successful and efficient management. A detailed account of it would be as technically wearisome and as potentially hypochondriac as taking one's blood pressure every morning before breakfast. The historian of the Heart of England must seek to catch the flavour of the years without reporting every tread on the staircase of escalated human and financial activity. At the 89th A.G.M. in April 1952 the Chairman, W. A. Homer, reported:- "The Society is fulfilling its function of promoting home ownership, 87% of our total mortgages relate to owner-occupied dwelling houses and are granted for the purpose of acquiring a home. Thrift may be a despised virtue but it is something that could lead our country back to financial stability, promote social contentment, and enable families to be brought up under the best conditions for health and happiness, and in this good work our Society is playing a worthy part." In 1953 an approach was made to the Walsall Permanent Building Society with a view to amalgamation. The Board of the Permanent were "not interested", but their decision meant delay, not cancellation and the amalgamation took place 14 years later in 1967. The Chairman had a telling point to make when speaking at the Annual Meeting in 1954: with hindsight one can see that had the country adhered to such financial rectitude we would have been spared the public expenditure crises of the 1970s and 1980. "There are three basic necessities of life and they are food, shelter and clothing. These should be the first charge upon a person's income. When these are provided money may safely be spent on other, less important things. But the tendency of many people today is to leave the provision of housing to others, and many of these people, by a careful rearrangement of their spending, could help themselves and solve their own housing problems."

By the end of 1954 increased business made it necessary to re-structure management arrangements and delegate more authority and responsibility to the executive. The Secretary became Manager and Secretary: the work of the Directors was increasingly done by sub-committees. The Society lost two senior Directors in early 1955. W. A. Homer, who had been Chairman from 1938-51 and a Director from 1933, died in January. His successor as Chairman in 1951 had been A .W. Cotterell and he died, still in office as Chairman in February. He had been a Director since 1937 and was Vice-Chairman throughout Homer's years as Chairman. It was at this time that Mr Frank Cooper's splendid service as Solicitor and Director reached fifty years; a dinner was held in his honour at the George Hotel to mark this rare distinction. Mr B. Baker was elected Chairman and Mr A. Fox as Vice-Chairman. They had joined the Board in June 1939, at the time when previous senior Directors had died in quick succession, and the class of 1939 had now come to power. In 1956 the Directors accepted a recommendation of the Finance Committee that a staff superannuation scheme be introduced, "for male members only." This seems late in the day to a generation accustomed to the pension arrangements of the 1970s and 1980s. It was however typical of its period and the previous absence of such arrangements – in society as a whole not merely in the building societies – explains why so many worked until life or health failed them. A prophetic link between 1956 and 1980 is contained in the Chairman's words at the Annual Meeting. "Drastic economy" said Mr Baker "in public expenditure and increased personal saving is the supreme need of the hour." He followed a year later with:- "Everybody, with justification in my view, complains about the penal taxation imposed in this country which most certainly is a powerful factor in the creation of the inflationary conditions which exist today." Truly, we have been slow to learn.

It was during this period that the Society reaped the benefit of the Lichfield Street purchase of many years ago. New office space was essential to the expanding Society. In February 1957 A. J. B. Llewellen agreed to vacate the first floor of the Bridge Street block. The next month a Premises Committee was formed to deal with the details of extension and expansion. It was no doubt encouraging to the Directors at this time to be told that "nationally only about 15% of Building Society shareholders were interest conscious to the extent of shifting their funds for higher yields." At the 95th Annual Meeting in 1958 the Chairman reported the development of the new offices on the corner of Bridge Street and Lichfield Street; he added that since the offices were last extended business had developed from 600 mortgages to 2,000 mortgages and 3,000 investors. Law and order were clearly not as yet social and political issues however for in July, 1958, the Directors minuted that "the provision of a burglar alarm was considered and deemed to be unnecessary." The new premises were taken over on 1st September, 1958 and an informal reception for Press and Guests was held on the evening of September 4th. The cost of the extension was £17,210.

The Society ended the 1950s in a strong financial position as the figures already quoted show. In May 1959 the Secretary reported that investments were flowing in at double the rate of a year ago. The problem of financial control was how to deal with a net inflow of funds; 15 years later of course the more difficult cash flow problem was how to manage with a net outflow. The 1960s were a period of continuous and considerable expansion and in November 1959 the Directors had already agreed in principle the need to develop branch offices. At that time the Society had 415 members in the Aldridge district and the first branch was sought there. The search for a suitable site took eight years and contracts for the purchase of 49 Anchor Road, Aldridge were not exchanged until March 1968. The first branch to be opened was therefore at Brownhills in September 1968, and the Aldridge Branch opened its doors in July, 1969. A dinner in Aldridge for one hundred people was judged to be a good public relations exercise. By this time priority was being given to Bloxwich and Cannock in the search for new branches. No. 27 Market Place, Cannock was acquired in March, 1971 and opened for business as the third branch office on April 2nd. In October 1971 No. 2 Conduit Street, Lichfield was bought for a branch office and opened on June 4th 1973. The policy of branch development was undoubtedly good for the Society for in January 1974 the Secretary reported that the branches were almost entirely responsible for the net investment inflow. As in February, 1974 withdrawals were 95% of new investments, the Society might have been in some trouble had it depended on Headquarters alone. The last branch to open before amalgamation was at 155 High Street, Bloxwich and the Society was brave enough to choose April 1st for the launch. Finally, in this story of property development, the Directors found that the 1957 expansion of headquarters was inadequate to cope with the boom conditions of the 1960s. In 1965 they decided to expand into the Lichfield Street shop frontage – they had already occupied the offices above – and this project was carried out during 1966. The present Directors of Heart of England must take much satisfaction from the acquisition and development of these properties before prices began to rise dramatically in the 1970s.

A necessarily brief examination of two other matters – the Centenary in 1963 and the financial problems of the 1960s and early 1970s – will complete this chapter. In May, 1961 John Richardson reported that demand for mortgages was rising faster than the inflow of funds and that new investment in the Society might have to be stimulated. He illustrated the potential by reference to a recent survey of investors:-

8% had money in a Building Society
31% had money in a Post Office Savings Bank
28% had money in Premium Bonds
27% had money in Bank Accounts.

The problem from May 1961 until amalgamation in 1974 was that the needs of investors and borrowers rarely matched. The Society was either grappling with a net outflow or a net inflow. It is a problem the Building Societies have still not solved and it makes them very vulnerable to political and social reaction.

At the 1961 A.G.M. the Chairman reported that the Society's margin of surplus was being eaten away. This was socially undesirable in a country where only 1/3rd of the population were owner occupiers compared with 2/3rd in the United States. A year later the Society's business had increased by 12½%. The average mortgage loan was £1,500 and this could be obtained by a person earning £12-£15 per week. During the following year 1,000 new accounts were opened and the Society was better able to meet all demands for mortgage loans. At the 101st A.G.M. in 1964 the Chairman spoke of a highly successful year of unprecedented growth. He commented that although the Government's budget was described as "expansion without inflation, the price of land and houses was increasing at an alarming rate." This of course was the last Budget of 13 Conservative years: a year later the Chairman could only comment that the First Labour Budget was "inflation without expansion." In 1968 the Walsall

Mutual took its blood pressure and compared it with that of the movement as a whole:-

	Movement	*Walsall*
Growth Rate	14.7%	21%
Management Costs	12.1½%	11/7d%
Surplus on Year	8/-%	8/-%

This was the year in which Mr B. Baker had to resign both as Chairman and Director on medical advice. He was one of the 1939 new boys – succeeded as Chairman by his contemporary, Austin Fox – and assets had risen from £1.5m to £10m during his chairmanship.

The next six years, 1968-74 were outstandingly successful. Under the Chairmanship first of Austin Fox and then of A. L. Wiggin F.C.A. the policy of local branch development increased assets from £9.4m to £22.8m. Mr Wiggin who became Chairman in 1972 was one of three directors who joined the Board at the time of the merger in 1967 with Walsall Permanent Building Society, of which he was Vice Chairman. Mr Frank Wootton M.B.E., Chairman of the Walsall Permanent since 1948 and a director since 1935, also gave valuable service during this expansionary period, until his death in 1973. One of the benefits of the 1967 merger of the two Walsall Societies was the added strength and experience that these two brought to the Board. They contributed in good measure to the 1968-74 progress and development.

The next year, 1969, was a good one for Building Societies. From June to December 1969 net investment in Unit Trusts was £71m, net investment in Building Societies £328m, and net dis-investment in National Savings was £222m. During 1969 3,500 new accounts were opened at Walsall head office and 500 at the branches. In May 1970 there was a record monthly net inflow of £201,000 and for three successive months investments exceeded £300,000. In September 1971 however the inflow and outflow of funds were in rough balance at £550,000 each and the problems which for a few days affected the Derbyshire Building Society, in connection with the liquidation of Rolls Royce, showed how important it was that the Walsall's investment portfolio contained a substantial proportion of quoted securities which could be realised immediately as opposed to local authority bonds, usually subject to six months notice. The resulting investment policy change was not without its own problems. By December 1973 the Walsall Mutual was again battling with the problem of a net outflow of funds. It therefore needed investments which were easily cashed not only as a buffer against a Derbyshire/Rolls Royce type of problem but also to provide funds to keep mortgage flowing. The Directors resolved that surpluses would henceforth go to readily marketable investments and in August 1973, because this type of investment had slumped in value, the Society along with others was subjected to some pressure upon its reserve ratios. A revaluation of the headquarters building corrected the imbalance. By the summer mortgage demand had become so heavy that the Society had to adopt a "members only" mortgage policy. By December 1973 therefore mortgage advances and business in hand were less than half of the high levels of a year ago. Repayments alone were adequate to meet this low level of demand. This was fortunate as in February 1974 withdrawals were 95% of new investment. In March they actually exceeded new investment for the first time – by £25,000. The outflow was temporary; in July there was a net inflow of £110,000. The net inflow of funds during the Walsall's final year was £1.4m, there was a 13.5% increase in assets and the Directors must have gone to their farewell dinner on September 10th 1974 with a sense of a job sustained throughout one hundred and eleven years and well ended by amalgamation with Rugby and Warwick on August 31st, 1794.

Eleven years earlier another dinner had signalled one hundred years of growth from a small gathering of enthusiasts in St. Matthew's Hall on February 19th, 1863 to a valued and respected part of the Walsall scene in 1963. On the exact anniversary telegrams were received from many well wishers. By then the anonymous author – undoubtedy General Manager John Richardson who had become a Director on reaching his personal 21st with the Society in 1971 – had produced the invaluable "1863, A Century of Interest 1963." Five thousand copies were printed of which 2,100 were sent to members, 400 to other Societies, and 1,000 to Walsall citizens who were not members of the Society. Eighty two invitations were sent for the Centenary Dinner and eighty accepted. Copies of "A Century of Interest" were available in the assembly area, but the temptation to place one with each table setting was resisted. The dinner was a Walsall and a Building Society occasion and taken with the farewell dinner eleven years later was a fitting tribute to what independence, initiative, self help and a willingness to shoulder one's own responsibilities can do for the spirit of a family and the quality of a nation.

Progress and Development: Oxford Building Society

Year	*Assets*	*Reserves*	*Chairman*	*Secretary*	*Address*
1878	£8,888	£230	G. Quelch	W. Woodward	64 George St.
1888	£18,030	£658	W. Parker	J. Richardson	11 George St.
1898	£33,076	£1,044	J. Nix	J. H. Darwood	21 George St.
1908	£56,249	£1,455	J. Nix	Chas Green	21 George St.
1918	£66,892	£1,301	A. Brooke	Chas Green	48 New Inn Hall Street
1928	£130,705	£2,617	W. M. Gray	Chas Green	Ditto
1938	£196,756	£6,518	C. G. Goldsworthy	Chas Green	Ditto
1948	£244,365	£11,491	M. F. Gray	S. W. Wren	Ditto
1958	£307,870	£13,978	M. F. Gray	S. W. Wren	Ditto
1968	£1,055,672	£54,858	J. Evans	S. W. Wren	154 Cowley Road
1974	£2,254,198	£101,919	J. Evans	S. W. Wren	Ditto

PLATE 23

Sydney Wren, Secretary, Oxford Industrial and Provident, 1946-74; Consultant (HEBS) 1974-79; Local Director (HEBS) 1979–.

PLATE 24

Treasurer Powell (Oxford Society) as seen by a local cartoonist.

PLATE 25

154 Cowley Rd., Oxford (early 1960s). Headquarters of Oxford Society, 1962-74. Now a branch of Heart of England.

PLATE 26

F. S. Pollard, Secretary, Coalville Society 1961-78; Consultant and Local Director (HEBS) 1978-80.

PLATE 27

Headquarters, Coalville Society, 1965-78. Now a branch of Heart of England.

CHAPTER TEN

The Oxford Industrial and Provident Land and Building Society Ltd: 1860-1974

THE HISTORY OF the Society, which in 1962 became the Oxford Provident Building Society, is encapsulated above. What the chart cannot show is that 1878 is the wrong base line; what it does not show is that the Society amalgamated with the Rugby and Warwick Society in 1974 and thus became part of the Heart of England Society in due course. The Oxford Industrial and Provident Land and Building Society Ltd. was in fact founded in 1860 and subsequently registered under the Industrial and Provident Societies Act of 1871. The first document which asserts these claims however is the Statement of Accounts for the year ending 31 December 1871. No earlier documents have survived and there is no information about the Society prior to that blotched, faded, tattered and repaired single sheet of paper. Moreover, unlike the other Societies in Heart of England, we have nothing but the Annual Statements of Accounts until February 18th, 1936 when the first surviving minute book of Directors' Meetings begins.

Oxford in 1860 was a lively place, dominated by its university. The arrival of the Land and Building Society can have made little impact on a university city which was still vigorously debating the report of the University Commission of 1850 and the resultant University Act of 1854. These had swept away the eighteenth century sleepy university and dragged it squealing into modern times. Professors were now "required to take a much more active part in teaching and the work of education"; the privileges of men of rank– "gentlemen commoners" – were abolished. In the same year that the Oxford Industrial and Provident was registered (1871) the abolition by Parliament of University Tests ended a long period when you had to be a member of the established Church of England to teach or study at Oxford. The history of the university is of course carefully documented; the early years of our building society have escaped through the wastepaper basket and the dust bin. But in 1980, if you stroll through Oxford within a radius of half a mile of Carfax, the branches of the building societies are as much a feature of the scene as the mediaeval architecture of the colleges.

In 1878, eighteen years after foundation, the reserves of the struggling Building Society were only £230 and of this small figure £3.10.0 represented the value of an iron safe, £7. 14. od the value of spare copies of the rules, and 7/6d the value of unused pass books. Loans on nine estates – a reminder that in those early days the Society was dealing in land as well as buildings – totalled £3,388. 7. 5. and loans on property were £5,265. 18. od. There were ten directors in addition to the Chairman. The office of the Society was in the centre of the city and of the university, in George Street, where it remained, although changing number, for forty years. It is doubtful whether the Society rented more than a room in the building, for this was a mini Society and was to remain so until it re-registered under the Building Societies Act in January 1963. As long as it was registered under the 1871 Act it was bound to remain small. For many years the maximum permitted investment per member was only £200 and at the time of re-registration it was still limited to £500. Before we leave these early years there is one other reasonable inference to be drawn from the table at the beginning of the chapter. Charles Green became Secretary in 1903 and still held that office when he died in June 1946. S. W. Wren, who had become a member of the Society in 1938, was appointed Assistant Secretary to Charles Green two months before the latter's death and succeeded him as Secretary. He retained the office until amalgamation with Rugby and Warwick in 1974 when he was appointed as 'Consultant' for the Oxford Area, and is still a Local Director of Heart of England in 1980. The Society enjoyed a continuity of seventy years through these two Secretaries and this must have been a considerable source of strength.

Charles Green had been Secretary for 33 years on February 18th 1936, the date of the earliest surviving minute of a Directors' meeting. These early records confirm that mortgage activities were strictly local. It is exceptional to find a loan on property outside

Oxford and the immediate neighbourhood; when money goes as far afield as Sedbergh or Bournemouth it is to people who had previously lived in Oxford. The fact that several houses in "Jericho" were in mortgage to the Society is not evidence of Middle Eastern empire building but a reminder of that part of Oxford with its fascinatingly inappropriate name. In February 1936 the Directors met in their office at 48 New Inn Hall Street opposite St. Peter's Hall (now St. Peter's College). They rented the property from St. Peter's who in their turn rented it from Brasenose College, to whom it belonged. Later, in the early 1960s, it was uncertainty and insecurity about the lease which led the Directors to buy 154 Cowley Road for £7,000, and become masters in their own house for the first time. In 1936 the Directors met weekly, immediately after the subscription meeting which was held each Monday from 5.30 p.m. to 7.30 p.m. This arrangement lasted until November 1942 when they decided to meet on alternate Tuesdays at 5.30 p.m. during the winter months from November to March. When March came the return to weekly meetings was unacceptable and they continued to meet roughly once a fortnight for the rest of their days. The Annual General Meetings were then held in the Masonic Rooms in High Street whence they had moved from Taphouse's Music Room in 1930. The 1939 A.G.M. was held in the Wesley Memorial Hall in New Inn Hall Street and it was there that the final Special Meeting of Shareholders was held on 15 January 1974.

The outbreak of war in September 1939 made little financial difference to a Society whose members were limited to such a small maximum investment. The Directors were aware of no cash flow problems and did not need to limit withdrawals. But the world wide crisis of aggression coincided with a constitutional crisis for the Society which remained unresolved until 1962. The Registrar of Friendly Societies drew the Directors attention to the fact that because the Society was registered under the 1871 Act, and not under Building Society legislation, they could not obtain the legal protection of the Prevention of Frauds (Investments) Act of 1939. He advised them to wind up the Society and re-form under Building Society regulations. In October 1939, with the whole future of western civilisation in the melting pot, it was too much for the Directors to contemplate. They were after all elderly and relatively humble folk – stall holder in the covered market, buyer for Elliston and Cavell's, supplier of linoleum to Government departments. They sought, and were given, permission to postpone the change until six months after the end of hostilities.

The remaining war years were relatively uneventful for the Society. In view of the investment in Jericho it is hardly surprising that in October 1940 the Secretary was negotiating with Mr Lazarus who wished to evacuate London and rent the three back rooms at 48 New Inn Hall Street, at a rental of £50 p.a. The Mayor of Oxford asked for a subscription to a fund to enable occupiers of business premises to carry out their obligations under the Fire Prevention Order 1941: one guinea was sent. The Secretary reported that a billeting order was served on him in April 1941, in connection with 48, New Inn Hall Street, but nothing seems to have come of it. In December 1941 £2,000 each was invested in National War Loan and in Savings Bonds. On 14 August, 1945 the Directors "realising that the end of the war was in sight, decided to brief H. G. Bullock, Solicitor of 4 George Street re the liquidation of this Society and its re-formation under the Building Societies Act." Mr Bullock was Senior Partner in the firm of H. F. Galpin & Co. About the same date the author of this history, newly out of Burma and waiting to invade Malaya, heaved a sigh of relief at the end of hostilities and turned his thoughts to home after four years in the Far East. By December, 1945 I was staying with my wife at the Mitre Hotel, less than three hundred yards from New Inn Hall Street and, for all I know, rubbing shoulders with Directors of the Oxford Industrial and Provident on the pavement of the High or Cornmarket.

It was another 17 years before the Society was dissolved and re-registered under the Building Societies Act of 1962. It did however bring a new Secretary. S. W. Wren had decided not to take up a senior military appointment in the Far East, but to return to his native Oxford. In June 1946 he was appointed Assistant Secretary to Charles Green and, like many other demobilised officers exchanged the rigours of war for the equal but different hardships of life in immediate post-war Britain. His appointment was no doubt precipitated by the Registrar's insistence upon a change, (of which he he was not told,) whereby the Society would come under the Building Societies Act. His working day began at 8.30 a.m. and his first daily task was to light the office coal fire. The Green/Wren partnership was short lived however and when Charles Green died suddenly in August 1946 he was succeeded by Sydney Wren. Nor did the coal fire last much longer. The minutes of the Directors' meeting on 3

September 1946 show that an electric fire had been installed in its place. Support staff for the new Secretary remained a problem throughout his tenure of office. A clerical assistant was appointed in September 1946 but by November he "had been given reasonable time to find another job" because "his work is not accurate enough." Mr R. Yates, Mr D. J. Ash, Mr Rex Whitaker and Mr W. M. Thody at later dates were excellent Assistant Secretaries, but Mr Ash left the Society for an appointment with Messrs. Crappers returning as successor to Mr Thody after several years away, and Mr Thody was taken seriously ill during the closing months of his appointment. Otherwise, junior clerks came and went with unsettling regularity. This led the Secretary to advise that the Directors should adopt salary scales which would allow professional progression and promotion within the Society, but they were unwilling and, in employment bouyant Oxford, staffing remained a problem.

The Directors continued to exercise a detailed and in some respects Dickensian control of the Society's finances. On May 6th, 1947, the Secretary asked "if the Board of Directors would, in view of the increase in business, consider improving the office by the purchase of two rugs and new lino in the reception office and also consider whether the offices could be redecorated. The carpets were approved and the decorating was left in the hands of Messrs. Gray and Pipkin. Mr Pipkin would also investigate the possibility of obtaining some second hand lino." If the Directors were saving money on second hand lino, the Secretary was saving them a much larger sum by offering remarkably prescient financial advice which they were sensible enough to accept. A minute of 17.6.47 reads:- "As the Society's reserve fund was invested in an undated stock (2½% Consols) the Secretary reported that the stock would be subject to a fairly heavy fall in price, should there be any weakening of the Government's position owing to a lack of productivity in Industry, and advised the Board that it would be a good time to sell in order to maintain the capital value of the investment and consolidate the profit in some other dated stock. This was approved." A Secretary who could forecast the movement of Consols, and foresee the future problems of industrial productivity, was worth his weight in gold – even at January 1980 prices. The profit realised was £2,711. 16. 8d and it was reinvested in 3% Savings 1960-70. Mr Wren was of course required to think small as well as big. On July 1st, 1947 he reported that the cost of the Annual Directors and Staff

Outing – the first to be held – was £1. 15. 8d per head and that the profit on the bar was 3/10d. These outings were a pleasant feature of the immediate post-war years – to the Isle of Wight, to Woodstock for a dinner, and so on. But when the local confectionery wholesaler, who generously gave chocolates, sweets and refreshment to the party, went bankrupt – perhaps through miscalculated generosity – the outings ceased.

So the Society moved through the fifteen immediate post-war years. A glance at the chart at the beginning of the chapter will show that financial progress was very modest between 1948 and 1958 and that reserves were actually lower in 1958 than they had been ten years earlier. The Society was effectively hamstrung by the investment limit. The ten years from 1958 to 1968 saw considerable financial growth however, largely a result of the re-formation of the Society as a Building Society from 1 January 1963. Christmas 1962 is a watershed in the post-war affairs of the Society for two reasons. Not only did it become a registered building society but it moved home from the tenanted 48 New Inn Hall Street to the owner occupied 154 Cowley Road. 1962 was a busy year for the Secretary and his Board of Directors.

Shortly before this period the Treasurer, Councillor F. J. Powell a Liberal member of the Oxford City Council, died at the Radcliffe Infirmary in his 86th year. He had been a director for 36 years and had served the Society well in that "limited vision" way which was typical of the Board at the time. He was a busy man, a great talker, and somewhat absent minded, at least in his latter years. A witty contemporary cartoon in the Oxford Mail showed him standing beside a donkey which was looking round with astonishment for a missing back leg. A passing R.S.P.C.A. Inspector seeks explanation from another by-stander and is told "if you ask me Inspector, the Councillor has been talking to it." Earlier, on March 11th 1958, the Directors proposed "that in view of the Treasurer's advancing years, and the danger to him personally of injury if attacked while conveying the Society's monies to the Bank, that arrangements be made for the use of the Bank's Night Safe." As so often with minutes, this one only tells half a story. The other half is that on the day following a subscription meeting the Treasurer was increasingly to be found going about his other business with the previous night's takings still firmly clutched in his right hand. Such were the Directors of the day: their type of strength had successfully carried the Society through

100 years of local history. It would have been inadequate in the Building Society movement of the 1970s and 1980s.

When 1960 arrived the Society did not celebrate its centenary partly no doubt because the records did not allow a precise date to be established. The only reference in the minutes that year is to receipt of a congratulatory letter from the Manager of the local branch of the Westminster Bank. Fifty years earlier one of his predecessors had similarly recognised the half century. The confusion of date is well shown by the fact that it was not until February 28th 1961 that the Oxford Mail published an excellent centenary article about the Society. But in February 1960 the Secretary was aware of a problem as potentially serious as the vulnerability of Consols. He urged the Directors to find a new headquarters "lest a new road, or widening in New Inn Hall Street might force a move." These were the days when Oxford roads, and the Christ Church Meadow Road Scheme in particular, were headlines in the national press. In January 1961 the Chairman, M. F. Gray died; he had been a director for 30 years and chairman for 15. Gray was Managing Director of Messrs. W. M. Gray & Sons, Builders, Decorators and Funeral Directors (and was a son of the late Alderman W. M. Gray, sometime Mayor of Oxford and Chairman of the Society in 1928). Both were ardent East Oxford Liberals and were highly respected.

M. F. Gray will be remembered for his humane compassion to others, his forward looking and impartial decisions which, coupled with the unbounding energy of Mr Wren, were instrumental in the progress of the Society during their long and happy partnership. At the 100th Annual General Meeting on 28 February 1961 members were told that a complete amendment of the rules was intended – they had last been printed in 1914. In August 1961 the Directors took a final decision to buy 154 Cowley Road for £7,000, and in October the Secretary reported a letter from the Registrar of Friendly Societies suggesting that during the next three years the Society should change to registration under the Building Societies Act. For the next two years at least, it was all go.

The disbandment of the Oxford Industrial and Provident Land and Building Society Limited (under the Industrial and Provident Societies Act 1871) and its re-creation as the Oxford Provident Building Society (Incorporated under the Building Societies Act, 1962) is the unique contribution of Oxford to the history of Heart of England. No other constituent society had this experience and it is therefore worth examining in some detail. When it was all over Mr Sydney Wren, who organised the change with considerable efficiency, read a paper to the Chiltern Centre of the Building Societies Institute (of which he was a past Chairman) explaining how it was done. The following account draws heavily on that paper and I am most grateful to Mr Wren for allowing me to see it. As we have already seen the Registrar of Friendly Societies, who is also Registrar of Building Societies, pressed for the change so that members would have greater legal protection against fraud. The problem for the Directors and their Secretary was that the Registrar could see only one way to effect the change – first to dissolve the Oxford Industrial and Provident and then to found its successor, the Oxford Provident. Mr Wren's concern was that the formal official notices dissolving the Society would have to be published in local newspapers and that in the ensuing uncertainty as to why the old Society had closed, there would be sufficient sense of failure to prevent the new Society launching successfully. The Directors decided to take Counsel's opinion, and were fortunate in the legal advice they received. They were encouraged to change two rules of the existing Society. This had to be done either at a Special Meeting of members or at the Annual Meeting. The alterations to the rules were put to the 101st Annual Meeting on February 27th, 1962 and because a Special Meeting had been avoided no alarm bells rang.

Rules 1 and 6 were the two vehicles of change. Rule 1 concerned the name and objects of the Society and the proposed change was to add one sentence, as follows:- "The Society may promote or form a Building Society for the purpose of acquiring all or any of the property rights and liabilities of the Society and may sell or dispose of the undertakings of the Society or any part thereof to a Building Society for such consideration as the Committee of Management of the Society in their absolute discretion may think fit and in particular for shares and/or deposits and/or cash of such Building Society." Rule 6, which concerned capital monies, was amended by adding the following two sentences:- "Should there be at any time more money in the Society's funds than can profitably be made use of, the Board of Directors shall have power in their absolute discretion to apply such money in paying off the shares of any member of the Society at the full sum paid upon such shares with interest. If a member who has received notice that the Board is prepared to pay such member off leaves the sum to be thus repaid in the hands of

Society, such member shall not be entitled to any interest thereon after the expiration of the time named in the notice of repayment." The effect of these changes is admirably stated by S. W. Wren:- "The significant points were as follows, that the new rule 1 would now permit the existing Society to form a Building Society, and the new rule 6 would allow the Society to pay off the shares of any member, thus allowing those who disagreed, if any, with the change and constitution of the new Building Society to be paid out."

Thirty one members attended the 101st Annual Meeting and after a careful explanation by the Secretary they voted in favour of the necessary change of rules. From then on it was constitutionally and legally plain sailing for the Directors and it was executively all hard grind for the Secretary and his clerical staff, and Mr Frank Ackerman (Personal Clerk to Mr Bullock, the Solicitor), who worked with the Secretary after hours on the legal documentation. The draft rules of the new Society were prepared and sent to the Registrar for comment. Although Mr Wren had made sure that each of the draft rules appeared somewhere amongst the rules of an existing Building Society, the Registrar nevertheless had alterations to suggest. The Directors chose 31 December 1962 as the date for incorporation under the Building Societies Act, 1962. It was particularly convenient because it was the end of the financial year: they were not to know when they decided on it that it would also coincide with the move from 48 New Inn Hall Street to 154 Cowley Road. The approved rules, printed but still in draft form, had to be submitted to a meeting of the intended first members of the new Building Society. One of the Registrar's requirements had been that at the Inaugural Meeting there must be ten members willing to invest £500 in the Society and leave it there for five years. The Directors of the old Society accepted this responsibility, invited themselves to an Inaugural Meeting of the Oxford Provident Building Society on 27 December 1962 at 6.00 p.m. and were then elected Directors of the new Society. The first Directors' Meeting followed immediately. The rules were approved and sent to the Registrar with the necessary fee. The new Society was born.

The Secretary could, and did, now write officially to every shareholder and depositor, and to every mortgage holder of the old Society, inviting them to transfer to the new. This was the anxious moment; it was to ensure virtually 100% transfer that such careful arrangements had been made to avoid any mistaken impression that the old Society was in trouble, financial or otherwise. Interest to members of the old Society had been paid gross whereas normal Building Society rules would govern the new one. There was consequent speculation that those who had not formed the habit of declaring their interest to the Inspector of Taxes might think it prudent to strike their financial tents and steal away through the darkness of transfer. But all went well. The administrative exercise continued through transfer of shares, deposits and mortgages to Loan Pass Books and Share Pass Books. The transfer of the Society's office premises was arranged by normal legal procedures and stamp duty of 10/- paid. The trustee investments were re-registered in the usual manner for any transfer of stock. The old Society's bank account was closed and the balance transferred to the new. The contracts of the staff were redrawn to show clearly that they were now employed by the Oxford Provident Building Society. The Secretary's special responsibilities were not quite over. His "tidying-up" operation is best described in his own words:- "The deeds which were registered in the Land Registry required an entry to be made showing the transfer from the old Society to the new Society. Our Solicitors therefore made an appointment with them and I personally delivered the deeds to them at Tunbridge Wells, Kent, on signature and collected them a month later. For the bulk service our solicitors obtained a special price instead of the usual charge of registration fee. When everything had been done or transferred that we considered ought to have been done, it was thought that it could still be possible for something to have been missed or overlooked and I instructed our solicitor to prepare and have executed by both Societies what we called an "Omnibus Deed" – this deed made effective the transfer of reserve funds from one Society to another – nothing remained but to ask the Registrar to remove the name of the Oxford Industrial and Provident Land and Building Society Ltd. from the Register. . . . The announcement caused no embarrassment to the Society."

By an accident of history the removal of the Society to new premises coincided with these constitutional changes. We have seen that in February 1960 the Secretary was justifiably worried that road development or other changes might deprive the Society of 48 New Inn Hall Street. In the event the street remained unaffected and in January 1980 has changed little from the 1930s when the author, as an Oxford undergraduate, knew it well. But Oxford University has changed considerably during those 50 years, and in particular student numbers have considerably increased. Mr Wren was right therefore in a second assumption – that the day must come when Brasenose or St. Peter's would want the building for undergraduate rooms and would refuse to renew the lease. By 1961 five year leases with virtual certainty of renewal had become six month leases with considerable uncertainty. The post war growth of Oxford University had far outstripped the growth in assets of the slumbering Oxford Industrial Provident.

Mr Wren realised that a move from a prime site in the city centre might have disadvantages when the reformed Society began to advertise for the first time in its history and was ready to expand. He therefore advocated a site in the centre of Headington, a growth area in Oxford economic life where there was as yet no building society branch. Two or three possibilities were investigated but nothing came of them. In the meantime Mr S. Bayliss, a principal in the Society's firm of auditors and joint owner of 154 Cowley Road, had drawn attention to its possibilities. In February 1961 the Directors inspected 154, decided that at £7,250 it was too expensive, and the Secretary minuted a decision that no further action would be taken. In May, 1961 however a further inspection was made and in the following month the Directors decided to offer £6,500. This was not acceptable and in August 1961 they offered £7,000 and a bargain was struck. At this stage the Society was in no hurry to move house; the necessary security of a permanent home should their lease be terminated was the real issue. The new offices needed a good deal of renovation and adaptation and in January 1962 the Directors allocated £3,000 for this work which was carried out by Benfield and Loxley a well known local builder. They were determined to be economical and in March 1962 decided that they could not afford £330 for a neon light name sign at 154. In June 1962 St. Peter's Hall added impetus to the building activities by giving the Society six months notice. The actual removal to 154 Cowley Road took place on December 24th 1962 and the new headquarters opened for business on December 27th, the date of the Inaugural Meeting of the new Society. By a happy arrangement the Directors were able to get planning permission to use the first floor and subsequently the second floor for additional offices and thus to offer a branch office to their solicitors. They were less happy about a G.P.O. telephone kiosk which stood on their land; those waiting to use it had a habit of "dumping rubbish and defacing the property". They gave the

Post Office notice to move their public facility and when they discovered that the kiosk would be moved only 16ft. the Secretary was instructed to "seek an interview". His silver tongue prevailed: the kiosk was removed to the next street (James Street) where it remains to this day.

The first year of the new Society was a potentially anxious period. During those twelve months the Society was not allowed under the Act to advertise for custom, but maximum investment per member was now £5,000 instead of £500 and potential for growth was there. By July 1963 the Directors were advised that they could not afford any more mortgage loans that year if they were to adhere to the 7½% liquidity rule. The Secretary's difficulties during this anxious period were increased in November 1963 by the serious illness – leading to resignation – of W. M. Thody, the Assistant Secretary. Fortunately a former Assistant Secretary, D. J. Ash, returned at the end of November and he was re-appointed Assistant to Mr Wren. At the time the offer was not accompanied by re-admission to the pension scheme, but that omission was later rectified. In April 1964 an application for permission to advertise was submitted to the Registrar; advertisements first appeared in the Oxford Mail in May 1965. Three other benefits of the Society's change of status remained to be harvested – trustee status, membership of the Building Societies Association, and membership of the Midland Association of Building Societies. Moreover they had to come in that order, for each depended on the achievement of the previous step. In August 1965 arrangements were made for the Chairman and Secretary to visit the Registrar in connection with trustee status. When it was granted the Directors applied for membership of the B.S.A. and were admitted in late October 1965. Admission to the Midland Association followed on November 7th 1965, and the Directors, through their Secretary, gained major benefits from the information, professional advice, and breadth of contact which thus came their way. The former Oxford Industrial and Provident Land and Building Society Limited was not eligible for admission to the B.S.A. or the Midland Association. The new Society was and there is little doubt that the climbing road from assets of £336,748 on re-registration on 1.1.63 to over £2m on amalgamation with Rugby and Warwick really began to rise steeply from the date of admission to the Midland Association of Building Societies.

The Oxford Provident Building Society existed as a separate

institution and legal entity from 1 January 1963 until 30 March 1974. The former Industrial and Provident Land and Building Society, with its strict limit on the amount a member could invest, had taken 102 years to achieve assets of £336,748. The new Society increased those assets by £1,663,000 in the ensuing eleven years. The amalgamation with Rugby and Warwick was thus undertaken from a position of strength by both Societies and by the Oxford Directors in the knowledge of a responsibility fully and properly discharged. Their Secretary, Sydney Wren, was able to complete his professional career with Heart of England, via Rugby and Warwick, and when retirement came at the age of 65 his wisdom and experience were still available to the Society in his capacity as a Local Director. The Oxford Society's assets passed £1 million in May 1968 and were celebrated with a full page advertisement in the Oxford Mail on May 21st. Later in the same year the considerable increase in business made the introduction of mechanised accounting essential, as also a proper internal communication system. Early in 1969 the Directors politely refused an invitation to amalgamate with a northern Building Society: they repeated their answer when approached by the same Society and many others in later years.

The major problem during these final years was in staff relations. The Directors, whose only experience was in the affairs of a tiny Society, were unable to understand the greatly increasing responsibility of their executive officers, especially the Secretary. They began well. In January, 1969 S. W. Wren was re-designated General Manager and Secretary. Although in April 1969 they had decided that the cost of a security screen "was out of all proportion", they fitted one a year later and increased the insurance cover for staff injured or killed during a hold up. In the summer of 1970 all the staff were sent on a decimal currency conversion course. But difficulties developed during the final three years. Perhaps their Secretary was unwise to tell them in July 1971 that the Registrar wanted a retirement age of 70 for all Building Society directors. Mr G. E. Tyrrell clearly took note for a month later he resigned his directorship on reaching the age of 90. Happily Mr S. W. Wren was elected to succeed him; he was by now a recognised spokesman on Building Society affairs in the Oxford area and was regularly interviewed on Oxford Radio during his term of office. One occasion was in connection with a new phenomenon which was making national headlines and bringing a new word 'gazumping' to our language. People had queued all night to buy new houses on offer in Radley for £5,250 and Sydney Wren was asked to read the portent of such an unusual event. Less happily, the General Manager was unable to agree with his fellow directors either over salary or pension arrangements. In February 1972 the Auditor told the Directors that Mr Wren's salary and car allowance were both "much too low". But there is no record in the minutes of subsequent meetings that this was corrected. In May 1972 the Board decided to make a substantial review of staff salaries from 1.7.72 but there is no evidence that the review took place. Instead, an ominous minute of 12.12.72 records that "the review of staff salaries was refused on the grounds of a Government freeze of all non-statutory contracted salaries." It must have been galling for the staff that a month later the Auditor reported that the Society was making "steady and excellent progress". The minute book is silent thereafter on the subject of staff salaries. The General Manager's pension scheme was discussed at three meetings in the summer of 1973 however, without reaching agreement. Mr Wren, on the advice of his solicitor, refused two alternative offers and there the matter rested. Staff salaries and pensions were unresolved problems taken over on amalgamation by the Rugby and Warwick, whose Directors were perhaps more experienced in these matters.

The amalgamation crept up rapidly on the Directors' minute book. It was first mentioned on 13 November 1973 in the context of a suggestion that the book entry of £12,420 for the value of 154 Cowley Road was much too low and that the property must be worth £30,000. A Special Meeting of Shareholders was held in the Wesley Memorial Hall, New Inn Hall Street on 15 January 1974 – attended by 6 directors and 38 members. The General Manager, at the Chairman's invitation, explained the points at issue. A resolution in favour of the transfer of engagements to Rugby and Warwick was moved. In the ensuing public discussion Herbert Walden answered questions and when the resolution was put there were 431 votes in favour and 35 against – massive support from the proxy vote. The final Board Meeting on 19 March 1974 dealt with nothing but routine business. The rest is silence – a silence heightened by the blank in the minutes of that March 19th meeting, an empty white space where the Chairman's signature should be. The Board never met again and the minutes of their final meeting were never confirmed.

Great things happened in the city and university of Oxford between 1860 and 1974. William Morris transformed our way of life when he began to manufacture motor cars instead of bicycles. He used his great wealth to help Oxford University become a great medical centre, and to found Nuffield College. Thomas Balogh influenced financial and economic thought, and thence the taxation system of our country. Oxford poets, philosophers and politicians fought and agonised in two world wars. My own college, Balliol, gave leaders to all three main political parties – Heath to the Conservatives, Grimond to the Liberals, and Jenkins and Healey to Labour. Oxford profoundly and extensively affected our national way of life and thought. The Oxford Industrial and Provident Land and Building Society Ltd and its successor The Oxford Provident Building Society, similarly affected the people of Oxford itself. From 1871 to 1892 the Society developed eight estates – the Glebe, St. Clement's, London Place, Iffley Road, Hayfield Road, Bartlemas, Fairacres, Stones and Southfield. Thereafter, ceasing to act as a Land Society, the Directors loaned money to countless Oxford citizens to buy their own homes. "No man is an island. . ."; we are all part of national and international life. But psychologically we each need our island, our patch of territory which we can defend like the robin, our house where we can shut the outer door as the Oxford undergraduate can "sport his oak". Many years ago, while still the Earl of Home, another Oxford Prime Minister said "We can build a house, but a home must grow." The Oxford Provident grew steadily for 100 years and rapidly for ten, and good Oxford homes grew with it. It thus helped to complete the circle which links every nuclear family cell with the destiny of the entire human family. For, to complete Lord Home's argument, – "Much can be done by collective action by the state, but by no means all. We can build a house, but religion and morality are founded on parental love and care. All home life is not good, but beyond question the good home is the foundation of the good society." Sydney Wren and his fellow directors were in the business of "good homes", and Oxford is the better for it.

Progress and Development: Coalville Building Society

Year	*Assets*	*Reserves*	*Chairman*	*Secretary*	*Address*
1922	£7,983	£102	W. Fellows	C. T. Walton	19 London Rd., Coalville
1932	£126,314	£4,780	J. R. Bennett	C. T. Walton	Ditto
1942	£154,512	£13,752	C. H. March	C. T. Walton	Ditto
1952	£246,437	£18,064	T. I. McCarthy	C. T. Walton	Ditto
1962	£753,313	£37,989	J. A. Walton	F. S. Pollard	Ditto
1972	£1,736,869	£89,629	A. D. Farmer	F. S. Pollard	42 High Street, Coalville
1977	£3,075,551	£185,050	A. D. Farmer	F. S. Pollard	Ditto

CHAPTER ELEVEN

The Coalville Permanent Building Society: 1912-1978

THE FIRST MEETING at which the formation of a building society in Coalville was discussed took place in May 1912. The first directors meeting was held in High Street, Coalville, on 16 January 1913. The Fiftieth Annual Report for the Jubilee Year ending 31st December, 1962 contains the following brief account of the first half century:-

"Having regard to the development of Coalville a number of local inhabitants considered the facilities offered by building societies for home ownership and a preliminary meeting to consider the possibilities of forming a society was held on 23 May, 1912. Apparently the position seemed promising, for a further meeting was held in the Adult School Hall on the evening of Wednesday the 27th September, 1912, presided over by a Mr W. Fellows who was a schoolmaster and a local councillor. Amongst those present at the meeting was a Mr W. Slater, a director of the Loughborough Building Society and it is interesting to note that he mentioned that his society had attempted to form a branch at Coalville some years previously but the time was not then opportune. A local solicitor, Mr C. E. Crane remarked that it was surprising that societies at Shepshed, Barrow, Quorn and Hathern had not opened branches in Coalville and he eventually moved the proposition that a society be formed to be called "The Coalville Permanent Benefit Building Society". This was seconded by Mr P. Goddard and carried unanimously. The business of the meeting then dealt with the acquisition of shares and it was decided that fifty shares were to be obtained before they proceeded with any legal formality. Twenty five shares were immediately taken up and this was regarded as an excellent start and those present at the meeting were asked to canvass their friends for the remainder.

The first Board of Directors was eventually appointed consisting of persons from various trades and professions: four schoolmasters, a builder, an architect, a solicitor, a plumber, a colliery cashier, and an under-manager, a loom designer and an insurance agent. The Society was incorporated under the Act of 1874 on the 11th December 1912, and at the first Board Meeting held on the 16th of the following month. Mr W. Fellows was appointed the first chairman.

The position of director was entirely honorary until 1933 when the first payment of directors' fees is recorded.

Less than two years after the Society was formed the war of 1914-1918 arose and although progress was necessarily limited, by the end of the war the assets had increased over 200%.

Steady development continued during the inter-war years and at the end of 1939 the total assets had increased to £154,270. In common with the majority of other societies, a policy of consolidation was carried out during the second war for at the end of 1945 the assets had only increased by £6,854 to £161,124, the reserves having increased by £3,671. Since the end of the war steady growth continued and at present the assets are over £750,000".

One of the most interesting features of the Coalville Society is its very existence. The other constituent parts of Heart of England developed in historic townships – Warwick, Rugby, Walsall and Oxford – each with a medium or large population and a multiplicity of business and economic activity. In 1912 Coalville was an overgrown village, largely dependent on coal mining. The first colliery opened in 1827. George Stephenson engineered a railway to move the coal to Leicester, 12 miles away. Cottages were built, miners arrived from Durham, and a small mining community grew up. By 1888, when the Leicester County Council was created, the population was large enough to justify its own urban council under the county. This local council provided the normal amenities of town life and by 1912 the area had increased by 300 acres and the population by 3,000 folk.

This was still a small community to support a building society. Moreover there were large societies in Leicester, Loughborough and Coventry – none very far away – and it would have been normal for one at least of these to establish a Coalville branch. As the quotation from the Jubilee Report shows, Loughborough had tried and found it impossible, which must be assumed to have discouraged the smaller local societies mentioned in the same report. So once more, in the history of the building society movement, local initiative provided the impetus and Coalville was midwife to its own building society. What other society one wonders had four schoolmasters on its first board! It is however a reasonable inference that it was not the four schoolmasters who were essential to the future of the Coalville Permanent Building Society but the one solicitor; when the directors met on 16 January 1913 it was in their Solicitor's office. Mr C. E. Crane was one of seven founder directors who were still in office at the outbreak of war in 1937. He succeeded another founder, T. I. McCarthy. as Chairman in 1951, held that office until 1960 and did not resign as a director until 1961 after almost 47 years service. Mr Crane set up in practice at his mother's house in Whitwick in 1908 and shortly afterwards moved his office to Coalville. He was the founder and senior partner of the law firm of Messrs. Crane and Walton with offices in Leicester, Coalville and Ashby. It was from their office in Coalville, that the Coalville Permanent operated until May 1965 when the Directors met for the first time in their own property – 42 High Street. C. T. Walton of the same firm was part-time secretary, on a virtually nominal salary, from 1913 until July 1961 when the first and only full-time Secretary. Mr F. S. Pollard took up his appointment. J. A. Walton, brother of C.T. but not a member of the firm of Crane & Walton, had succeeded C. E. Crane as Chairman in April 1960 and was still Chairman when he died in 1966. There seems no doubt that this firm of solicitors, corporately as well as through certain individuals, played a major part in the foundation, growth and success of the Society. It was a fine contribution to the social history of Coalville and the welfare of its people.

The historian's problem is always one of selection and rejection. Original documents and source material provide a great deal of information of which only a fraction can be used. The lack of some early records of the Coalville Permanent, coupled with the fact that its separate existence was only about half as long as that of the other constituent members of Heart of England, has therefore one advantage. There is space to comment on the early rules of the Society and, in a later section, to analyse some of the mortgage business transacted.

My copy of the rules was printed in Coalville by A. Wilkins &

Sons, Printers and contains a copy of the Certificate of Incorporation dated 11 December 1912. It is signed G.S.R.– Sir George Stuart Robertson K.C. was Chief Registrar from 1912 to 1937 – and carries the seal of the Registrar of Friendly Societies, Central Office. Rule 1 provided that the Chief Office should be at High Street, Coalville, "or at such other place where intoxicating liquors are not sold." Rule 3 established the Officers of the Society as twelve Directors, a Secretary, two Auditors, and a Solicitor. The Directors were to be shareholders and would constitute the Board of Management. Rule 4, which dealt with subscriptions on unadvanced shares, required "every member on entering the Society shall pay an Entrance Fee of sixpence per share on every unadvanced share and threepence on a half share, and a Monthly Subscription of five shillings per share." The weekly wage of a coal miner in 1912 was barely adequate to cover such a monthly subscription. Rule 7 provided for all subscriptions to be paid at the office of the Society on the second Monday in every month "between the hours of six and nine o'clock in the evening". Rule 8 set out the arrangement for Annual Meetings of Shareholders and Rule 9 governed the "Mode of Voting", allowing the Chairman a casting vote where necessary. A detailed Rule 12 dealt with the unfortunate possibility of "Shareholders becoming Lunatic" and required a twelve month "get well" period before an attorney could act. Rule 13 provided for the more inevitable eventually of "Death of Shareholders". Rule 17 stipulated that buildings mortgaged to the Society should be insured against fire:- "Every shareholder executing a mortgage to the Society, shall within two days of such execution, give to the Secretary a written statement of any trade carried on, or the existence of any stove or furnace. . . .; and default thereof the shareholder shall pay a fine of ten shillings per week for every week that such statement is withheld."

Rules 19-22 gave the Directors power to borrow money, invest surplus funds and, once every three years, to transfer surplus profits to the Reserve Fund. Rule 24 allowed each Director to hold office for four years, or the unexpired portion of his predecessor's term, and one third of the Board was to retire each year. Failure to attend a Board Meeting for six months meant "he shall forthwith cease to hold office as a Director". The duties of the Directors are set out in great detail in Rule 25, those of the Secretary in Rule 28 and those of the Solicitor in Rule 30. There could be no plea of ignorance in the event of carelessness or failure of duty. To ensure adequate local knowledge there was a requirement that all Directors and Officers of the Society should live within ten miles radius of Coalville. Rule 33 sets out the arrangements for termination of the Society; it could only be dissolved with the consent of "three fourths of the members holding not less than two thirds of the number of shares in the Society, testified by their signature on an instrument of dissolution." The final rule, Number 36, was entitled "Losses. How to be met". In these days of Government warnings about the tar content of cigarettes there seems to be a case for similar warnings about "reading the small print". Losses were to be met – "in the first place out of the Reserve Fund Account, and if this proves insufficient, then out of the profits of the year, then out of the profit already credited to the Investing Shares, and lastly, from the generally subscribed funds of the Society". How many shareholders stopped to think that those generally subscribed funds were more clearly described as their money.

At their first meeting in January 1913 the twelve directors elected W. Fellows as their Chairman and J. R. Bennett as Vice-Chairman. Ashton Glover was appointed Secretary. His resignation on 13 November, 1913 because of pressure of work led to the appointment of C. T. Walton who remained in office until April 1961. The directors decided to meet on the third Monday of each month at 7.00 p.m. and authorised the necessary office equipment, including a deed box which cost £1. 3. 3d. Mr Crane offered office accommodation until the Society was permanently settled – a process which took fifty two years. The first monthly pay night was arranged for 10 February, 1913. At the February directors' meeting the Nottingham and Notts. Banking Company was appointed banker to the Society and Messrs. Major & Co., Chartered Accountants, as auditors. A sub-committee of Messrs. Crane, Bennett and the Secretary was appointed to open the post – a wise precaution in view of the future experience of the Grays Building Society. A brass plate was ordered and arrangements made to advertise in the Coalville Times once a week throughout the year, at the cost of 1/- per week.

The directors were already publicity conscious. On 21 April, 1913: "The Chairman, in order to get outsiders interested in the Society, offered a prize of a value of not less than ten shillings, to the member who introduced the most new members between now and 31 March, 1914, provided that the member introduced not less than five, such proposal not to include paid agents". In August 1913 the Society had sufficient funds to justify offering mortgage advances and the first was approved in October – £225 on a house in Melbourne Road, Ibstock. This was a controversial decision however and the Ibstock agent resigned in December because the advance had been limited to £225 instead of the whole £275 asked. The decision might have surprised him less had he known that the Society was still so short of funds that the directors agreed to pay from their own pockets for the cost of printing one hundred copies of the report for the first Annual Meeting held on 30 March 1914 in the Adult School Hall.

By the outbreak of war in August, 1914, two more mortgages had been granted. In September:- "it was resolved that should any member of the Society be called up to the War, no fines would be imposed during the cessation of payment of contribution." In July, 1915, a director George Glover, was given leave of absence as he had been appointed an Officer of the V.A.D. In May, 1916, the Secretary, C. T. Walton, joined the Army and C. E. Crane was appointed temporarily to succeed him. Two years later, in October 1918, :- "Mr Crane reported that Mr Walton, the Secretary, had been home on leave from France and that he had withdrawn a deposit of £10 with interest and had been paid the Secretary's salary from the time of his joining the Army to date. It was resolved that the Directors express their appreciation of Mr Crane's action in carrying on the work of the Secretary for the latter's benefit during his absence".

C. T. Walton resumed as part-time Secretary in October, 1917. The Society was now approving two or three mortgages per month and must have been funding them by borrowing from the bank. In April, 1920 the overdraft was £1,107. 9. 7d and the Bank asked the Society to open a loan account to cover the overdraft. By January, 1923, the overdraft had increased to £2,500 and in October of the same year the bank agreed to £5,000, requiring a deposit of deeds to the value of £5,025. By now the directors dealt with an average of seven monthly applications, most of them for mortgages in the £250-£350 range. In April, 1924, borrowing power was increased to £10,000 but when the directors asked for £20,000 only six months later, the bank jibbed. The only solution for the Society was to shop around, with the result that on 31 December, 1924 the bankers became the Midland and the overdraft £15,000. In September, 1927 the Midland agreed to £20,000, as long as it was reduced to £17,500 by the end of the year. This was the highest point in the practice of lending on mortgage by borrowing from the bank, although an

Insurance Company loan of £4,000 in October, 1926, was clearly very useful. By May, 1932 the debt at the bank was down to £3,878. 9. 6d and £2,000 of the insurance loan had been repaid. By December, 1936, the Society was in credit with the bank to the total of £3,136. 12. 9d. Although there are no copies of Annual Accounts to confirm it, the impression is that mortgage repayments now more than covered the ten to fifteen monthly applications, and thus steadily reduced the overdraft. Once however the bank borrowing ceased, the amount of money available each month brought the Society back to an average monthly approval of two or three mortgages.

When the Secretary made his first entry in the Society's fourth minute book, on January 18, 1937 seven of the twelve original directors were still members of the Board. The five whose resignations had taken place during the intervening twenty five years were the first Chairman, W. Fellows (19 July 1926), the second J. R. Bennett (July 1935), W. Birrell, A. Knowles, and L. G. Widdowson. As we have seen C. T. Walton, brother of J.A., had been Secretary since 1913. Thus the Society had been fortunate in its continuity of management and direction during the first quarter century. The five new directors were C. H. March, who succeeded Bennett as Chairman, E. J. Holmes, J. W. Horne, F. Goddard and J. A. Walton (brother of C.T.) The financial statement for January 1937 showed a credit balance of £2,246. 11. 8. Applications for three mortgages were considered, two approved and one referred back for further enquiries. The two approved were for £50 on a property in Silver Street, Whitwick and £350 for a newly erected house in Bardon Road, Coalville. The Secretary reported disposal of Mr X's property for £400; Mr X, who had presumably been in arrears with his payments, received 10/2d from the sale. Applications to invest in paid-up-shares were considered and one only accepted; the others were to be told "that at the present no further money could be taken up but as and when money was required they would be informed". Finally, the draft accounts for the year to 31 December, 1936 and the Auditor's Report were "fully discussed". It was decided to recommend to the shareholders at the Annual Meeting that £500 be placed to the Special Reserve Fund. Thus the impression from Directors' minutes at this time is of a safe, financially secure, conservative local society which was well advised by its officers – financially, legally and sociologically. But what building society in the 1980s would consider three mortgage applications in a month and accept only one shareholder! It was indeed a different world, only forty years ago.

These bare bones of the Coalville Permanent Building Society are best fleshed out by recording the chief events in the monthly directors' minutes between January 1937 and the outbreak of war in September 1939. The March 1937 minutes confirm that the Society had joined the new Building Societies Association (August 1936) and the Midland Association of Building Societies. In April the Secretary's salary was increased to £300 p.a.: from it he paid his Assistant Secretary. In May 1937 the same Secretary was congratulated on winning the Captain's Prize in the Golf Tournament held during the Annual Conference of the B.S.A. at Brighton. In May 1937 the Society had spare cash and the Board decided to invest £3,000 in 3% Conversion Loan. The Directors were being careful of their pence however and in August 1938 they decided not to subscribe to the testimonial to Sir Enoch Hill. In October 1938 the Registrar requested that all fire insurance premiums should be paid direct to the Society and not through Crane and Walton. In March 1937 Directors' fees were minuted as £13. 12. 0d for the Chairman and £7. 12. 0d for each other director; they had first received payment in 1933, when the shareholders awarded them a total of £100. It is perhaps worth recording here that the final fees agreed in December 1977 were – Chairman £284, Vice-Chairman £278, and £272 for each of the other four directors. In June 1937 a new brochure was under consideration and in August the Assistant Secretary (A. Kenrick) and the Clerk (R. H. Neal) were sent to a Midland Association Weekend School, held in conjunction with the B.S.I., in Liverpool. In December 1938 F. J. Bayliss, a founder director, had not attended a directors' meeting since January through "permanent illness" and his office was declared vacant. In February 1937 the Brighton and Sussex Building Society suggested a merger and received the same answer they were to get from Walsall Mutual a little later. In August 1937 there was a very reasonable request that the notice of directors' meetings should be accompanied by an agenda. In September 1937 the outbreak of war caused the Board to set up an Emergency Committee of five and led them to agree that during the emergency the policy of the directors would be guided by that of the B.S.A.

A final glimpse of the pre-Second War Society is given by the mortgage business considered at the September 1937 Board Meeting. It must be remembered that before 1962 there was no delegation to an applications committee or to the Officers of the Society. All applications were brought before the full monthly meeting. This month there were seven applications; six were approved and one deferred. The total cost was £765 and the deferred application was for £100. Two of the loans granted were first advances, one of £600 on a house in Stafford Leys Road, Leicester, and the other of £300 on a new house in Meadow Lane, Coalville. The other approvals were all further advances of £10, £10, £20 and £25 respectively on houses in Coalville, Ellistown, Ibstock and Bagworth. The deferred application was for a further advance of £100 on a house in Whitehill Road, Ellistown. A decision would be made after the Surveyor, Mr T. I. McCarthy, had inspected and reported.

In common with other building societies the Coalville Permanent had little opportunity to expand between 1939 and 1945. As we have seen, during the six years of war assets increased by only £6,854 and Reserves by £3,691. There were several monthly Board Meetings when no application for mortgage was submitted. In January 1940 it was decided to close the monthly Monday subscription days at 7.00 p.m. instead of 8.00 p.m. – the black-out again! During the winter months Directors' Meetings began at 3.00 p.m. on the third Wednesday instead of at 6.00 p.m. on the third Monday. In common with the other constituents of Heart of England, the Coalville Permanent had spare money to invest and did so in National Defence Bonds (£3,000), Salute the Soldier Week (£3,000), the Leicester T.S.B. (£2,000), Coalville War Weapons Week (£6,000), Coalville Warships Week (£2,500) and Coalville Wings for Victory Week (£4,500). One of the directors, Mr F. Goddard, was excused attendance throughout the period of the war; he was serving as a member of the War Damage Commission.

The minutes of November 18th, 1942 record:- "A letter from the Ministry of Works relating to compensation payable to mortgagors for iron fences was read, and the Secretary was instructed to inform the Ministry that the Society had no objection to the Ministry paying compensation direct to the Mortgagor, up to a limit of £5." In January 1944 the Secretary's salary was reorganised so that £300 was paid to the Secretary and £50 to the Assistant Secretary and a year later the Auditor's fee was increased to ten guineas. Finally, in August 1945 as the war ended, the directors found themselves involved in negotiations which were to drag on for some years. These negotiations are mentioned on August 20th, 1945 under the heading "Property at Woodville". The minute reads:- "A letter from the Deputy Clerk to Woodville Parish Council asking whether the Society would be willing to present the site to the Council was read, and the Secretary was instructed to send a suitable reply". One imagines that the "suitable reply" made clear that the Coalville Permanent Building Society was not a charity.

The story had in fact begun in October, 1929, when Messrs. F. Heath & Sons were granted a mortgage of £2,000 on their pottery at Woodville. By December, 1932, the Company was in difficulty and the Society accepted the surrender of Mr Heath's life insurance policy for £150. In February, 1933, Heath & Sons went into voluntary liquidation and the Society acquired a problem which took them many years to solve. In June, 1933, the pottery was unsuccessfully offered for sale, but in February 1934 a part was leased to a new tenant. In August, 1936 the Secretary reported that Hartshorne Pottery at Woodville was being demolished and there the matter rested until the war was over. In September, 1945 the Directors indicated their willingness to sell for £2,000 and in October the Repton R.D.C. replied that they were not interested and wanted the site cleared. At the same time it is clear that in addition to the site of the former pottery there was at least one adjoining house and shop. The directors were eventually to get their £2,000 but they had to serve a hard apprenticeship and wait a long time for their money. In 1947 they were surprised to discover that tenants were occupying part of their property – the house and the shop – and that no rent had been paid since 1935. Arrangements were made to collect arrears and first results were encouraging. At this point however one tenant decided that he was not really responsible for rent because he "probably" owned the property. The Society disputed his contention but after careful searches their Solicitor advised that they would be unable to prove a title; thereafter this small part of the Woodville property disappears from the Society's records. In November 1951 the Directors were offered 1/6d a yard for the Woodville property but their minimum price was 3/6d. In October 1952 they accepted £300 for part of the land and responded to an enquiry about the remainder by offering to sell for £1,200. Luckily for them this was too much for the purchaser, for in September 1955 an offer of £2,000 was forthcoming and was accepted. Finally, therefore, a matter which had occupied the directors' time at least once a quarter and often month after month, was favourably resolved and in 1955 they received the £2,000 they had asked in 1945, in addition to the £300 paid in 1952. Happily the rate of inflation during those ten years was low.

If proof were needed of the steady, undramatic progress of the Society from the end of the war in 1945 until the appointment of F. S. Pollard as full-time Secretary in 1961, Heath's Pottery provides it. Take it out of the record of those 16 years and not much remains. There are in fact only two subjects worthy of comment. One is the determination of the directors to advertise on a purely local basis and the other is the changes in personnel at the top. It will also be useful at some stage to look again at the type of mortgage business being done, but this will come in the final period – the seventeen Pollard years, 1961-78.

The bulk of the Society's advertising was carried by the local paper, the Coalville Times. In June 1946 however the Directors decided to advertise in two local cinemas, by means of slides. In April, 1947 they sent a guinea to a local reporter in appreciation of his attendance at the Annual General Meeting and the report he wrote. In November 1947 the advertising in the Coalville Times was increased to 2″ per week; two years later it was increased to 3″ and the cost met by discontinuing the slides in the two local cinemas. During the same year, in May 1951, there is reference to advertising in the Coalville and Whitwick parish magazines and this use of church magazines became a feature of the Society's advertising thereafter. Over the years Hugglescote, Ravenstone, and Ashby parish magazines were added to the list. So was the Newbridge High School magazine (1969) and the Coalville Chamber of Trade "Shoppers' Guide to Coalville" (1973). The Board's approach to parish magazines was broad church, for in November 1769 "It was reported that the Catholic Church of St. Wilfred of York did not issue a Parish Magazine, but had a Church Diary published and it was authorised that an advertisement be placed in the Diary for the ensuing year". The policy of local advertisement was strictly maintained. The Midland Association of Building Societies regularly pressed the Directors to take part in their collective advertising scheme. They invariably refused, even when John Richardson, future colleague in the Heart of England, was Chairman of M.A.B.S. and wrote urging them to change their decision.

When the war ended in August 1945 C. H. March was still Chairman of Directors with T. I. McCarthy, the Society's Surveyor, as his deputy. The total of Directors' fees paid for the following year, 1946, was £100. March's death was reported at the Directors' meeting in February 1947 and on April 19th, 1947 T. I. McCarthy was elected to succeed him with C. E. Crane as Vice-Chairman; each was a founder director, first elected in 1912. Chairman McCarthy died in office in February 1951 and in April of that year C. E. Crane was elected Chairman and J. A. Walton, brother of the Secretary, Vice-Chairman. In March 1953 the Auditor, E. P. Major of Birmingham, resigned and was succeeded by his son, G. S. Major. In January and February 1955 both the Chairman and the Vice-Chairman sent their apologies for non-attendance at the monthly directors' meeting. Thereafter C. E. Crane was as often absent as present until July, 1957 when he was taken seriously ill. From that month his apologies were almost continuous until he was replaced by J. A. Walton as Chairman in April, 1960 and retired as a director in 1961 after 49 years on the Board. He was 29 years old when he first became a director, 68 when elected Chairman and 74 when he first began to have difficulty in attending directors' meeting. He remained Chairman until he was 77 years old, resigned his directorship at the age of 78 and died on 4 September 1966 when he was half way through his 84th year. It was fitting that the Service of Thanksgiving held in Holy Trinity Church, Ashby-de-la-Zouch included the sentence "Let not your heart be troubled: ye believe in God, believe also in me. In my Father's house are many mansions". Charles Edmund Crane and his fellow leaders of the Coalville Permanent Building Society had voluntarily given many days, weeks and months of their time and talents to ensure that there were also some reasonable homes and houses in their Father's kingdom on Earth. Crane was succeeded by J. A. Walton and A. D. Farmer was elected Vice-Chairman. E. A. Crane, son of C. E. Crane, and T. R. C. Hunt – both partners in the firm – served on the Board for many years. About this time the Secretary's salary was increased to £1,200 p.a. and in February 1961, the same meeting at which C. E. Crane's resignation as a director was reported, the Board decided to advertise for a full-time Secretary. As the door finally closed on the era of the founding directors, and on C. T. Walton their Secretary who had joined them in 1913, it opened on the seventeen years of full-time secretaryship during which the Assets increased from £663,370 to £3,075,551.

The decision to appoint a full time Secretary meant a break from Crane and Walton, who had so admirably administered the Society for half a century. The Directors decided to advertise for their new Secretary in the Building Societies Gazette, the Leicester Mercury and Evening Mart, and the Coalville Times. They negotiated with Crane and Walton for the continued use of their accommodation and it was agreed that the Society should have the secretary's office, the pay office, joint use of the strong room, heating and lighting for an annual rent of £156 p.a. inclusive of rates. In April 1961 the appointment of Mr F. S. Pollard as Secretary was confirmed and he held that office until amalgamation with Heart of England in February 1978. Mr Pollard's appointment inevitably led to re-organisation and to new structures. New accounting procedures were discussed with the Auditor. A separate telephone line with two extensions was installed in the offices, so that the Society would appear in the local telephone directory. As Mr A. Kenrick was no longer required as Assistant Secretary he was declared redundant and Mr Pollard began to recruit junior clerical staff, not without some difficulty. A new adding machine was bought, the Auditors were found to be homeless in the more restricted accommodation and arrangements were made for them to work in the nearby Masonic Hall. Office hours were left to the Secretary's discretion but Board Meetings would be held on the first Tuesday of each month. In these and other minor ways the Society adjusted from part-time to full-time management.

The new Secretary was hardly in office before he enquired (21.8.61), "how the Golden Jubilee was to be marked?". A Jubilee Committee met for the first time on April 9th 1961 and recommended that the "fifty not-out" should be acclaimed by advertising in the Coalville Times and the Ashby Parish magazine during May and June 1961. At their second meeting they completed the Jubilee plans by arranging to subsidize special "Bounty Accounts". A paid-up share account would be credited with £1 as a free gift to children born between 1 July and 31 December 1962 on condition that the amount remain with the Society for five years, the parents live within a radius of ten miles of the Chief Office, and the totality of the gifts to be limited to the first two hundred claimants. This was an imaginative way of spending £200 on advertising, and a happy alternative to the more typical dinner with speeches.

As soon as these arrangements were agreed, in May 1962, the Secretary and Directors turned their attention to a quite different problem. The third item on the Agenda of the Annual General Meeting held on 26 March 1963 read:- "To appoint Messrs. Elverstone, March & Co., Chartered Accountants of Coalville, as the Society's auditors in place of Mr G. S. Major and Mr L. F. Elverstone who have resigned". On 4 September 1962 the Secretary had been instructed to write to Mr G. S. Major whose practice was in Birmingham, to say that the Directors were considering a change because they wished to make much greater use of "on the spot audits." Mr Major met the Board on 19 September 1962 and during a long and amicable discussion agreed that "auditors round the corner" could offer service which it was not so easy for him to maintain from Birmingham. Moreover the 1962 Building Societies Act had relaxed the Rule 3 requirement that there be two separate Auditors. Finally, after he had answered a number of questions, it was agreed that Mr Major should attend the Board Meeting on 5 February, 1963. A discussion took place with Mr Elverstone, both Auditors placed their resignations in the hands of the Board, and at the A.G.M. in March 1963 the change from two Auditors to one was decided by vote of the shareholders and formalised.

Of all the changes carried out in the early 1960s there is no doubt that the most beneficial to the Society, after the appointment of a full time Secretary, was the move from rented, improvised accommodation in London Road to permanent and purpose-adapted offices in High Street. The minutes of the 3rd July, 1962 summarise the Directors' view at that time – "Although present arrangements were quite satisfactory it was thought that accommodation nearer the centre of Coalville would be to the Society's advantage and the question was to be kept in mind." On 2nd April 1963, after J. A. Walton had been re-elected Chairman and A. D. Farmer Vice-Chairman, it was reported "that 42 High Street, Coalville was for sale and Mr Collings (Surveyor) was authorised to make a thorough investigation and report to the Board at the next meeting." On April 18th Collings reported to a special Board Meeting that although 42 High Street was not ideal, "accommodation could be made on the ground floor and the upper floor converted to separate offices, the total cost including the purchase would be in the region of £15,000". Confusingly, No. 24 High Street came on the market in May 1963 and at first sight this seemed to the Directors and their Surveyor to be a more convenient and suitable property; they opened negotiations at £6,000. On 28th May, 1963 however "a letter was read from Boots the Chemists in reply to the Society's previous offer of £6,000 in which they stated that it would be pointless to continue negotiations unless the Board offered to increase the sum of £8,500. Having regard to the fact the 42 High Street, Coalville had not yet been sold the Secretary was authorised to submit an offer of £8,500 for that property". At the Board Meeting on 2 July, 1963 it was reported that the offer of £8,500 had been accepted and a sub-committee of Chairman, Vice-Chairman, Surveyor and two others was appointed to consider plans for the lay-out of the offices. The contract was signed on 29 October, 1963 with completion on 31st January 1964.

The Society then encountered a "planning approval" problem with which many of its shareholders were no doubt already familiar. It is best described by quoting verbatim the minutes of an Emergency Board Meeting on 8 May, 1964.

"Mr Collings (Surveyor) reported as follows:

Mr Collings first telephoned Mr Sharpe in July last year and asked him whether or not there would be any objection to converting the shop premises at 42 High Street into Building Society offices. Mr Sharpe was doubtful and could not give a decision.

This was followed by a letter dated 16th July to Mr Sharpe of the Leicestershire C.C. planning department stating in principle that the scheme was to modernise the front and to provide accommodation on the first floor. Mr Collings had a letter from the Planning Officer dated 21st August stating the proposals had been considered but a final plan should be submitted.

Formal application was made immediately and approval in principle to the proposals was obtained on 10th October, 1963.

The property was purchased on the strength of that approval.

Mr Collings then made a formal application for bye-law and planning approval in February, 1964 and bye-law approval was obtained in March. In view of the recent planning approval in principle it seemed reasonably safe to proceed with demolition and clearing of the site in order to save time whilst waiting for the formal approval.

Mr Bixby of the planning department telephoned Mr Collings on 7th May to say that there had been a complete change in the policy regarding the centre of Coalville and our proposals fell within this scheme. It was quite possible that we should not receive final planning approval to the plan submitted. Mr Collings immediately telephoned Mr Sharpe, who confirmed this and added that it might be some time before a decision would be made.

The work on 42 High Street was closed down and the approximate cost of demolition would be in the region of £375".

There followed a meeting between the representatives of the Society and of the County Planning Authority in Leicester on 24 June, 1964. "The meeting was extremely cordial and the representatives of the County Planning Authority were most sympathetic over the position which had arisen concerning the Society. The upshot was that the Planning Authority hinted at a five year planning approval which might well be extended, and suggested that the Society should reduce capital expenditure by submitting a modified scheme for the new offices". Such a scheme was approved at the Board Meeting on 7 July 1964, and the plan formally submitted for approval. That approval was granted in September 1964 and the Society was now free to consider moving house. This they did in May 1965 and the minutes of the Directors' meeting held on 4 May, 1965 record with satisfaction the "first time the Society had held a Board Meeting in its own offices." The official opening by the Chairman was on Tuesday June 1st, 1965. Mr Walton made graceful reference to Mr C. E. Crane – "probably the originator of the idea that a local Society would be beneficial to the Town and surrounding district" - and less happy comment that "the Building Society Movement had been receiving plenty of undeserved publicity recently", and then formally declared the Offices open. They are today the offices of the Heart of England Building Society in Coalville, but on June 1st, 1965 that change of name was still almost 13 years away.

Those remaining thirteen years were a period of steady and healthy development. Financially the Assets of the Society grew considerably; in October 1965 they passed £1 million, in 1974 they exceeded £2 million and during the final year of separate existence (1977) they reached £3 million. In 1965 when the Society moved to its new home, the Chairman was J. A. Walton and the Vice-Chairman A. D. Farmer. Chairman Walton's death was reported in February, 1966 – his brother C.T. had died on April 4th 1964 – and J. A. Walton was succeeded as Chairman by A. D. Farmer, with E. A. Crane as his Vice-Chairman. These two continued unchanged in office until amalgamation; the minutes of the final Board Meeting in February 1978 were signed by A. D. Farmer, who had been authorised by the meeting to do so. In September, 1970 the Society obtained unconditional planning approval for the occupation of its offices. The records give a clear picture of a popular, well managed, local Society where the clients enjoyed a good personal relationship with the staff and valued the Society as an important local institution. The Directors for their part were sufficiently confident of the value of their Society to refuse all offers of amalgamation until they found the arguments of Herbert Walden and his colleagues irresistible.

Before recounting that amalgamation let us look again at the type of mortgage business the Society was undertaking. Until 31 December, 1963 applications for mortgage are listed in detail in the minutes of each monthly Directors' meeting. Thereafter the Board minutes only give the names of the applicants and thence the total number of applications for the month. Details were recorded in a separate book and confirmed by the Board. At their meeting on 3rd December, 1963 the Directors considered 23 applications, 20 more than they considered at the January meeting in 1937. The majority – 17 – were approved, but 5 were declined and 1 deferred. In all cases the property was local; 6 of the houses were in Coalville, 5 in Whitwick, 3 in Hugglescote and 3 in Nottingham. The total approved was £21,990 and the average mortgage was therefore just over £1,290. The highest advance was in fact £2,675 on a bungalow on the Ashby Park Estate; the lowest was £50 as a further advance on a house in Forrest Road, Hugglescote. Those were still the days when £50 would buy something! The monthly number of mortgage applications continued at or slightly below this level for the next decade. In December, 1973 exactly ten years later, there were only 7; the dramatic rise in house prices during the past 18 months had led to a shortage of funds and a restriction on the number of applications that could be considered. In May 1974 however there were 31 applicants, 29 in May 1975, 22 in May 1976 and 15 in May 1977.

By May 1978 the Coalville Permanent Building Society had transferred its engagements to the Heart of England. Such a possibility was first discussed formally by the Board on 28th September, 1977. "A special meeting of the Board was convened in order to consider certain proposals from the Heart of England Building Society in relation to a merger, and that this could be considered in depth, Mr H. R. Walden, the General Manager and Secretary had also been asked to attend." The Directors held a short meeting before Mr Walden joined them, were "re-acquainted with the suggested proposals" and told that another Society was also interested in a merger. Mr Walden was then "warmly welcomed by the Chairman on behalf of the Directors. Mr Walden replied suitably, thanking the Board for their courtesy in extending to him the opportunity of meeting them." After these niceties, serious discussion began. Similar discussions had also been held with other Societies. The Directors were assured that "there would not be any detriment suffered to existing members of staff in any way" and that the proposed bonus to shareholders might possibly be increased. It was suggested that a convenient date for the merger might be 1 March, 1978, the beginning of a new Heart of England financial year. Mr Walden retired whilst the Directors reached their decision and on his return was told of their unanimous resolve "To proceed with negotiations with the Heart of England Building Society, (provided that the terms are satisfactory to both societies and that the bonus to shareholders is not less than 1½%)." Mr Walden promised to inform his Board and hoped that Mr F. S. Pollard and he might see the Registrar on either October 6th or 12th.

On 17th October 1977 the Directors learned that the Board of the Heart of England Society had agreed to the bonus of 1½%. They then examined a copy of the Instrument of Transfer dated 17th December, 1973 between the Oxford Provident and the Rugby and Warwick Societies and suggested that the Instrument of Transfer for the Coalville Society should be on similar lines. Mr Pollard gave details of his visit with Mr Walden to the Registrar on October 12th and the Directors were glad to note the Registrar's approval in principle and in detail. All the Directors, with the exception of Mr F. S. Pollard, agreed to accept compensation for loss of Office on the merger. Mr Pollard of course continued as an officer of Heart of England. He was Area Consultant until his retirement on 31 December, 1979, and a member of the Local Board until his sadly early death at the age of sixty on 15 July, 1980. His major professional work was to adapt the Coalville Society to modern conditions and to bring it firmly into Heart of England. Both tasks were well planned and carried through successfully.

The final meeting of the Board of the Coalville Permanent Building Society was held on 20th February, 1978, 65 years after foundation. There were now six Directors only and all were present. Eighteen applications for mortgage were considered. The Board agreed to repay a term share, on the holder's death, without the usual six month's notice, and reduced the rate of interest applicable to a particular mortgage because the property had been modernised. There remained only two other items of business. The Directors agreed that compensation should be divided equally between them, and authorised their chairman to sign the minutes "without further reference to the Board". This he did on March 9th, 1978, by which date the Coalville Permanent had ceased to exist. For the Directors, the change meant that they were no longer responsible for a small and deliberately local building society. The staff now had the career, conditions of service and promotion prospects of a much larger Society. For the shareholders there was the pleasure of a $1\frac{1}{2}\%$ bonus, but otherwise the least change of all. The Coalville Permanent was still their Society, the staff were still their friends, even if the name over the door was now Heart of England. Intense competition for scarce funds means that the day of the small building society is over. That being so, and the strong local feeling of Coalville people being what it is, they were fortunate to amalgamate with Heart of England with its strong local loyalties and its "feel" for the sense of community which is so important in Midland towns.

CHAPTER TWELVE

The Rugby and Warwick Building Society: 1967-1974

THE UNION OF the Rugby and Warwick Societies brought together two institutions with strong local affiliations, and the strong men who led them. George Smith and Herbert Walden had both served their professional apprenticeships with their respective Societies, had risen through their efforts and abilities, and each was now a Director and General Manager. L. T. Goodway had been Chairman of Rugby since 1965 and R. S. Squires of Warwick since 1960. Sir Hubert Rance succeeded P. H. B. Lyon as President of Rugby in 1956 and P. E. Kennard became President of Warwick on H. J. Ansell's death in 1962. The men responsible for the new Society had many problems to solve, especially those which result from geography, working methods, and seniority in office.

The problems of personal precedence and title were however quickly solved. Sir Hubert Rance became President with P. E. Kennard as his Vice-President. The Directors elected Goodway as their Chairman and Squires as his Deputy. But the personal relationship which was absolutely crucial was that between George Smith and Herbert Walden. Each had known the other well in the Midland Association of Building Societies and therein lay the basis of their judgement that they could work together. For nearly five years, until Mr Smith retired as Joint Managing Director in July, 1972, they fully justified that belief. They jointly formed a new Society from two intensely local and separate Societies. They collaborate still, for after his retirement Mr Smith continued as a Director, first of Rugby and Warwick and then of Heart of England and in 1980, when he was elected Chairman of Directors, the Society still benefits from the advice of a man who joined the staff of the Rugby Society in 1928 and who has rendered tremendous service.

Although the Rugby and Warwick Society was a separate entity for only seven years, they were busy and eventful years of significant progress. The two major developments were in financial activity and in the acquisition of new premises, and the Board quickly recognised this by establishing a Finance Committee and a Premises Committee to advise them. They also established Local Boards for Rugby and Warwick, of which more later. I propose first to look at the history of Rugby and Warwick in financial terms, then secondly through the ever growing web of branch development, and finally through all those miscellaneous matters which breathe life into the structure.

The assets of the two Societies on amalgamation were £17 million. In the ensuing seven years those assets more than doubled so that Rugby and Warwick's asset contribution to Heart of England was £38 million. Not surprisingly, the biggest annual increase was £5 million in 1971-72, the year when house prices began their considerable and seemingly inexorable rise. In fact, £14 million of the £17 million increase was harvested between 1971 and 1974. From 1967 to 1970 the lending policy was based on a monthly average of £500,000, and it was not until January 1972 that the first waves of the coming flood began to lap against the account books. In that month £621,810 was loaned; in July the figure was £1,396,765 and in August £1,111,784. The September 1972 quota was reduced to £800,000 but promises already made pushed the November figure to £1,335,078. Corrective action inevitably followed and the December 1972 figure was £266,589. Only in three months in 1972 – July, August and November – did the Rugby and Warwick Building Society lend more than £1,000,000 in a month. From January, 1973, although there were fluctuations, monthly lending averaged between £600,000 and £700,000. The real change was of course, as it is today in 1980, personal and social rather than financial. In July 1968 lending £594,405 serviced 188 mortgages. In March 1974 only 139 mortgages flowed from lending £844,312. In short, an increase of 42% in the amount of money available for mortgages was matched by a reduction of 26% in the number of properties mortgaged.

The new Society had also to give serious thought to its accounting system and methods of audit. There was a steady pressure to reduce the number of accounts in arrears. In February 1969 the position was:-

Arrears of less than £40	300 accounts
Arrears of £40 to £100	300 accounts
Arrears of over £100	160 accounts

As a result of regular checks and persistent pressure the position steadily improved. In February 1970 lending policy was based on 2.75 times the husband's gross salary for a twenty five year mortgage, 2.50 times gross salary for a twenty year mortgage and a 2.25 times gross salary for a fifteen year term. In addition half the husband's income from regular overtime would be counted and the wife's income could increase the total loan by £500. Two years later the multiplication factor was increased by .25 and consideration of the wife's income was established on a much more liberal basis. The latter policy, followed by all building societies, was to lead in the next decade to a society in which wives could not afford to be out of paid employment and yet there was not enough of it for all husbands and wives who wished to be bread winners. It is arguable that the cost of houses, the effects of inflation, and the expectation of a high standard of living are all leading to an exploitation of women and a neglect of children comparable to periods of nineteenth century poverty.

The necessary improvement in accounting systems was sought through computerisation. The task of amalgamating the accounts of two separate societies in time for the first Annual Meeting of the joint Society required weeks of detailed and difficult work. The Directors accepted a recommendation from the Joint General Managers that a national firm of Chartered Accountants:- "be asked to consider the Society's present accounting system in all its aspects, and to advise generally on any steps the Society might take to ensure that smooth and up to date running occurs." These discussions continued throughout 1968, led to an invaluable examination in depth of accounting methods and enabled the new Society to adopt the best contemporary practice at an early stage of its united existence. On 13 February, 1969 the Board records show that "The Joint General Managers were complimented on the satisfactory completion of the 1968 Audit and Accounts and were requested to convey the Board's thanks and appreciation to all members of Staff for their co-operation." During the course of 1968 the Computer Accounts Department had acquired one Burroughs' E2154 machine as well as a new Auto Reader and an additional panel for the E2190. Three years later, on 21 October, 1971, the Joint General Managers were able to report "that all investment balances had been transferred to Centre-File and balanced to existing controls as at 30 September 1971." (By 1981 the Heart of England will have its own computer). The accounting system of the Rugby and Warwick had been both modernised and computerised, to the considerable benefit of the customers. Those customers received one further, unexpected benefit. The staff of Rugby and Warwick were so well trained in computer use that they came to understand that mistakes are not made by computers but by the humans who inform them. As a customer of Heart of England therefore you will not be fobbed off with the classic contemporary excuse – "blame the computer." You will receive a polite apology for a human error. To err is human: to forgive is to be a computer?

The Society had to attract investment money as a necessary preliminary to proper accounting systems or wise policies for mortgage lending. This was done by following national policy with regard to investment rates, by keeping a close eye on local competition for funds, and by developing new branches or branch agencies whenever possible. The introduction of bonus shares in October, 1968 was a calculated reaction to local competition. During the first month they attracted £484,000 and two months later the total was £900,000. Branch development necessarily happened more slowly, but the Premises Committee actively pursued such a policy throughout the seven years. In May 1969 the Board decided to investigate branch possibilities in the following towns, given in order of priority: Kidderminster, Worcester, Sutton Coldfield, Redditch, Oxford and Birmingham. In September of the same year priority had changed to Kidderminster, Bromsgrove, Sutton Coldfield and Redditch. By January, 1971 real progress had been made in Kidderminster and Redditch. At that date the Society owned twelve headquarter or branch buildings insured for a total of £503,000, as follows:-

Temple Buildings, Rugby	£100,000
22-26 Jury Street, Warwick	£120,000
18 Jury Street, Warwick	£20,000
1B, Castle Lane, Warwick	£8,000
26, High Street, Banbury	£75,000
53, Broad Street, Banbury	£15,000
24, Sheep Street, Rugby	£50,000

PLATE 28
L. T. Goodway, Chairman, Rugby, 1965-67; Chairman, Rugby and Warwick, 1967-70.

PLATE 29
R. S. Squires, Chairman, Warwick, 1960-67; Chairman, Rugby and Warwick, 1970-73.

PLATE 30
R. H. M. Burton, Chairman, Rugby and Warwick, 1973-74; President, Heart of England, 1974-80.

PLATE 31
T. D. Kelly, Chairman, Rugby and Warwick, 1974; Chairman, Heart of England, 1974-78.

PLATE 32
Rear view (circa 1900) of present Redditch branch.

PLATE 33
Interior of Redditch branch, opened by Rugby and Warwick in 1972.

PLATE 34

Mr Tom Coyne opens Erdington branch of Rugby and Warwick in 1973.

PLATE 35
Kidderminster branch, opened by Rugby and Warwick in 1971.

PLATE 36
Queen St., Oxford branch opened by Heart of England in 1978.

PLATE 37
Southam branch opened by Heart of England in 1978.

PLATE 38
Stow-on-the-Wold branch opened by Heart of England in 1978.

PLATE 39
Ledbury branch opened by Heart of England in 1978.

PLATE 40
Willenhall branch opened by Heart of England in 1979.

PLATE 41

Senior Executives, Heart of England Building Society, 1980. Left to right:-
J. T. Norman *(Assistant Gen. Manager)*, B. H. Froggatt *(Assistant Gen. Manager)*, H. R. Walden *(Gen. Manager)*, C. E. S. MacIntyre *(Deputy Gen. Manager)*, P. A. Coogan *(Assistant Gen. Manager)*.

PLATE 42

The Board of Directors, Heart of England Building Society, 1980. Left to right:- L. T. Goodway; C. E. S. MacIntyre *(D.G.M.)*; H. R. Walden; H. B. Duggins; E. H. Page *(Chairman,* 1978-80*)*, H. J. Prince; G. Smith; J. Richardson; T. D. Kelly.

18 Victoria Terrace, Leamington	£45,000
4, High Street, Lutterworth	£18,000
41, High Street, Daventry	£8,000
53 Henley Street, Stratford-upon-Avon	£40,000
Cottages, Railway Terrace, Rugby	£4,500

The first branch to be opened by the Rugby and Warwick Building Society was in fact 18 Worcester Street, Kidderminster, opened on 2 September, 1971 by Lady Eddy in the presence of the Mayor and Mayoress and eighty invited guests. She received in return "a suitable piece of bone china". In May of that same year 20 Jury Street, Warwick, was bought, thus removing a cuckoo from the Warwick headquarters nest. The purchase of 13 Church Green East, Redditch, was completed on 15 April, 1971. When Sir Edward Thompson opened it on 30 June, 1972, £30,000 had been spent on adapting it to a branch office. Three months later the Society initiated a move into Birmingham by buying 258, High Street, Erdington. The building cost £20,000 to adapt and was opened by Tom Coyne on 22nd March, 1973. The final major building activity of the seven years was the adaptation of the Jury Street, Warwick buildings to form an administrative headquarters. This considerable undertaking, costing £230,000 was admirably executed. The result both retains the visual contribution made by the Society's buildings to that part of Warwick and provides the necessary environment for management control of the Society. Other alternatives, including Temple Buildings, Rugby, had been considered but on 18 April, 1974 the Directors met in their new Board Room in Warwick for the first time. They met there on five occasions before they amalgamated with Walsall and changed title once more. There was no official opening ceremony for the new headquarters. Originally it was to have been christened, and names such as Avon, Unity, Castle, Temple, or Warwick House were bandied about. Finally it was thought wise to call it the Administrative Centre.

Assets, cash flow, accounting and branch development were the major responsibilities and activities of the Rugby and Warwick Building Society during those seven years. Records and source material offer the historian the merest glimpse of the real lives of the men and women who were responsible for policy or for its execution. Nine of the twelve original Board members were still directors when the final meeting of the Rugby and Warwick Board took place on

22 August, 1974. Goodway and Squires, although still Directors, were no longer Chairman and Vice-Chairman; the period of office was now normally three years. Goodway did not stand for re-election to the chair in 1970 and was succeeded by Squires. When Squires became Chairman R. H. M. Burton was elected Vice-Chairman, subsequently succeeding as Chairman in 1973. At that time H. J. Prince was elected Vice-Chairman. In May 1974 Burton, who proposed to retire from the Board when the merger became effective, stood down as Chairman and proposed for this office T. D. Kelly who had already been designated as Chairman elect of the new Heart of England Society. The other changes at Board level all happened between 1971 and 1973. In March 1971 the death of P. E. Kennard, the Vice-President who with his father had served the Warwick and Warwickshire Society for so many decades, was a matter of great sorrow. So too was the resignation through ill-health two months later of the President, Sir Hubert Rance, who had held such office with either Rugby or Rugby and Warwick for fifteen years. W. C. Everard died in August, 1971, D. Edyvean-Walker resigned through ill-health in May, and D. Mitchell died on 30 December, 1971. These three directors were not replaced and their colleagues expressed their appreciation of many years of supportive service and their sorrow at the personal tragedy. In May, 1973 a member of the Local Board, C. G. Richards, died. As we have seen he had rendered exceptional service to the Rugby Building Society of which he was a director from 1934-67, and Chairman from 1945-59. His history of the first hundred years of the Rugby Society is a fitting memorial to him and I have quoted extensively from it in this book. His successor as Chairman was E. R. Marshall who was a Director of Rugby from 1940-67 and Chairman from 1959-62. Like Richards he had joined the Local Board in 1967, judging that the Main Board needed younger men. He died in October, 1973. The Rugby Society in particular and the Building Society movement generally owed much to men such as these.

Mr George Smith retired as Joint General Manager, but not as a director, in July, 1972. He had joined the Rugby Society in 1928, became its General Manager in December, 1950, held leading positions in the Midland Association of Building Societies, and was appointed Joint General Manager of Rugby and Warwick on amalgamation. He made a tremendous contribution to the Rugby Building Society, but he may well feel that his highest achievement was the successful launch of the amalgamated Society. Certainly, when he retired, he knew that he and Herbert Walden had jointly achieved that success. Mr Walden was at the same time gaining national recognition in the Building Societies Movement. In February 1969 he was elected Hon. Secretary of the Midland Association of Building Societies. He became Deputy Chairman in April, 1971 and Chairman in April, 1972. In May, 1974 he was elected to the Council of the Building Societies Association and in 1980 he is a leading member of the Council as Chairman of the Practice Committee and a member of the Chairman's Committee. His service and experience at national level have been of incalculable value to the national movement and to Rugby and Warwick and its successor, Heart of England.

What else were the people of the Rugby and Warwick Building Society doing during these seven years. The members of the cross country team were involved in a great deal of disciplined training, as they still are. In 1968 they won the Inter-Society cross country race. D. G. Davey was placed second and V. G. Bridges fourth in the 1972 race. These were outstanding successes by a team from one of the smallest Societies in the competition. The initial plan to have Local Boards of Directors for Rugby and for Warwick was modified in May, 1969 when they joined together as one Local Board. In June 1972 meetings became quarterly, centred upon a working buffet lunch, and the Joint General Managers were able to keep the Main Board well informed of the opinions on local affairs of former directors of the separate Rugby and Warwick Societies. The Directors sought to encourage all members of their staff to feel involved in the policies and management of the Society. In May, 1973, Mrs E. A. Measures won a prize for a suggested savings incentive scheme "aimed at young potential first-time buyers . . . giving additional interest if an account was subsequently used as a deposit when applying for a mortgage." Two years later the staff were invited to suggest names for the new administrative centre in Warwick, and prizes were awarded. Finally, it was the corporate unhappiness of the staff about any of the suggested names that led to the choice of the functional "Administration Centre."

Successful advertising was important during a difficult period, when investment money was becoming increasingly mobile. The best advertisement the Rugby and Warwick Building Society – and later Heart of England – ever had is its staff. It has always been a pleasure to do business with them, their approach to their customers is personal as well as professional and one visits a branch of the Society to meet old friends as well as to manage money. To attract new customers however, the Society increasingly used professional advertising, controlled by the Directors in terms of an advertising budget and by their executives in terms of content.

As always, the official records conceal as much as they reveal about the earliest discussions between two Societies with regard to amalgamation. This is understandable, for these are delicate matters. No doubt senior directors and senior executives must have explored possibilities unofficially. An historian is not a fly on the wall and he would not write history if he were. On 20 December, 1973 however the Directors received a report dated 10 December from their General Manager. They authorised him to have further talks with John Richardson, General Manager of the Walsall Mutual Building Society, and to report. This he did on 17 January, 1974 in a nine page document, with sixteen recommendations. The most important of these provided:-

(a) for the transfer of engagements from Rugby and Warwick to Walsall: by this method of amalgamation there would be an estimated tax saving of £120,000.
(b) that tax saving was the only reason for choosing this method, and that the merger must not appear as a take-over by either side. The suggested title for the new Society was "Heart of England".
(c) That the Main Board would be limited to ten members.
(d) that Mr Herbert Walden and Mr John Richardson would be Joint General Managers until 28 February, 1976 when Mr Richardson would retire.
(e) that Mr C. E. S. MacIntyre would be Deputy General Manager and Mr J. T. Smith, Mr B. H. Froggatt and Mr P. A. Coogan, Assistant General Managers.

All these recommendations were approved by the Board, with very minor amendments. The Chairman of the negotiating committee, R. H. M. Burton, was congratulated on "the unselfish and generous leadership shown" which "had resulted in an extremely amicable tone being set," Mr Burton was to become the first President of the new Society, succeeding Sir J. Cliff Tibbits who died before he could assume office. He served with distinction as the first President of the

Heart of England Building Society, until his death in October, 1980. A Special General Meeting of the Rugby and Warwick Building Society was held at the Administration Centre on 4 July, 1974. Eight directors, three local board members, and fifteen members were present. Many proxy votes had been received in advance. The Chairman moved and R. H. M. Burton seconded:- "That the Rugby and Warwick Building Society do transfer its engagements to Walsall Mutual Building Society in accordance with the terms of an Instrument of Transfer of Engagements dated 14 May, 1974." There were 3,783 votes in favour and 225 against; there were no spoilt papers. The proposed name of the new Society – Heart of England – was a happy choice. It was suggested by Mr Walden, accepted by the Directors, and received favourable mention from Margaret Stone in the Times.

Joseph gained much material advantage by correctly interpreting that Pharaoh's dream foretold seven fat years followed by seven lean. The seven years of the Rugby and Warwick Building Society were prosperous and successful. Fortunately, as we shall see in the next chapter, the man set to music by Andrew Lloyd Webber was no longer around with his long range economic forecasts and the heart of England has already built six more years of success on the seven of the Rugby and Warwick. Rugby and Warwick succeeded because the two merging Societies had a century of experience in the Heart of England behind them. More especially they succeeded because George Smith and Herbert Walden, the heirs to that "century of interest", made quite certain that they could and would. As current Chairman of Directors and General Manager respectively of Heart of England they are a guarantee of future success and command much trust and respect.

CHAPTER THIRTEEN

The Heart of England Building Society: 1974 —

FOR SOME OF the leaders of the new Heart of England Building Society the events of 1974 were a re-run of those of 1967. Six members of the new Board of Directors – H. B. Duggins, L. T. Goodway, T. D. Kelly, H. J. Prince, G. Smith and H. R. Walden – had been actively involved in the union of the Rugby and Warwick Societies. So had many of the senior executives, and C. E. S. MacIntyre, who became Deputy General Manager of Heart of England, played a major supporting role in the success of Rugby and Warwick and in the creation of the new Society. On 20 May, 1974 the minutes of the Joint Steering Committee note that "Mr John Richardson expressed thanks to Mr H. R. Walden and Mr C. E. S. MacIntyre for the detailed work they had carried out on the drafts and printing preparations". At the first Heart of England Board meeting on 3 September, 1974 "Mr John Richardson paid tribute to the work carried out by Mr H. R. Walden, Mr C. E. S. MacIntyre and Mr P. A. Coogan in relation to the integration problems relating to the merger." The knowledge and expertise gained in 1967 was invaluable in 1974 and the six former Rugby and Warwick leaders and their four fellow Board members from the Walsall Society were fortunate in that respect, as they were also in the support of Charles MacIntyre and other senior executives like him. Finally, the new Board – completed by E. H. Page, H. Perry, J. Richardson and A. L. Wiggin from Walsall – was unusually blessed with experience in that three of its members were past or present General Managers. John Richardson of Walsall, George Smith of Rugby and Herbert Walden of Warwick were trained and successful professional managers, with extensive experience of the region in which Heart of England hoped to be strongest.

As with Rugby and Warwick in 1967, the first priority of the Heart of England Board was to determine financial policy. They decided upon an initial monthly mortgage quota of £765,000. They noted that the former Walsall Mutual had forward mortgage commitments of £1 million and the former Rugby and Warwick of £1.7 million. Since the end of the previous financial year the actual lending of the Rugby and Warwick had been £4.15 million (8 month period) and of Walsall Mutual £1.7 million (6 month period). Total assets on amalgamation were £66 million of which £11.4 million or 17.27% were liquid assets. It was anticipated that at the end of the financial year on 28 February 1975 assets would be about £70 million: they were in fact £72 million. On February 28, 1976 they had increased to £82 million; in 1977 they were £91 million; in 1978 they were £109 million, in 1979 the total was £128 million and in 1980 £149 million. The monthly mortgage figure fixed in August, 1974, proved too low. From then until the end of February, 1975 the lowest monthly lending figure was £889,161 and the highest, in October 1974, was £981,046. The monthly quota for the financial year 1975-76 was therefore set at £1,050,000. For 1976-77 the quota was £1,650,000 per month; for 1977-78 it was £1,470,000, followed by £2,250,000 per month in 1978-79 and £2,550,000 in 1979-80. It is moreover most heartening to record that inflation did not entirely neutralise the increase in lending. In September 1974 lending of £921,121 produced 137 mortgages. In January 1979 loans totalling £2,377,551 enabled 270 people to buy houses. In its first fifty three months, from September 1974 to January 1979, the Heart of England Building Society provided money for 12,405 mortgages.

The greatest activity during these first six years was however in branch development. When the two Societies merged the Rugby and Warwick Building Society operated from thirteen headquarter or branch offices. The Walsall had five branches, in addition to the headquarters at 41-43 Bridge Street, Walsall. During the next five years, eleven further branch offices were opened and in addition 27 Market Place, Cannock was converted from leasehold to freehold. In September 1975 the Directors accepted a recommendation from the Premises Committee that they should look for a branch in either Brackley or Chipping Norton, to be a sub-office of Banbury. In March 1976 the Board first discussed the possibility of buying 29

Queen Street, Oxford, to give a second Oxford branch in the heart of the city, and 26/27 Sheep Street, Rugby, which would form the main Rugby office with Temple Buildings as a branch. They also approved in principle the plan for a second Leamington branch and the search for suitable property began. The branch at 26/27 Sheep Street, Rugby was bought in May 1976 and 29 Queen Street, Oxford in July of the same year. It was nearly a year later, in April, 1977, that 70/72 Warwick Street, Leamington was first identified as a suitable branch office and opened in October 1978.

In November 1977 the long search for a branch office in Kenilworth had been brought to a satisfactory conclusion. The Warwick and Warwickshire Society had first considered a Kenilworth branch in the previous century. The Rugby and Warwick made persistent but unsuccessful attempts, but now 27 Warwick Road, Kenilworth became available as a leasehold. Like other recent acquisitions it is in the main shopping area and is a most suitable site. The next year, 1978, brought particularly active branch development. It resulted from a Board decision in June 1977 that a capital sum of £1,000,000 should be available over a 3 year period for purchases, that a central office should be found in the Black Country, and that a branch in Stow-on-the-Wold was a priority. The new Rugby office in Sheep Street opened for business early in 1978. This was followed on May 12th by the official opening of 29 Queen Street, Oxford, subsequently one of the most successful branches. The branch in Church Street, Stow-on-the-Wold received its first customers on August 18th. The second Leamington branch, in Warwick Street, opened on 5 October, and 1978, a true annus mirabilis for the Society, ended with a flurry of activity. At the Board meeting on 21 December, 1978 the General Manager reported that 83 Stafford Street, Willenhall would be ready in twenty four weeks, that 18 Market Street, Brackley had opened successfully on 18 December, 1978, that a tender had been accepted for 27 Bridge Street, Stourport and that tenders for 22 High Street, Ledbury would be opened on 13 February, 1979. In four and a half years the Heart of England Building Society had so extended its branches – an increase of 81 % – that it could justifiably claim to be providing some important capillaries to feed the artery which kept the financial heart of England beating.

Who were the people who planned and achieved these developments? The policy was determined by the Board, professionally advised by their Joint General Managers who were of course fellow directors. At their first meeting on 3 September, 1974, T. D. Kelly of Warwick was elected Chairman and A. L. Wiggin of Sutton Coldfield, Vice Chairman. The other directors were H. B. Duggins of Leamington, L. T. Goodway of Rugby, E. H. Page of Walsall, H. Perry of Walsall, H. J. Prince of Warwick, J. Richardson of Walsall, G. Smith of Rugby and H. R. Walden of Warwick. The oldest member of the Board was sixty four and the youngest, the Chairman, forty seven. The Vice Chairman, who had come to the Board of the Walsall Mutual from that of the Walsall Permanent on amalgamation, resigned as a director in July 1976 and was warmly thanked for many years of service. He was succeeded as a director, in September 1976, by D. Linford of Rugely; at the age of forty two he was the youngest board member. On 1 July, 1976 E. H. Page was elected Vice-Chairman in anticipation of Mr Wiggin's retirement. He served as Vice-Chairman to Mr Kelly until 27 July 1978 when the first Chairman of Heart of England – a man who had made a distinguished contribution to its success – retired from that office but not from the Board. Tribute was paid to him at the time in the following terms: "At the time of the merger it was agreed to continue the established practice of the constitituent Societies to rotate the chairmanship of the Society. In July Mr T. D. Kelly was succeeded in that office by Mr E. Harold Page. His colleagues pay warm tribute to the service rendered by Mr Kelly as Chairman during a momentous period in the Society's history which saw the achievement of the mergers which formed Heart of England, the attainment of £100 million of assets, the grant of Armorial Ensigns and the naming of a rose after the Society. His contribution was outstanding and it is most gratifying that his services and wise counsel are still available to the Society as a director". Mr Page was then elected Chairman with Mr George Smith, the former Joint General Manager of Rugby and Warwick as his Vice-Chairman.

The only other change in the Main Board – a reduction in number – followed from the death of Mr H. Perry on 12 March 1978. The Chairman, T. D. Kelly "referred to the death of Mr Harold Perry on 12 March 1978, spoke in warm terms of his valued service to the Society and to the former Walsall Mutual Society since his appointment as a Director in 1971 and said he would be greatly missed both as a colleague and as a good friend. The members of the Board stood in silence as a token of his memory." During this period a former

Director and a member of the Local Board both died and the Directors recorded their considerable appreciation of the qualities they had brought to the Society. Mr A. R. Tatham who died on 15 November 1975, had been a member of the Rugby Board from 1950-67 and of the Board of Rugby and Warwick from 1967-74. Mr A. J. Waddington, who died on 1 July 1978, had been a member of the Warwick Board from 1961 and of the Local Boards from 1967. The other major change fortunately did not deprive the Society of an important personality, for John Richardson continued as a director after his retirement as Joint General Manager. He retired from executive office at the end of February 1976 and the members of the Board offered "Mr John Richardson an expression of their high appreciation of the careful attention which he had devoted to his various duties since his appointment as the first full-time Secretary of the Walsall Mutual Building Society on 1 December 1949 and as General Manager on 1 January 1968 and also since his appointment as Joint General Manager of Heart of England Building Society on 31 August 1974, of their recognition of his success in those various offices and of their gratitude for his unfailing courtesy and kindness, and that he be asked to accept the very best wishes of his Co-Directors for a long and happy retirement from executive office."

The Rugby and Warwick cross country runners took their competitive spirit with them into Heart of England. In 1976, 1977 and 1979 they won the Inter-Society race previously won by Rugby and Warwick in 1968. Heart of England was the smallest Society taking part, and such distinguished results were made possible by hard and systematic training and fine team spirit. In 1977 the road relay team won that competition; Heart of England fielded three of the nine teams entered. In 1980 these same athletes raised £6,500 for the British Heart Foundation by running a sponsored 337 miles round the heartland of England. J. T. Smith, one of the three Assistant General Managers, retired on 31 December 1976 after valuable service, especially to the former Rugby Society; his successor was Mr J. T. Norman. On 28 April 1977 Herbert Walden, once again and for the third time sole General Manager of a Building Society, was re-elected unopposed to the B.S.A. Council and elected to serve on the Chairman's Committee of Council, the body which represents the Association on the Joint Advisory Committee for discussions with Government. No previous leader of the Heart of England or one of its constituent Societies has achieved such distinction in the national building society movement. In October 1980 he completed 40 years with Warwick: Rugby and Warwick: Heart of England and his journey from office junior to chief executive was celebrated by his senior colleagues and acclaimed in the local press. None of these leading personalities would doubt however that the success of their policies and plans depended on the quality of the staff of Heart of England. In 1976 there were 107 full time and 40 part time staff. A year later the number of full-timers had increased to 119 and the number of part-timers reduced to 36. Staff relationships were an important priority of the Board, new conditions of service were agreed when the Heart of England Society was formed, and great care was taken to maintain quick and clear communications throughout the hierarchy. It remains an inescapable fact that to members of the general public the Heart of England Building Society means the voice that answers the telephone, the personality on the other side of the counter in branch or banking hall, the officer who discusses the mortgage application – a request which carries the hopes and fears of many a married or engaged couple. The Heart of England Building Society is well served by all these various members of staff.

As we have seen in the previous chapter, the staff can only respond when people contact them. The purpose of organised advertising is to encourage the initial contact, to cause you and me to think "Heart of England" when we think "Building Society". This account of the first six years of Heart of England ends with the story of that advertising in action. Routine advertising of course continued all the time, but the Society, guided by their specialist advertisers and by their General Manager, created or made use of a number of special opportunities. In November, 1975 the Directors approved a House tie, with the Heart of England logo as a crest, and two hundred were ordered. It was in 1977 and 1978 however that policies and events conspired most closely to provide opportunities for bringing public and Society together. On 26 June 1977 the Heart of England rose was well reported in the Sunday Times. In 1978 the rose was successfully launched at the Royal Show at Stoneleigh and Prince Charles accepted a gift of twelve for his gardens at Chevening. This rose is now an established part of the English summer scene, emphasising the essential Englishness of its parent and namesake Society. In June 1980, as I write, beds of that rose are coming into bloom in each town where there is a branch of the Society.

The achievement of Assets of £100 million in the autumn of 1977 was naturally and properly an occasion for much publicity. The Directors decided that October 17th would be the formal date and arranged a Press release for that day. They also authorised a local advertising campaign lasting four or five weeks and beginning on 29 October: it was to include television advertising. Special cards and posters were provided for each of the Society's offices, there was a special franking design for the postal machine and small stickers to attach to all Heart of England literature. A social event was planned for each local branch area; a commemorative Royal Worcester china bowl was ordered. Finally, emphasising their view of the important role played by the staff in this achievement, the Directors decided on a staff bonus. It was one hundred and twenty four years since the foundation of the first constituent Society, Warwick and Warwickshire, with a subscription of £17. 1. 8d at the first meeting. One hundred million pounds of assets would have been a fairy tale, prospector's gold, to those earnest mid-nineteenth century pioneers. It was indeed an achievement worth celebrating, a tale worth telling, a success story of significance to English social and economic history during a century and a quarter.

In the meantime, the Heart of England rose had proved an excellent ambassador and had extended its influence. In December 1977 250 bottles of rose petal wine were made. No doubt this unusual form of advertising was appreciated by some of those wine connoisseurs who were actual or potential members of the Society. Moreover, nine months later, there was a welcome and unexpected spin-off. The rose, in transit from the grower, was protected by a stiff paper sack. In September 1978 the paper sack produced for the Heart of England rose won the "Sack of the Year" award presented by the Paper Sack Development Association. The advertisers were quick to make use of such a splendid opportunity.

By the summer of 1978 the new Heart of England Building Society was successfully established and its name was in the public eye. It so happened that in July George Smith, former General Manager of Rugby and Warwick, Vice-Chairman of Directors of Heart of England, completed fifty years service with the Society, via the Rugby Building Society. This was not a subject for advertising but for rejoicing, although it naturally brought some welcome publicity to Heart of England. So too did the grant of Armorial Ensigns, negotiated after consultation with Richmond Herald. The presentation took place on 13 June, 1978 in the presence of Her Majesty's

Lord Lieutenant of Warwickshire, Mr C. M. T. Smith-Ryland. The account of that presentation and a description of the Armorial Ensigns are given as an appendix to this chapter.

Here we leave the first six years of the Heart of England. The events of those years from 1974-80 are current affairs, not history. One cannot appraise historically the Heart of England Building Society or the men and women who lead it. But it is possible to assert as historical fact that it is successfully established. It thus follows that the Warwick and Warwickshire Building Society, the Rugby Benefit Building Society, the Walsall Mutual Building Society, the Oxford Provident Building Society and the Coalville Permanent Building Society each and all completed their separate histories by feeding and nourishing the Heart of England Society. Each made a unique contribution, each complemented the other. In the final chapter I shall hope to bring these tributaries together and examine the strength and direction of the main stream. As this story ends, yet another Society – the South Birmingham Savings Society Limited - has joined the Heart of England. That however must be the subject of a chapter when the next volume of history is written.

Appendix to Chapter Thirteen

HEART OF ENGLAND BUILDING SOCIETY

On Tuesday 13th June 1978 a distinguished company assembled at the Lord Leycester Hospital, Warwick, for a Ceremony of Presentation of Letters Patent granting Armorial Ensigns to the Society by Her Majesty's Lord Lieutenant for the County of Warwick (C. M. T. Smith-Ryland, Esq.) attended by Richmond Herald of Arms in Ordinary to the Queen (J. P. Brooke-Little, Esq. MVO MA FSA).

The guests assembled at 11.15 a.m. At 11.30 a.m. the platform party consisting of:

The Lord Lieutenant
Richmond Herald
The High Sheriff
The Chairman of Warwickshire County Council
The Chairman of the Society
The Chairman of Warwick District Council
The President of the Society
The Mayor of Warwick

The General Manager of the Society

proceeded to the dais.

The Chairman of the Society (T. D. G. Kelly, Esq. FCA) welcomed all the guests and introduced Richmond Herald of Arms (J. P. Brooke-Little, Esq. MVO, MA, FSA).

Richmond Herald then read the document of Letters Patent to the assembled company, handed it to the Lord Lieutenant who then formally presented it to the Chairman of the Society.

The Chairman made a speech of acceptance on behalf of the Society.

Photographs were then taken and the company adjourned to Alderson House, 23 High Street, Warwick, for a reception and luncheon.

After the luncheon, the Lord Lieutenant proposed the Loyal Toast and the Society's General Manager (H. R. Walden, Esq. FCIS, FBS.) proposed the toast of "Our Guests" to which the High Sheriff (The Hon. H. A. Feilding, MC) responded.

The Chairman thanked all the guests for their support and declared the proceedings to be at an end.

Grant of Armorial Ensigns

The Blazon (or description) of the Arms is as follows:

Arms:	Gules within a Heart voided a Chevron Or on a Chief double enarched of the last a Griffin passant of the field beaked and armed Azure
Crest:	On a Wreath Argent and Gules A demi-Bear Sable armed Gules muzzled charged on the body with a Pale couped raguly and resting his forepaws on a Heart voided therein a Chevron Or
Mantled:	Sable doubled Or
Supporters:	Upon a Compartment composed of Thrift growing upon a Grassy Mound proper on the dexter side a Lion Or and on the sinister an Ox Gules armed langued tufted and unguled Or about the neck of each pendent from a Cord a Heart voided therein a Chevron that on the Lion Gules and that on the Ox Or
Badge:	A Heart voided therein a Chevron Or

INTERPRETATION

The Heart of England Building Society originally adopted an attractive and symbolic *logo,* namely, the outline of a house within a heart.

When the Society decided to petition for a grant of armorial bearings, it naturally wanted to retain this logo in some form. Fortunately, it was possible to do this with a very minor alteration; a chevron, the heraldic symbol for a house, being the shape of the eaves, replaced the outline of the house.

A Heart voided therein a Chevron Or (i.e. gold) is the main motif on the shield of arms, forms the badge of the Society, and appears

PLATE 43

Grant of Armorial Ensigns to Heart of England Building Society, 1978. Left to right:-
K. A. Evans Esq. *(Artist who illustrated Letters Patent)*; J. P. Brooke-Little Esq., MVO., MA., FSA., *(Richmond Herald of Arms in ordinary to The Queen)*. C. M. T. Smith-Ryland Esq., *(Her Majesty's Lord Lieutenant for the County of Warwick)*; H. R. Walden Esq., FCIS., FCBSI., *(Director and General Manager)*; T. D. G. Kelly Esq., FCA., *(Chairman of Directors)*.

PLATE 44

George Smith, Secretary, Rugby, 1950-67; Director, 1961-67; Director and Joint General Manager, Rugby and Warwick, 1967-72; Director Rugby and Warwick, 1972-4, and Heart of England, 1974- . Chairman of Directors, Heart of England, 1980- .

PLATE 45

Headquarters (Jury St., Warwick) of Heart of England Building Society, 1980. H. R. Walden, Assistant Secretary, 1955-57; Joint Secretary 1957-62; Director and Chief Executive, Warwick and Warwickshire 1962-67. Director and Joint General Manager, Rugby and Warwick 1967-72; Director and General Manager, Rugby and Warwick, 1972-74. Director and Joint General Manager, Heart of England 1974-76; Director and General Manager, Heart of England 1976– .

in the crest and, suspended from cords, about the necks of the supporters. On the lion supporter the emblem has to be red because, the lion being gold, it would not be easily recognisable if it were also gold. Also on the shield is a golden chief double enarched which follows the line of the top of the heart.

The point of having a chief (the top division of the shield) is to exhibit the red griffin 'beaked and armed Azure'; that is, with blue beak and claws. The griffin, a mythical beast, half eagle, half lion, is the guardian of treasure and also forms the crest of The Building Societies Association, of which the Society is a member.

Above the shield is the closed steel helm, appropriate to a corporate body. The helm is to display the crest, a subsidiary device which became popular at the end of the 13th century. The crest itself is a black bear with a golden muzzle, charged on the body with a golden ragged staff and resting its forepaws on the badge of the Society. The bear and ragged staff are ancient emblems of the Earls of Warwick and have been used extensively in Warwickshire heraldry. They occur in the arms used by the towns of Warwick, Walsall and Rugby and so symbolise the Rugby Building Society and the Warwick Building Society which united to form Rugby and Warwick Building Society in 1967 and subsequently merged in 1974 with Walsall Mutual Building Society to form Heart of England Building Society. The traditional wreath round the base of the crest is silver and red, the colours of England and the mantling (the cloak attached to the helm, possibly to deaden the effect of sword blows on the neck) continues the gold and black of the crest.

Certain corporations, because of their size, or pre-eminence, are accorded the special honour of having supporters on either side of the shield.

The Society qualified for such a distinction and has a golden lion for the dexter (right) supporter symbolising England, and also referring to Walsall, which has a lion supporter, and a red Ox with golden hooves, horns and tail tuft is the sinister (left) supporter.

The Ox occurs in the arms of Oxford and refers to the fact that the Oxford Provident Building Society was incorporated in the Heart of England Building Society.

Both supporters are adorned with the badge of the Society and stand on a compartment consisting of a grassy mound on which thrift grows. The grass symbolises land, as building societies originally existed to help people to buy land; the thrift needs no explanation.

The motto, on the scroll beneath the compartment, does not form part of the grant of arms, but it is customary to have a motto. The Society has chosen a Latin motto which refers to its name and badge *Cordibus Fortibus,* with strong hearts.

CHAPTER FOURTEEN

Reflections

IN A LONELY spot in the Massif Central you can listen to the birds and breathe the flower scented air at the source of the River Loire. High in the Alps you can walk on the Rhone glacier, where the mighty Rhone begins as a freezingly cold milkwhite trickle. Not far from Cirencester in the heartland of England you can search for the source of the Thames and find it invisible, below ground. Wordsworth's magnificent sonnet, together with Westminster Bridge and the Palace of Westminster, seem momentarily the stuff of dreams, tricking reality into non-existence.

The river bed of the Heart of England Building Society flows through history, not through geography as do those of the Loire, Rhone and Thames. In historical terms its source must be the meeting in Warwick on 10 November 1853. During the remaining 46 years of the nineteenth century local initiative led to the foundation of four other societies whose history would later flow with that of Warwick – Oxford in 1860, Walsall in 1863, Rugby in 1866 and Daventry in 1883. During the first half of the twentieth century Coalville was founded, in 1912, and Rugby established branches at Banbury in 1927 and Lutterworth in 1945. Thus six societies and two branches were established during the first 108 years. During the remaining 18 years of our journey, ending with the Annual Meeting of June 1980, a further 21 branches were opened as follows:-

1961	Banbury	by Warwick
1962	Leamington Spa	by Rugby
1962	Stratford-upon-Avon	by Warwick (1965 by Rugby)
1968	Brownhills	by Walsall
1969	Aldridge	by Walsall

1971	Cannock	by Walsall
1971	Kidderminster	by Rugby & Warwick
1972	Redditch	by Rugby & Warwick
1973	Erdington	by Rugby & Warwick
1973	Lichfield	by Walsall
1974	Bloxwich	by Walsall
1978	Oxford (Queen St.)	by Heart of England
1978	Stow-on-the-Wold	by do do
1978	Southam	by do do
1978	Leamington Spa (Warwick St.)	by do do
1978	Ledbury	by do do
1978	Rugby (26/7 Sheep St.)	by do do
1978	Brackley	by do do
1979	Darlaston	by do do
1979	Kenilworth	by do do
1979	Willenhall	by do do
1979	Stourport	by do do
1980	Chase Terrace	by do do

Those dates, those buildings, the people who worked in them, the people who borrowed, the people who invested, the capital assets engendered (now totalling more than £170m) show us the growing flood of the Heart of England Building Society as clearly as we may see the Loire flowing through Warwick's twin town of Saumur or past some of the finest chateaux in France. As we look back along the historical river bed we see that people are the living element, its water of life. Without their initiative, their realisation of the need for better housing, their co-operative understanding of how lender and borrower could help one another, their skill in money management, there could have been no Heart of England today. The tiny streams started more than one hundred years ago would simply have run into the sand. Those nineteenth century pioneers were helped and encouraged by the civic leaders and authorities in whose areas they operated. They were helped by parliamentary legislation, stimulated by the pressures exerted on M.P.s by the National Association of Building Societies and later by the B.S.A. They were disciples of Samuel Smiles and firmly believed that they would build a better society and a better country if the British were encouraged to own their houses. In consequence, Britain has a much higher proportion of owner occupation than any other European country. Reflected in the waters of history we can see the men who pioneered the Heart of England; Temple, Wratislaw and Fisher in Rugby; Thomas Davies and Sallaway in Warwick; Joseph Dixon and John Smith in Walsall; Charles Green in Oxford and C. E. Crane and W. Fellows in Coalville; differing widely in their professional skills and social background but with a common purpose. We see their successors; Purser with his determination to hold everything in his own control and Ansell who in the end was too big a man for Purser. We see the younger Fisher, and C. G. Richards, excellent historian of Rugby's first century. The Llewellens, father and son, swim strongly with the growing stream as the rising current of Walsall sweeps by. C. T. Walton, Treasurer Powell and similar organisers and initiators help carve out the river bed through the countryside of history. Finally, as the tributaries flow together and the river broadens on its way, it is professionals such as George Smith, Herbert Walden, John Richardson, Sydney Wren and Frank Pollard who strengthened the river banks against the growing weight of water and thus saw the powerful Heart of England river moving purposefully forward.

History is written and read for pleasure, for scholarly study and intellectual exercise, for a better understanding of human behaviour and above all for its revelations and its insights into why the present is as it is. I have spent three years reading source material and documents about the separate building societies which today comprise the Heart of England Building Society. The material was not written for a future historian of course, but for business purposes. But, within that limitation, I have sought to identify the chief events and major personalities and to select material which will support a story line true both in fact and in spirit. I am aware that I have left out fifty times as much as I have put in. During those three years my life, as a retired schoolmaster, has also been occupied by my commitments as a county councillor, magistrate, chairman of an agricultural working party, lay reader, honorary secretary of a national benevolent association, family man and holiday maker. These other activities have given me ample opportunity to get outside my research and my writing and to think about it. Where do the building societies stand now, and where are they going? Although I believe that my three years study of the history of Heart of England helps me put the present in perspective, I make no claim to be able to forecast the future, and any idle speculation I now offer should be treated as such. The opinions offered are entirely my own.

"On Friday 17 March 1978, Harold Percy Jaggard, the 79 year old Chairman and Secretary of the Grays' Building Society was found dead in his bath at home . . . ." (Investigation under Section 110 of the Building Societies Act, 1962.) One hundred and fifty years earlier, in 1828, building societies were hardly more significant in their communities than the local bowls club. But no bowls club secretary could have caused a deficiency in excess of £7m in his club accounts between 1938 and 1978. Harold Jaggard could and did; and the Grays' Building Society was a relatively small one. Building societies are now big business, not only in their own regions but nationally. They feature extensively in the Report of the Wilson Committee on the Functioning of Financial Institutions. Modern building societies are convenient and useful, and like any darling of the public they attract politicians as does a honey pot the bees.

It has always been pleasant to own your own house, but only recently has it become financially compelling. I lived in headmaster's tied houses from 1952 until 1977. I monitored the movement of house prices year by year and invested sufficient to buy my retirement home when the time came. It was not until 1972 that it became clear that no other investment could keep up with investment in houses and that I must therefore buy a house, even though I could not live in it. The house I bought in 1972 would have cost me 2½ times as much in 1977. It is however young people, young marrieds, who experience most dramatically the need to get on the housing escalator before it passes them by for ever. The mortgage payment is thereafter a major budget element for them and an increase in mortgage rate is therefore inescapably a national political issue. There is great pressure on the societies to provide funds for house purchase and to provide them cheaply.

But if I take off my house buyer's hat and substitute my senior citizen's panama, why should I invest my retirement nest egg in a building society? In November 1979 I could have placed money in both the gilt edged market and the building societies at 15%. A gilt edged investment would have either guaranteed me 15% for the rest of my life, if I held the stocks, or capital appreciation if I sold them as MLR came down. The building society could give me no guarantee how long the 15% would last, and common sense suggested that the rate of interest must decline. Moreover, if I happened to be one of those senior citizens, or young people, not liable for the standard rate of income tax, I would not be receiving 15% on my building society investment, but 10.5%. At first sight I might argue that any money I placed with my friendly building society was in part a charitable donation in recognition of long and faithful service.

But I need ready money somewhere – that £2,000 for the rainy day, or the miscalculation at bingo, or the sudden call to relatives in Dallas, Texas. The building society offers me a service which I can use almost like a bank account, except for the payment of standing orders. Moreover it pays me the going rate of interest on my daily credit balance. If only it could offer me 15% in perpetuity, as an extension of the present term share system, it might have picked up all my capital for the rest of my life. Not surprisingly the competition between bank and building society is hotting up, especially in the business of mortgage loans. The banks are now making considerable sums available.

In the meantime the young married house buyer, beset on the one hand by high interest rates and big mortgage payments, is belaboured on the other by those who consider that he receives unfair preferential treatment. When his parents die he will receive his share of the considerable capital sum produced by the sale of their home. He will in fact be a member of the first generation to receive this inherited house price bonus. In addition he receives tax relief on his mortgage payments, at his top rate of tax, and his investment has one of the best examples of gearing in the investment scene. Yet his daily budget is so stretched financially when mortgage rates are high that the B.S.A. dare not recommend a mortgage rate which would be fair to investors, bring in the money, cut the mortgage queues and housing chains and keep the flexibility in the housing market which is so essential to a mobile industrial society and its work force. Because of these uncompetitive rates the working population of this country has become almost static and applications for vacancies which two years ago would have commanded a national field come today only from those who live nearby and would not have to move house.

These are some of the reasons why building society leaders must think and plan carefully. Their societies are bridge builders as well as house builders. They bridge the financial institutions, they bridge the ground between those institutions and housing policy which means homes for the people, they bridge the troubled area of building society liquidity ratios and the funding of government debt through sales of gilt edged stock. The societies have become too important for their own comfort. They can no longer expect to be left alone by politicians. They must avoid managing their affairs insensitively or inefficiently. They must not provoke a public outcry which the politicians could not ignore, lest the time should come when parliament takes more control over the building society movement.

A building society is a typical product of free enterprise activity. Each constituent society of the Heart of England owes its existence to men who believed in self-help, initiative, entrepreneurial activity, freedom of economic choice and, above all, competition. These men understood that they must band together as borrower and lender if they wished to emulate the rich and own their own houses. In one respect only have the societies eschewed competition and operated a price fixing cartel. Generally the societies accept the B.S.A.'s recommendations for mortgage and investment rates and do so in the belief that it is in their client's best interests that they should. The B.S.A.'s Major Evidence to the Wilson Committee commented as follows on interest rates:-

"Societies recognised that some disadvantages can be claimed for the relative lack of competition between them on interest rates. They are convinced, however, that any major discrepancy in the rates offered to investors by the large societies would quickly be eliminated and that in any foreseeable circumstances free competition would result in a generally higher level of interest rates. Societies consider that, on balance, stability and order are preferable to the uncertainty in the minds of millions of borrowers which unbridled competition would bring".

In June 1978, two years later, the Wilson Committee replied:-

"The interest rate cartel produces doubtful benefits and, by encouraging non-price competition, is wasteful of resources. The only way to provide a competitive spur to building societies is to end the recommended rate system and the Committee recommends its abolition. Pressure to set competitive rates should encourage administrative efficiency and cutting costs. The Committee recognised that the mortgage rate would probably rise. However the housing market and the construction industry would benefit."

The dilemma faced by the building societies, the decisions they must take, are at present being debated in financial terms. I believe that this is wrong and that the debate should be about people. It should include a serious survey, in the form of an enquiry of those people about what they expect from their building societies. Non-price competition leads to a proliferation of building society branches in our towns. These branches are small, they are staffed by local people, and above all they are friendly. It has been easy, and a pleasure, to pay tribute to the staff of the Heart of England as the best advertisement the Society has. When borrowing and lending rates are fixed nationally it is only through friendly staff and neighbourhood branches that the societies can compete with one another and with other financial institutions for the limited supply of funds. We pay for everything. Too often during the past thirty years we have paid for a more economical product with a reduction in the quality of life. Is, for example, the modern housewife really grateful for the competition of the super-market? or would she rather that it had never been invented and that she still dealt with her friendly neighbourhood shopkeeper, who might even taken an order and deliver it. The recommendations of the Wilson Committee might temporarily produce a higher investment rate, but at what cost in human terms?

Investment rate price competition, as opposed to the present non-price competition, would greatly increase the pressure on societies to amalgamate. By the end of the century we might well find that the building society movement had joined those national enterprises which have sought supposed economics of scale by reorganising on a basis of few and big. John Bull shows signs of realising that the freedom to shop around may be no less important than those political and philosophical freedoms hard won during the past five hundred years. The Heart of England Building Society remains local both in Warwick, Rugby, Walsall, Coalville and Oxford and throughout a region which is clearly identifiable as England's heartland. The little shops with their personal service are enjoying a new lease of life. The customer will pay for a smile and a comment on the weather. This I believe is the message for the Heart of England and the whole building society movement.

In 1919 the Chairman of the Building Societies Association argued that the post-war houses so desperately needed should be built through the concerted efforts of small builders and local building societies:- ". . . .By such economies he can build at a price with which the local authorities could not compete. Building Society managers especially know and appreciate the point. The houses will be purchased for occupation by the owner, and one cannot but feel that a few thousand people owning their own houses would be a better asset to a town than the same number of tenants occupying municipal houses".

This local involvement, translated into 1980 terms, should remain the aim and purpose of the building societies. The Wilson recommendations would push them rapidly into a cannibalism which would end in a few national societies, heavily involved in national economic and financial considerations, ripe for nationalisation/denationalisation, and quite unrecognisable by their founders. This is not their role. They are a product of British ingenuity, individuality and self-help. They believe that each human being is greater than the sum of all human beings and that the purpose of political, financial and economic activity is to give such individuals as much freedom and freedom of choice as possible. Building societies should not build financial empires they should build houses – castles for Englishmen, where the British love of home, family and freedom may continue to be nourished and enriched. The Heart of England Building Society encapsulates the issues faced by the whole movement. It has evolved and expanded greatly during the past 130 years but it is still rooted in Midland soil, with the Heart of England rose as a fitting emblem of that relationship. Can it respond to the national pressures upon the building society movement and yet retain its local identity and personal involvement?

Index